Northwest Indiana

Craig Berg ▼

Jon L. Hendricks ▼

NWI Symphony Orchestra ▼

region*ality*

Sand, Steel & Soul

Published by:

THE TIMES

Northwest Indiana
Newspapers

Northwest Indiana

region

John Watkins

Tom Hocker

ality

Sand, Steel & Soul

Written by Julia Versau ■ Photo Editing by Kirk John Mitchell ■ Art Direction by Tom Kacius

Craig Berg ▼

Publisher
Northwest Indiana Newspapers

Executive Project Director
Marc Leuthart

Project Directors
George Carl
Michael Donley
Joe Gurnak
Amy Owens
Lisa Tatina

Art Director
Tom Kacius

Editor
Julia Versau

Photography Editor
Kirk John Mitchell

Page Designers
Ami Reese
Dave Savage

Lead Profile Photographer
Jon L. Hendricks

Digital Color Technicians
Barbara Chapman
Kirk John Mitchell

Administrative Coordinator
Claudia White

Special Project Intern
Phillip Dietrich

Northwest Indiana Newspapers
2080 North Main Street
Crown Point, Indiana 46307

ISBN 0-9704756-0-8
Library of Congress Card No. 00-110678

Contents

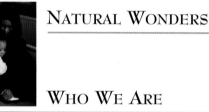

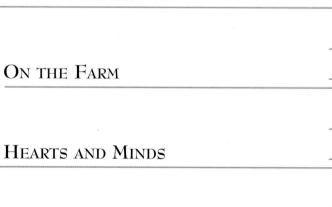

Geoff Black ▼

John Luke ▼

*T*HAT NORTHWEST INDIANA IS A DISTINCT TERRITORY WITH A PERSONALITY ALL ITS OWN MIGHT ESCAPE AN OUTSIDER. A BOOMERANG-SHAPED STRIP OF LAND HUGGING LAKE MICHIGAN FROM ITS BORDER WITH CHICAGO ON THE WEST TO MICHIGAN CITY ON THE EAST, THE TURF IS A MYSTERY TO MANY WHO WHIZ ALONG ITS EXPRESSWAYS WITHOUT STOPPING. PEOPLE USUALLY KNOW ONE THING OR ANOTHER ABOUT NORTHWEST INDIANA—BUT NOT BOTH.   BY JULIA VERSAU

One sees a scion of steel, its factory stacks blowing smoke rings into the sky. Another, a Shangri-La of sand, each dune testimony to the region's natural inheritance. No one can say whether more grains of sand have been carried out in tiny bottles after summer vacations spent at the lake or more ingots of steel have been shipped out to the world's makers of cars and refrigerators. Visitors who do get off the expressway, in Miller Beach, or Portage, or Michigan City, marvel at the juxtaposition: millions of grains of sand moments from the massive mills, the natural serenity of the place skin to skin with the gritty, manmade commotion of factories and machine shops.

*S*toppers-by marvel at other things not easily gleaned from the window of a speeding car or train. Tucked one after another into Indiana's lakefront region, through the counties of Lake, Porter, and LaPorte, are a series of cities and towns with unique histories and charms. Here one moves past sand and steel to the soul of the region. On a summer's night in Washington Township, nervous teens promenade sheep past 4-H judges hoping for a blue ribbon, the sounds of an old-fashioned

▶ Jon L. Hendricks

◀ G. Kelly Harrison

county fair echoing just outside the barn. In Whiting, merry citizens make new memories of their shared history when residents of eastern European descent take to the streets in July for Pierogi Fest. Throngs turn out to greet the arrival of the Slicers, the city of

LaPorte's championship high school baseball team. Perennial pros in America's beloved sport, they get a welcome worthy of a president. The only time northwest Indiana seems like anyplace else is when it feels like Kansas, but that only lasts for a day when 200

Tony Bruno ▼

Dorothys in blue gingham dresses and sparkling red shoes march in Chesterton's Oz Fest parade.

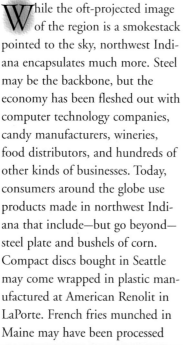
Michael Gard ◀

While the oft-projected image of the region is a smokestack pointed to the sky, northwest Indiana encapsulates much more. Steel may be the backbone, but the economy has been fleshed out with computer technology companies, candy manufacturers, wineries, food distributors, and hundreds of other kinds of businesses. Today, consumers around the globe use products made in northwest Indiana that include—but go beyond— steel plate and bushels of corn. Compact discs bought in Seattle may come wrapped in plastic manufactured at American Renolit in LaPorte. French fries munched in Maine may have been processed with industrial food equipment built by Urschel Laboratories in Valparaiso. A cozy temperature in the visitor center at Mount Rushmore is a credit to Michigan City boiler maker Weil-McLain. Tough car batteries and delicate crystal alike get their strength from lead compounds produced by Hammond Group, Inc.

Northwest Indiana was in many ways ground zero for the industrial revolution. In the new millennium, cities like East Chicago, Gary, and Hammond—built by steel and heavy industry—are working to create economies that strike a balance between what has come before and what is now arriving. An established network of highways, rail lines, and cargo shipping via the Great Lakes is being augmented by the critically important fiber optic cable and satellite systems required of players in the information age. In Porter and LaPorte counties, farms, dairies, and wineries still underscore the region's importance as a part of the national breadbasket stretching from Pennsylvania through the plains to the Rockies.

Once a crossroads, always a crossroads. The U.S. Highway Administration in the 1920s built the first transcontinental expressway—Lincoln Highway—through northwest Indiana, placing the region smack dab at the center of the nation's comings and goings. If the region's leaders and residents have their say, northwest Indiana will remain at the center of things.

In an Internet chat room, a person from the region will say he lives in Indiana. Pressed for more

Craig Berg ▼

Jon L. Hendricks ▼

Oregionality

specifics, the answer is usually either "right by the lake" or "about an hour southeast of Chicago." The region is definitely in the Hoosier state, where Purdue and Notre Dame and Indiana University flags fly free. Nonetheless, the region keeps time with its neighbor Chicago. And not just of the daylight savings sort. Its citizens tend to root for the Bears, and many more visit "the windy city" on a regular basis than make the trek to the state capitol in Indianapolis. Municipalities in northwest Indiana relish this accident of birth that has allowed their cozy, picturesque downtowns and neighborhoods to exist only an hour away from the delights a huge metropolis offers.

It has made a difference to people on both sides of the border. Chicagoans, especially from the south side of the city, fought hard to save the Indiana Dunes and preserve what is now roundly considered northwest Indiana's most redeeming feature. It was to Chicago department store Marshall Field's that a gawky Hoosier in a bow tie turned in 1970 for a chance to display his new brand of popcorn. Valparaiso, where the entrepreneur set up his factory, still honors Orville Redenbacher each September with its annual Popcorn Festival.

The region gives back. The 40-foot tall Picasso sculpture gracing Daley Plaza in Chicago, it should be known, was fabricated by a steel company in Gary. Northwest Indiana fans hooted and hollered to help a local boy make history on the court, and now smile when Valparaiso University's Bryce Drew dons his Chicago Bulls jersey. In 1935, northwest Indiana gave Chicago's Goodman Theatre a young Serbian lad named Mladen Sekulovich, who made both locales proud as actor Karl Malden.

For decades after the turn of the twentieth century, northwest Indiana was a playground for prominent Chicagoans and famous actors who escaped to places like Cedar Lake and Miller Beach for vacations and respite. One person known to have desired a speedy retreat out of the region was legendary bank robber John Dillinger, who vamoosed from an "escape-proof" jail in Crown Point in 1934. Contrary to popular thought, Dillinger wasn't born in northwest Indiana. But like many other men and women (who were, thankfully, possessed of nobler bents) he discovered the region can be a good place to build a name for oneself.

Kirk John Mitchell

Robert Kauffman

S A N D ,   S T E E L   &   S O U L

History and location made flexibility of allegiances a necessity. Northwest Indiana citizens constitute a diverse lot who pay homage all around: to a city block, the neighborhood, "da region," the big city next door, the state, the old country.

The area was built by Germans, Irish, Italians, African-Americans, Hispanics, Greeks, Poles, Serbs, and a host of other peoples who found not only freedom here, but also the means to earn one's bread. Strong hands were needed to build the railroads that in the 1880s carved a path through the swampy lakefront from cities in the east to the burgeoning metropolis of Chicago. After the tracks were laid, there were new opportunities. A man from any corner of the globe speaking any tongue could find work at John D. Rockefeller's Standard Oil refinery in Whiting, or at U.S. Steel Corp., a marvel of industry that set up shop in 1906 and then proceeded to build the City of Gary as a hometown for its workers. Diversity still sets the tone in northwest Indiana, where the smelting pot led to a cultural melting pot. The town of Merrillville spoke for itself—and also the region—

when it created its municipal slogan: "Where everyone is welcome." Though often portrayed by national media as behind the ball, often the region is quite ahead of it. It was Gary that in 1967 elected a black man, Richard G. Hatcher, the first African-American mayor of a major metropolitan city, years before Detroit, Los Angeles, or New York would boast of crossing that racial divide.

O regionality is a look at life in northwest Indiana. Those who peruse its pages will discover the delightful juxtapositions that often go unknown, or uncelebrated. Farm and factory. Urban and rural. Black and white. New and old. Sand and steel and soul. We started with "regional" as mission and map. The "O" we took from the common refrain one hears when northwest Indiana is truly described: "Oh! I didn't know that." The "ity" is up to the reader who might choose among an ample list of adjectives: diversity, personality, ingenuity, originality, vitality. Our good look at the region got us thinking that we needed to invent a whole new word. And so we did.

Oregionality

Natural Wonders

Craig Berg

Craig Berg

The heart of the region beats quietly and beautifully in the Indiana Dunes. Located approximately 50 miles southeast of Chicago in the counties of Lake, Porter, and LaPorte in northwest Indiana, the national lakeshore runs for nearly 25 miles along southern Lake Michigan, bordered by Michigan City on the east and Gary on the west. The park contains approximately 15,000 acres, including 2,182 located in Indiana Dunes State Park.

Ellen Skye ▼

Christopher A. Meyers ▼

Michael Gard ▼

Oregionality

rains may outnumber guests of the dunes, but not by so many. Since the Indiana Dunes Lakeshore was designated a national park in 1966, thousands of tourists have left footprints in the sand.

▼ Ellen Skye

▼ Kirk John Mitchell

▼ Lyn Wellsand

This sign (top) no longer exists but the amenities it extols— like the Indiana State Park bathhouse (bottom)—still do.

Oregionality

Climbing Mount Baldy, one of the dunes' prize peaks, is a challenge few visitors pass up.

MT. BALDY

INDIANA DUNES NATIONAL LAKESHORE

SMOKING DUNE

Mt. Baldy, one of the largest dunes on the southern shore of Lake Michigan, is 123 feet tall and is advancing inland at a rate of 4 to 5 feet per year. Northwest winds move Mt. Baldy inland, slowly burying the forest just south of the dune.

Winds pick up sand grains from the beach and blow them inland. The sand grains roll and bounce along in a process referred to as "saltation." As the wind speed increases, the sand is picked up and carried. Viewed from a distance, the sand blowing off the top of Mt. Baldy appears as wisps of smoke, thus the term "smoking dune."

Tony Bruno ▼

▲ Robert Huffman ▼

Indiana Dunes State Park was the site of the Zoy Run from 1984 to 1997. When participants swelled from a handful to several hundred, damage to the dunes was deemed too great. Many still return the first Sunday of each November for an informal trek across the sand and through ice-cold Dunes Creek.

▶ Carol Banach

▶ John Rzepka

O r e g i o n a l i t y

ind, waves, and water: for residents, life in the region is often a day at the beach.

▼ Craig Berg

▼ Gregg Gearhart

▼ April Grisham

Richard Loslo ▼

P oised for the plunge, a young
girl dips her toes in Whihala
Beach in Whiting.

4

Oregionality

G ary's historic Aquatorium features majestic architecture replete with grand staircases and ornate columns.

O r e g i o n a l i t y

▼ John Niemann

▼ Craig Berg

▼ Craig Berg

Those who battled to save the dunes won the war, keeping a northwest Indiana treasure intact for future generations.

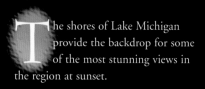

The shores of Lake Michigan provide the backdrop for some of the most stunning views in the region at sunset.

Dennis Hodges ▼

Craig Berg ▼

Oregionality

▼ Carol Banach

▼ Tony Bruno

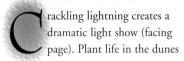

Crackling lightning creates a dramatic light show (facing page). Plant life in the dunes ranges from sand-stabilizing Marram grass to beech maples, black gum trees, and dainty daisies.

The landscape provides focal points for monitoring the revolution of time. Northwest Indiana is colorful in every season.

Kirk John Mitchell

Robert Kauffman

Robert Kauffman

Robert Kauffman

Oregionality

Larry A. Brechner

Jon L. Hendricks

Pristine prairie: Oak Ridge, a park in Griffith, provides a tranquil respite for hikers, bird watchers, and nature enthusiasts.

Tracy McPherson ▼

Kirk John Mitchell ▼

Toyell Thomas ▼

Dianne Sprehe ▼

O ff the beaten track, flowers stretch fresh faces to the sun: Bleeding Hearts at Deep River Park in Hobart (bottom right), wild lilies at Lake George (top left), and blossoms and butterflies along trails at the Indiana Dunes.

Oregionality

Jim Golembieski

Kirk John Mitchell

Justeen Schultz

Citizens of the region share space with both the feathered and the furry.

Judy Smith ▼

Kirk John Mitchell ▼

William Longfellow ▼

Oregionality

Places to rest and restore one's spirit abound. Pictured are Wilhelm Road in northern LaPorte County (top) and serene spots in Cedar Lake (bottom). Facing page: Lake LaLumiere in LaPorte County (top) and the Indiana Dunes State Park (bottom).

Judy Smith

Tony Bruno

Kirk John Mitchell

Zookeepers in Michigan City manage quite a menagerie. A popular destination for school field trips, the Michigan City Zoo is a draw for visitors from throughout the midwest.

Oregionality

No two snowflakes are alike, and perhaps no two deer. This one stopped along a wintry path and shared a moment with Terry Swanson, whose photograph of the encounter won him first place in the Oregionality photo contest. A once busy barn (facing page) lies nestled in snowy splendor.

W inter's snow and ice appear as decorations on the natural and the built. Jesse Josleyn's photograph of one winter scene (facing page top) won him the Photographer of the Year award in the 2001 Professional Photographers of Indiana Association competition and a prize in the Oregionality photo contest.

S topping in the woods on a snowy evening: Hidden Lake Park in Merrillville (left) and Deep River County Park in Hobart.

Oregionality

Icy scenes are a counterpoint to summer's white-capped waves at the lighthouse in Michigan City (facing page) and the Indiana Dunes National Lakeshore.

Michael Connors

Kirk John Mitchell

O r e g i o n a l i t y

Jesse Josleyn

A father and son brave the elements in search of the perfect Christmas tree.

Who We Are

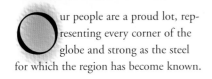

Our people are a proud lot, representing every corner of the globe and strong as the steel for which the region has become known.

Gregg Gearhart ▶

Tracy Albano ▶

Kirk John Mitchell ▶

Gregg Gearhart ▶

Regional sports heroes push forward—and give back. Lloyd McClendon (top left), who played baseball at Valparaiso University and was named manager of the Pittsburgh Pirates in 2000, helps youngsters at a youth camp. Ron Kittle (bottom left), former Chicago White Sox slugger, established Indiana Sports Charities to support cancer research. Glenn Robinson (top right) was a hoopster at Roosevelt High School in Gary before joining the NBA's Milwaukee Bucks. Shane Power (bottom right), an Andrean High School powerhouse, proves caring starts young. He won the IHSAA Trester Award—open only to state finalist team members—for his efforts both on and off the court.

Oregionality

Zbigniew Bzdak

The ring of success: legendary Hobart Brickies football coach Donald Howell, one of the region's winningest coaches, was repected for his drive to develop all-around individuals. Howell suffered a heart attack and died in November, 1999 after lifting weights with players and just nine months after his retirement.

idespread fame and a bevy of book awards have flowed to Walter Wangerin (top), writer-in-residence at Valparaiso University, featured columnist for *The Lutheran* magazine, and author of more than 60 titles including 1980's American Book Award winner, *Book of the Dun Cow*. Saw-master Steve Franek (bottom) serves as president of the Northwest Indiana Woodworkers Association.

Oregionality

L ife in the region can be hair-raising, whether one's into reveling or rebellion—or simply some unruly chocolate ice cream.

THE REBEL

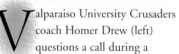
Valparaiso University Crusaders coach Homer Drew (left) questions a call during a basketball game. With equal emotion, conductor Albert Jackson (right) directs the South Suburban Chorale.

Sam Riche ▼

Melisa Goh ▼

Oregionality

sther "Rusty" Kristoff (left) learned the Girl Scout law as a youngster and today is a veteran leader. Judge Karen Freeman-Wilson mastered many laws and now metes out justice in Gary.

Celebrated storyteller Art Willing (facing page) spins tales to the delight of audiences throughout northwest Indiana. At historic sites like Bailly Homestead in Porter (bottom), schoolchildren from Bibich Elementary School in Dyer hear stories from a ranger about the region's first residents and early settlers.

▶ Carol Banach

▶ John Niemann

▶ Tom Kay

▶ Tom Kay

L ife is a journey full of ups
and downs, leaps, and happy
endings whether the landing
is in finger paint or pudding.

▼ Steven Harper

▼ Susan Cher

▼ Gregg Gearhart

▼ Tamara Bell

There is proof one should avoid judging a book by its cover. Beneath the tough exterior (and tattoos) are well-meaning motor cyclists who organize an annual charity ride to support the Muscular Dystrophy Association.

▼ Cary Best

▼ LaPorte County Convention & Visitors Bureau

▼ Melisa Goh

Pleasures of the past are relived at eateries and events in the region. The annual Jim Dandy's 1950s Car Show and Street Dance in Portage (top left) brings back poodle skirts while the Temple News Agency in Michigan City (top right) keeps the malted trade alive. Car Cruise Night in Schererville (bottom) is a hit with young and old.

W hether young at heart in a garden (top) or the very flower of youth (bottom), joy is perennial.

Susan Hurley

Jesse Joslyn

O r e g i o n a l i t y

Zachary Ellis of Hobart plays in a water fountain during the city's riverfront festival (top). Frank Olivarri of Lake Station (bottom) sticks to the straight and narrow as a member of the Deep River Bowmen Archery Club.

Photo credits: Melisa Goh, Melisa Goh, Times File Photo

NASA astronaut and Crown Point native son Jerry Ross (top) shares stories with Lowell High School students. The music may be too much for Alex Jow of Schererville (left), but sounds just right to actor Karl Malden (right), born Mladen Sekulovich in Gary in 1914.

Kirk John Mitchell

Northwest Indiana has had its share of "pop." The Jackson 5 were born and raised in Gary and are still local icons (left). Orville Redenbacher (right, shown with grandson Gary Fish) made his brand of Hoosier popcorn—and bow ties, too—famous worldwide from headquarters in Valparaiso.

A king and a queen: Betsy Bobel (top) of Chesterton shows a queen's duties are countless as she tries to amuse Hope Hurley of Portage at a fundraising event in Chesterton. Bobel represented Indiana in the 2000 Miss USA contest. Mayor Scott King (bottom) addresses reporters at a press conference in Gary. King was instrumental in bringing the Miss USA pageant to Gary for a three year run starting in 2001.

Melisa Goh ▲

Natalie Bataglia ▼

Seniors in the region live life to the fullest. Retired railroader Gordon Ashley (top) pursues a train hobby; looking for an ace at the Pruzin Senior Center in Merrillville (center); Mayor Robert Pastrick (bottom), a senior and a tireless leader, has been mayor of East Chicago since 1972.

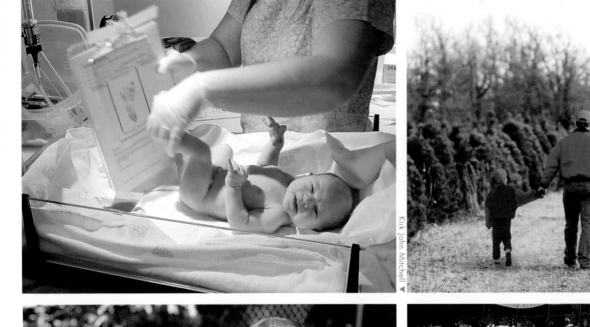

Moments captured: a first game of "This Little Piggie," hunting down a perfect tree, a summer buzz cut, learning to get along with girls.

Oregionality

Zbigniew Bzdak

C eleste may be pint-sized, but she stops champion boxer Angel Manfredy cold during his practice at the Police Athletic Club gym in Gary. To Celeste, Manfredy is not only a dynamo, he's also her dad.

L ift your eyes, raise your arms:
children respond with exuberance to the thrills of a balloon
race, water park fun, a spelling bee
win, and a parade.

Oregionality

▼ John Luke

▼ Natalie Bataglia

Northwest Indiana grew quickly after construction of rail lines that connected points east with the bustling city of Chicago (above, Broad Street Station in Griffith). Since the late 1800s, trains have served as a major locomotive of progress in the region.

The Chicago South Shore Line ferries passengers to and from the region daily, stopping in cities from Hammond (this page) and Chesterton (facing page) to South Bend.

Brian Rossin ▼

John Niemann ▼

Oregionality

John Niemann

Cheryl Milchak

Kirk John Mitchell ▼

Oregionality

All aboard at Beverly Shores.
At night, the neon light casts
a golden glow.

Cheryl Milchak

Gregg Gearhart

Kirk John Mitchell

O r e g i o n a l i t y

There's nothing nicer than a new car, unless it's an old one in tip-top condition. Visitors to the region ogle antique autos like Bentleys and Citroens—and a rare Tucker of movie fame—at the Door Prairie Auto Museum in LaPorte. Parades of classic cars are staples at the Chesterton Hometown Picnic (facing page left) and the Crown Point Festival Days Kobe Cup Race (bottom left).

Oregionality

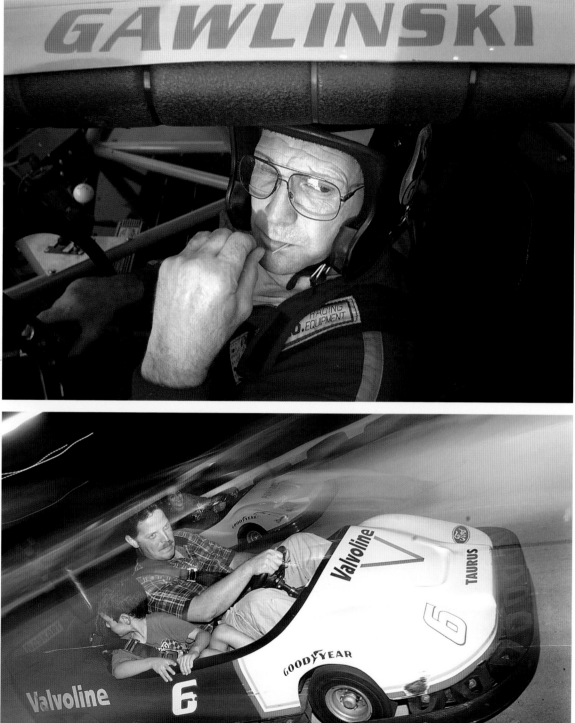

GAWLINSKI

▼ Wes Pope

▼ Jon L. Hendricks

The region gets revved at Illiana Motor Speedway in Crown Point. Pit crew members Joe Gensel of Lowell (left) and Ron Watroba of Lansing (right) cheer for driver Mike White as crew chief Tom Rose of Hammond (center) maintains radio contact with White (facing page top). Frank Gawlinski of Lynwood (top) is a seasoned veteran at Illiana.

Other local races, like those at Schererville's Brickyard Raceway, feature smaller cars at safer speeds (bottom).

Gary's annual Air and Water Show lures the Red Baron team (top) and the U.S. Navy's Blue Angels.

John Watkins ▲

John Watkins ▲

Oregionality

The USAF Thunderbirds (top) are always crowd-pleasers, while area fans of flight honor the aviation studies Octave Chanute conducted at the dunes with some radio-controlled fun of their own.

▼ John Watkins

▼ Tracy Albano

Oregionality

▼ John Niemann

One if by land, two if by sea: on the go in northwest Indiana often means making one's way through water. A jet skier braves the waves at a Michigan City Beach (left); others get wet on foot.

Oregionality

Craig Berg

Craig Berg

Craig Berg

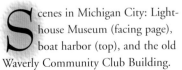

Scenes in Michigan City: Light-house Museum (facing page), boat harbor (top), and the old Waverly Community Club Building.

O ur love affair with lakes—
sunrise, sunset, and anytime
in between—is undisputed.

Carol Banach ▼

Oregionality

Dee Tripp

Carol Banach

Kirk John Mitchell

ugging Lake Michigan from Hammond to Michigan City, northwest Indiana is a perfect place to get some wind in one's sails. The crew of the Mischief heads out on the lake. Sailors of all sorts earn stripes at Cedar Lake (facing page top) and Wolf Lake (facing page bottom).

Oregionality

SAND, STEEL & SOUL

ichigan City was host city for a tour of a replica Nina of pilgrim's passage fame (bottom right). Residents and tourists alike flock to Lake Michigan's shores to take in regattas (top)—or a little relaxation (bottom left).

Kirk John Mitchell ▼

Times File Photo ▼

Gregg Gearhart ▼

Oregionality

The Hammond Marina as seen by seagulls. An enlarged marina and new lakefront parks have been a boon to development in Hammond.

or some folks, "on the go" means spokes. A solitary bicyclist peddles up a Hebron road. Bikes are welcome modes of transportation in the dunes (facing page top), along the Erie Lackawanna Bicycle Trail (facing page, bottom left), or to meet up with other sets of wheels.

Jesse Josleyn ▼

Oregionality

▼ Cheryl Milchak

▼ Tom Kay

▼ Jean Gehrig

Jesse Josleyn ▼

John Niemann ◄

Kirk John Mitchell ▼

Then again, "on the go" could spell snow. Seasons spent at sunny beaches are counterbalanced by winter months of white. Sliders swoosh down a sledding ridge at Indiana Dunes State Park in Chesterton (left); learning how far to lean at Lemon Lake in Crown Point (top), and traveling by ski at the Pines in Valparaiso (bottom).

Regional fortitude is forged on the few days each year when getting anywhere at all is difficult—or frankly impossible.

Oregionality

Keeping the Faith

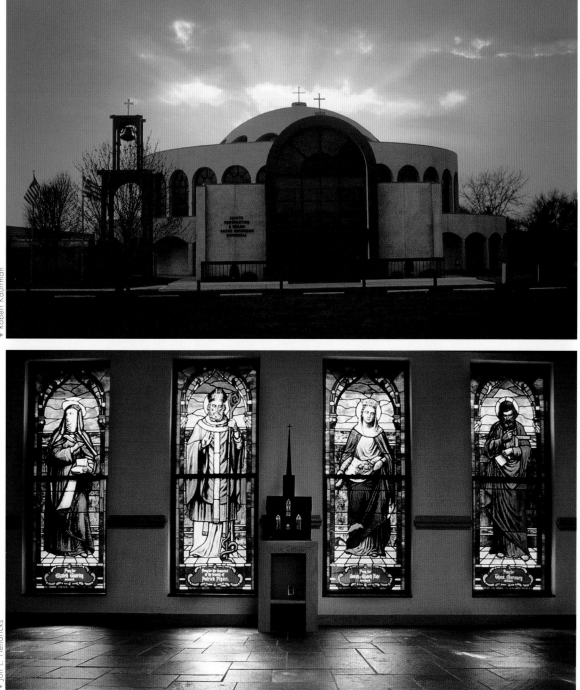

Robert Kauffman

Jon L. Hendricks

The faces of faith are many in northwest Indiana. Christians, Jews, Eastern Orthodox, and Muslims live in harmony and help each other. Pictured: a Serbian woman clutches her prayer book (facing page); St. Constantine & Helen Greek Orthodox Cathedral in Merrillville (top); St. Patrick Catholic Church in Chesterton.

et there be light: for many, spirituality is the foundation of family and community life.

▶John Niemann

oseph Henry Ganda, an archish-
op from Sierra Leone, celebrates
mass at St. Anthony Medical
Center's Corpus Christi Chapel.

Oregionality

rthodox Christians from throughout eastern Europe settled in the region beginning in the early 1900s. The upheavel of World War II, as well as economic opportunities in the region's mills and factories, brought high numbers to northwest Indiana.

The spire and the cross: communities across the region boast religious buildings of breathtaking beauty. Immigrant neighborhoods often raised funds first for a church, then worried about other building needs.

СРПСКА ПРАВОСЛАВНА ЦРКВА АО. СВ. ГЕОРГИЈЕ.1912.

Robin Perez

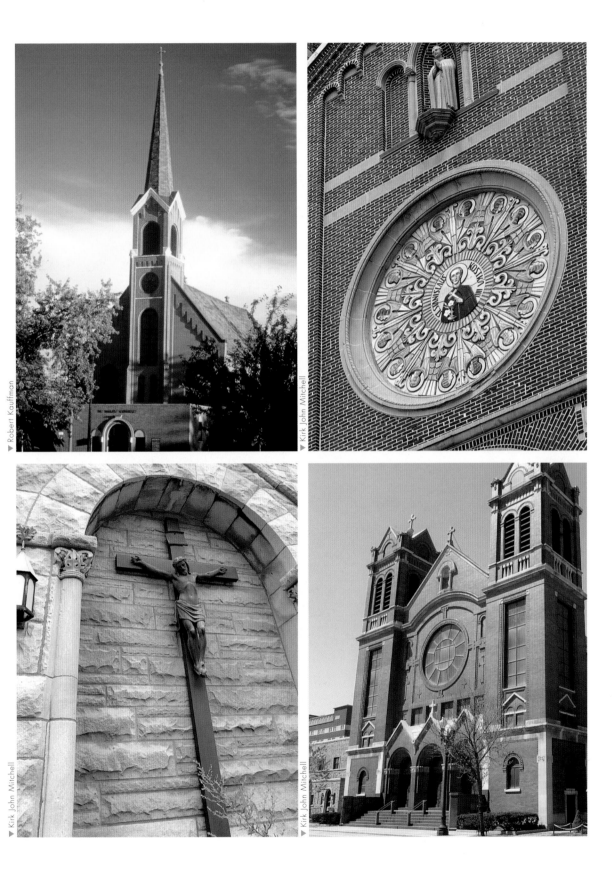

Robert Kauffman

Kirk John Mitchell

Kirk John Mitchell

Kirk John Mitchell

One of the region's magnificent landmarks, St. Sava Serbian Orthodox Church in Merrillville was consecrated in 1991. Its five domes form the shape of a cross.

Oregionality

Kirk John Mitchell

Robin Perez

Jon L. Hendricks

Churches, synagogues, and mosques encompass the traditional and the modern, the old and the new.

B ell, book, and candle:
worshippers find many
ways to express faith in prayer
and in action.

John Niemann ▼

Gregg Gearhart ▼

O regionality

Angela Scanlon ▼

Marie Trgovich ▼

Cynthia Dywan ▼

Oregionality

Living faith is expressed in stone statuary throughout the region. At the Discalced Carmelite Fathers Monastery in Munster (bottom), monks live a life of prayer and contemplation.

John Watkins ▶

P eople who know how to hold their heads up proudly also know when to bow them in prayer.

O r e g i o n a l i t y

Jon L. Hendricks ▼

Oregionality

Jon L. Hendricks

Natalie Bataglia

Geoff Black

The signs of faith are many: singing praises at Family Christian Church (facing page) and lighting the menorah at Temple Beth-El in Munster (left); praying at a Sikh service at the Northwest Indiana Islamic Center (top right); blessing of the cornerstone for Tree of Life Church in Gary.

ister Celine Tomasic of the Poor Handmaids of Jesus Christ nuzzles a kindergartner (top); nuns celebrate mass in the chapel at St. Margaret Mercy Health Center in Hammond (bottom left); Mary Ann Bibat of Whiting and her sons get a head start on hymns at St. John the Baptist Church.

Oregionality

Zbigniew Bzdak

John Watkins

Geoff Black

Bishop Dale J. Melczek of the Diocese of Gary celebrates mass (top left) and officiates at ordination ceremonies (bottom).

Archbishop Stefan and Bishop Kiril conduct mass at St. Peter & Paul Macedonian Orthodox Church in Crown Point (top right).

The photo credits read (vertically): Natalie Bataglia, Tracy Albano, Tracy Albano.

T he life, passion, and crucifixion of Christ are acted by the Hispanic Ministries in East Chicago (top) and by the Family Christian Church in Munster (bottom). The productions draw thousands of patrons each Easter season.

Oregionality

▼ Natalie bataglia

▼ Natalie Bataglia

▶ Lake Hills Baptist Church

Mike Salinas plays the role of Jesus Christ during the Hispanic Ministries' Living Stations of the Cross on Good Friday (top and bottom left); a live Nativity scene is conducted at Lake Hills Baptist Church in Schererville.

INRI

cts of charity large and small are daily duty in northwest Indiana, where citizens young and old prove it is better to give than to receive.

Natalie Bataglia ▼

Natalie Bataglia ▼

Natalie Bataglia ▼

Oregionality

sharing is caring

GOD bless you...

THE SALVATION ARMY

Need has no season

"BELL RINGER"

▼ Tasos Katopodis

▼ Kirk John Mitchell

Holy cow! When it comes to preening for the camera, a heifer milks it for all its worth (facing page). Mark Riley and his quarterhorse ham it up at the Porter County Fair (top); a Chellberg Farm rooster (bottom) struts his stuff.

armers in the region know
how much the machinery
of their trade has changed.
At Chellberg Farm in Porter (top),
history buffs can see the horse and
plow method as practiced when
Swedish immigrants settled the
80-acre spread in 1874.

Oregionality

The Wolf family of Wanatah (top) runs state-of-the-art equipment including tractors outfitted with air conditioning and CD players, a far cry from the primitive tractors (facing page bottom) and early steam-powered plows (bottom) of yore.

A large number of farms in northwest Indiana have survived to see the 21st century. Bucolic vistas abound: a tractor sits idle until dawn (top); rolled hay, looking like giant biscuits of Shredded Wheat, awaits the next day's loading trucks.

Oregionality

Wheat reaches upward in a fertile field in Crown Point (bottom). In the fall, processors like this one in Hammond (top) will prepare the harvest for use locally or shipment to a buyer in the U.S. or abroad.

Oh, yes, we have no bananas. But northwest Indiana farmers are known for their bumper crops of corn, peppers, soybeans, pumpkins, tomatoes, beans, and more.

Tom Hocker

Larry A. Brechner

Brett Reierson

Rich soil and steady stewardship are in ample supply, so farmers—as ever—mostly worry about the weather. When all goes well, the crop can astound with prize winners like a 443-pound squash (bottom right).

A utumn comes wearing many colors, but goes heavy on the orange. Pumpkin-picking is a high art as practiced at County Line Orchard in Hobart.

O r e g i o n a l i t y

For those who live in northwest Indiana and those who often visit, it's clear there's no better place to seek out perfect pumpkins, model mums, or ideal Indian corn and plop them in the wagon.

Following page: round barns stand as reminders of times past. Of the approximately 226 built in Indiana, about 96 are extant, including several in the region. The first round barns built in the U.S. were constructed by Shakers. Why round? Shakers believed the curved shape protected them from ever being trapped in a corner by the devil.

arly settlers included carpenters and shopkeepers, but most earned their daily bread as farmers. Though the region is known more for steel than soybeans, it's still just a short drive to a field rippling with tall corn or a tranquil pasture of grazing sheep.

Oregionality

Photographers have a field day with rich imagery found around every corner: antique tractors, once-proud grain silos, and retired, ivy-covered barns bestow a sense of history and are a feast for the eyes.

Larry A. Brechner

Rebecca Hutchins

Kirk John Mitchell

A dandelion gone to seed, a silo in the sun: a lazy summer day settles in at a Cedar Lake Farm.

Oregionality

From Lake to Porter to LaPorte County, tours of the region boast a bevy of beautiful barns. Barn history buffs can find relics of the past: paned windows, intricate detailing, and haylofts from before the advent of mechanized balers.

Matthew Hewlett

Judy Smith

Robert Kauffman

At a livestock auction in Lowell, the herdsmen drive hard bargains—only the animals can afford to act sheepish.

Katie Thomas ▼

Katie Thomas ▼

Oregionality

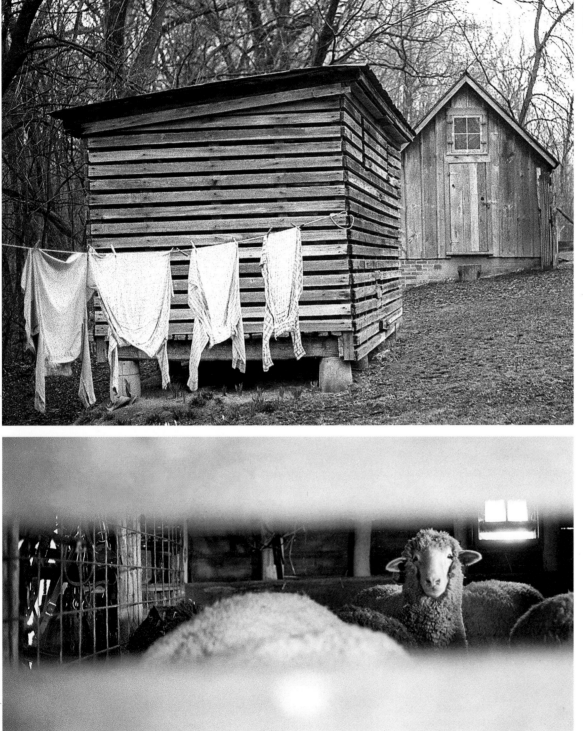

hellberg Farm in Porter is maintained as a working turn of the 20th century farm by the Indiana Dunes National Lakeshore. Two annual events at Chellberg, the Duneland Harvest Festival and Maple Sugar Time Festival, draw thousands of visitors from throughout the midwest.

Cheryl Milchak

Cheryl Milchak

Youth in the region keep 4-H ideals alive and learn valuable skills in everything from livestock care and horsemanship to flower arranging, cooking, and photography. Penny Hineline of Chesterton (top) coaxes her cow into the 4-H barn at the Porter County Fair, while Steven Sharp waits to show a lamb named Braveheart (bottom left). Alan Duttlinger of Lowell (bottom right) has his hands full at the Lake County Fair with a sow and 13 piglets.

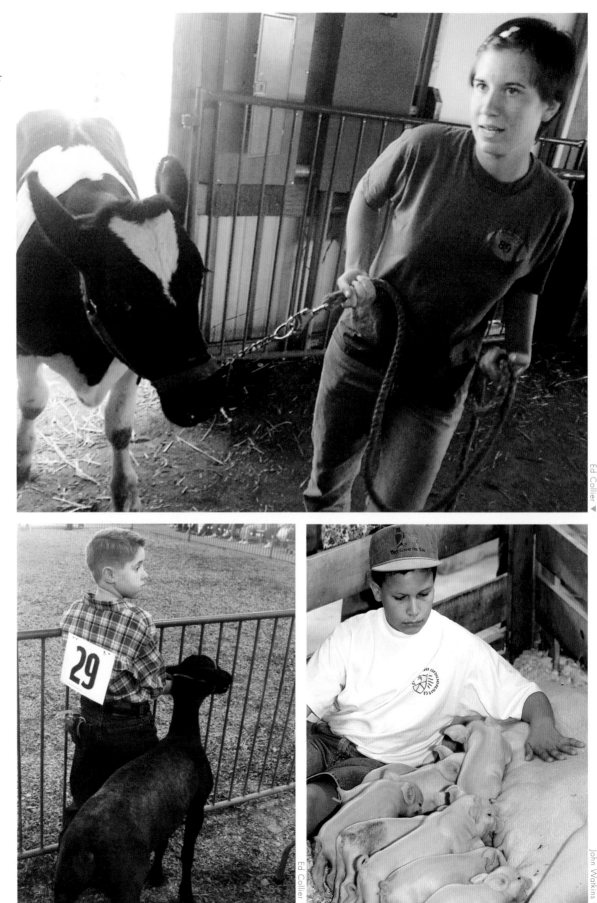

Ed Collier ▼

Ed Collier ▼

John Watkins ▼

Oregionality

The annual 4-H Agricultural Fun Fair, sponsored by the Purdue Cooperative Extension Service, introduces students from Blessed Sacrament School in Gary (top) to the pleasures of animal husbandry. Fun is the watchword, but horsing around was risky for Rebecca Boznak during an equestrian contest at the fair.

O r e g i o n a l i t y

The road less traveled: country roads in the region offer up pastoral scenes and leave each passerby with a sense of peace.

▼ Laura Nagai

▼ Ali Ido

Oregionality

▼ Deborah Mosca

E questrians compete for blue ribbons at the fair. Contest day is the culmination of months of hard work for 4-H members. A man enjoys a moment away from the merry mayhem at the Lake County Fair (facing page).

Hearts & Minds

Therese Horn

▼ Therese Horn

Music director Kirk Muspratt (facing page) conducts the Northwest Indiana Symphony Orchestra, established in 1940 and beloved by serious music lovers in the region and beyond. Griffith students (above) perform in a spring concert.

If music be the food of love, as Shakespeare opined, we're absolutely smitten. Pictured: contestants wait their turn to play at the Indiana State School Music Association regional competition (top); violins wait their turn to be selected by a music student (bottom); the Northwest Indiana Symphony Orchestra performs at Star Plaza Theatre (facing page).

Oregionality

For many students in the region, music mastery is a highlight of their high school careers. The Whiting High School band plays at a football game (top) and proves some guys have prowess both on the field and on the sidelines. Rick Davis of Lake Central High School (bottom left) toots his own horn; the Valparaiso High School band (bottom right) plays in the city's annual Popcorn Festival parade.

Oregionality

▼ Tamara Bell

Recognized statewide for superior achievement, the Valparaiso High School Chamber Orchestra violin section makes the strings sing.

The Star Plaza Theatre in Merrillville is the venue for the Northwest Indiana Symphony Orchestra as well as national tours by theatre companies and musicians.

Oregionality

Roy Ferrer

Roy Ferrer

John Watkins

John Watkins

From blues to rock to country, Star Plaza Theatre has the hottest tickets in the region.

B.B. King, Ringo Starr, Tim McGraw, and Donna Summer have all played the Star Plaza stage.

Dancers with the LaPorte Little Theatre's Canterbury Troupe create magic with movement and color.

▼ Melisa Goh

C rown Point ballerinas check their make-up before tip-toe-ing on stage for a production of Sleeping Beauty.

Chinese artists (top) perform a traditional dance during Purdue University Calumet's International Night. Ballet Folklorico (bottom), a group of 26 boys and girls who perform Mexican dances, rehearses at Central High School in East Chicago.

Dennis Hodges

Natalie Battaglia

Oregionality

A dancer with Gary's Alyo Children's Dance Theatre (top) wows audiences during Black History Month celebrations at the Genesis Convention Center. Few pass up the opportunity to take in the Northwest Indiana Ballet Theatre's annual production of The Nutcracker (bottom).

▼ Natalie Battaglia

▼ Tasos Katopodis

The Center for Visual and
Performing Arts in Munster is
a cultural treasure. Actors guild
performers and regional thespians present an annual program of top-notch
productions. Recent offerings have
included My Fair Lady (top) and
Hansel and Gretel (bottom left).
Players at the Family Christian Center
in Munster get into the act with a performance of Scrooge (bottom right).

Larry A. Brechner

Larry A. Brechner

Jon L. Hendricks

Oregionality

ohn Payonk plays the lead character in a production of Finian's
Rainbow at the Center for Visual
and Performing Arts.

There's always something exciting on the program when it comes to northwest Indiana theatre. A chorus line struts to "Hey, Big Spender" at the Center for Visual and Performing Arts (top); a traveling company presents the time-honored musical Brigadoon (center); the Main Square Players perform in Joseph and the Amazing Technicolor Dreamcoat (bottom).

Energy and creativity are hall-marks of performances by young people in the region. Students from Emerson School for the Visual and Performing Arts in Gary learn practice makes perfect; an "Up With People" production (bottom) invigorates students at Valparaiso University.

Northern Indiana Arts Association

Ed Collier

Northern Indiana Arts Association

John G. Blanc Center for the Arts

Museums keep history and art at the forefront. The skeleton of a mastodon (facing page), discovered in a farmer's field in Porter County, was reconstructed and put on display at the Jailhouse Museum in Valparaiso. Permanent collections and traveling exhibits delight art aficionados at the William J. Bachman Gallery at the Center for Visual and Performing Arts in Munster (left), the Brauer Museum of Art at Valparaiso University (top right), and at the John G. Blank Center for the Arts in Michigan City (bottom right).

Oregionality

John Watkins

Gregg Gearhart

Tracy Albano

Portraits in paint: a section of a mural in downtown Hammond (facing page); a performer in Crown Point dots all the eyes (top left); a Salvador Dali painting (top right) is hung at the Brauer Museum; Mike Chelich (bottom), chosen to paint the official portrait of Indiana Governor Frank O'Bannon, focuses on brushwork in his Hammond studio.

A major attraction in the region, Griffith's Art in the Park (top, facing page) show and sale draws some of the midwest's most accomplished artists. Sculptures by Portage artist Bob Witt (center) bring art and viewer eye to eye at the Chesterton Arts and Crafts Fair. An Indian Arts Expo in Hammond (bottom) featured Cherokee drawings on drums and blankets.

Kirk John Mitchell ▼▼

Michael Gard ▼

Melisa Goh

KNOWLEDGE IS POWER

A frieze above the entry of a former library in Gary proclaims "knowledge is power." The art deco building on 5th Avenue will soon be renovated for office space.

Tracy Albano

Viktor Pejic

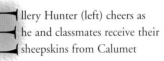 llery Hunter (left) cheers as he and classmates receive their sheepskins from Calumet College in Whiting. Smiling seniors are thumbs up about graduation ceremonies at Chesterton High School (right).

Aldino Gallo ▼

John Luke ▼

Aldino Gallo ▼

Elementary students on the move in Merrillville (top); Washington Township second graders enjoy a field trip to County Line Orchard (bottom).

Jon L. Hendricks

Zbigniew Bzdak

Zbigniew Bzdak

Reading, writing, and arithmetic may be at the top of the list, but the region's youngsters learn other lessons, too, like when to stop (left), how to imitate a face in the school yearbook (top right), and how to stay safe (bottom right).

Youngsters definitely "get spacey" at the Challenger Space Center in Hammond. The NASA-inspired center teaches science in a creative, hands-on environment.

Jon L. Hendricks ▼

Diane Sprehe ▼

Jon L. Hendricks ▼

Oregionality

Learning's twice as nice when there's some fun: Porter Lakes Elementary students wear costumes for a Mercer Mayer parade (top); Portage first grader Kaitlin Winowitch (bottom left) thinks the Cat in the Hat is a hit; preschoolers get physical at Gymboree in Dyer (bottom right).

▼ Michael Gard

▼ Michael Gard

▼ Jon L. Hendricks

Zbigniew Bzdak

Bishop Dale Melczek of the Catholic Diocese of Gary goes one on one with Ashley Ubik of St. John the Baptist School in Whiting. Melczek happily accepts a basketball during a "symbolic gifts" mass where students offered up crayons, dolls, skates, and other gifts.

Gregg Gearhart

Judy Smith

Melisa Goh

Brett Reierson

Northwest Indiana students are top performers in the state, benefiting from investments in talented teachers, cutting edge equipment, and enhanced environments. Students in Gary perform liquid density experiments (top left); high schoolers at LaLumiere School in LaPorte take a walk around the idyllic campus (top right); preschoolers at the Chinese School in Munster rehearse for a Chinese New Year's celebration (bottom left); Lowell High School student Rosa Salazar (bottom right) does homework with a colorful mural as backdrop.

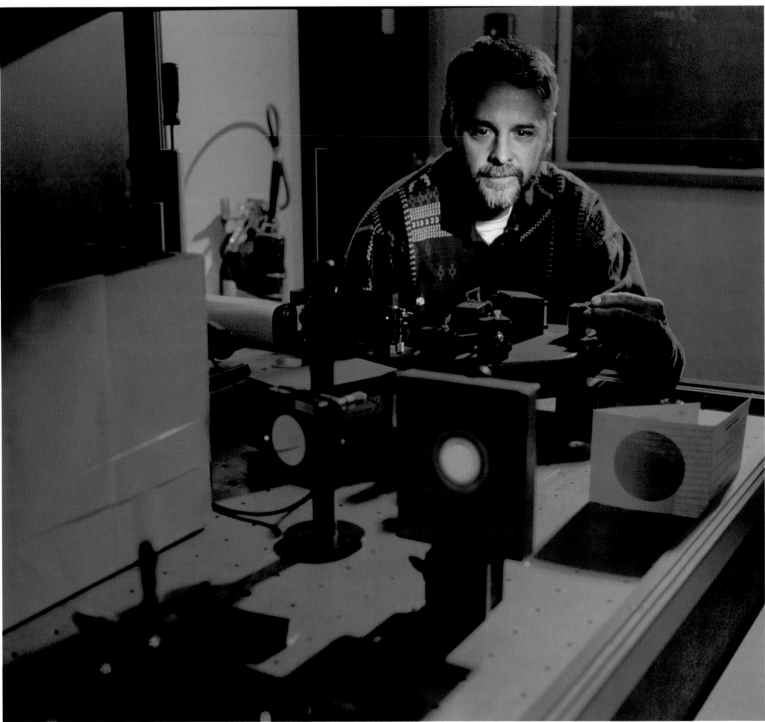

Professors at northwest Indiana colleges and universities are helping train young minds for careers in the information age.

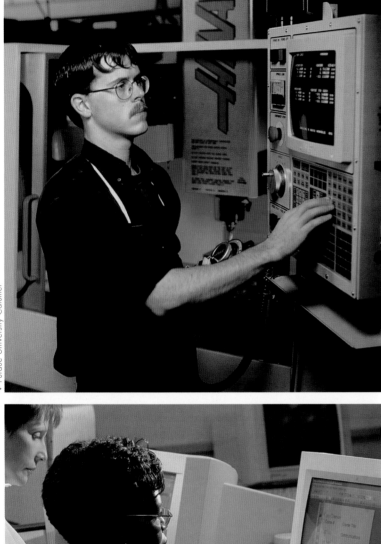

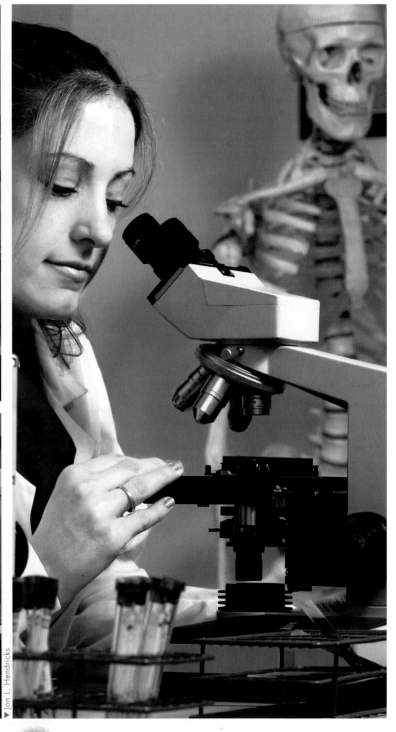

Schools of higher learning in the region include Calumet College, Indiana University Northwest, Ivy Tech State College, Purdue University Calumet (top left), and Valparaiso University, as well as business and technical schools such as Commonwealth Business College, Davenport University, and Sawyer College (bottom left, right).

Aside from academics, college is a time for developing a sense of self and honing social skills. Students at Indiana University Northwest (top, bottom right) and Hyles-Anderson College (bottom left) enjoy respite from the rigors of the classroom.

Indiana University Northwest ▼

Jon L. Hendricks ▼

Indiana University Northwest ▼

sculpture of praying hands at Graceland Cemetery, across a highway and visible from the Valparaiso University campus, is a daily reminder of the value of time.

Celebrating & Remembering

Natlaie Bataglia

Natlaie Bataglia

Natlaie Bataglia

Fireworks fill the sky with starbursts at Hidden Lake in Merrillville (facing page). All-American spirit is on display at Cedar Lake's Fourth of July celebration (top); the music is sweet and so is the cotton candy at Gary's Gospel Fest (bottom left); man's best friend gets into the act at the Whiting Fourth of July parade (bottom right).

Heartland America survives in small town celebrations in the region: Lowell gets fired up for Labor Day (top); Mr. Pierogi is a hot dish at Whiting's annual Pierogi Fest (bottom left); girls dolled up to look like Dorothy know they're not in Kansas, but at Chesterton's popular Oz Fest (bottom right).

Oregionality

Ed Collier

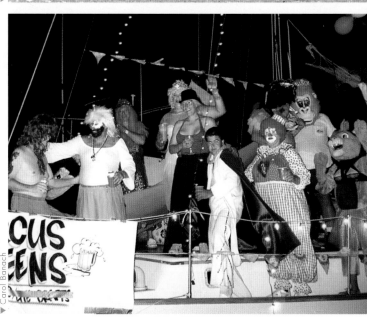

Carol Banach

Kirk John Mitchell

Hear no evil: Katelyn Spencer, Alyss Zimmerman, and Mackenzie Dykes (top, l to r) cover their ears during Civil War re-enactment musket fire at Valparaiso's Popcorn Festival parade, while Caroline Dykes decides to just holler. Clowns have a nose for fun at community festivals in Whiting (bottom left) and Chesterton (bottom right).

A swirl of light on a summer night. County fairs in northwest Indiana are extravaganzas of old-fashioned fun with busy 4-H barns, mesmerizing midways, and grandstand acts that offer rock-and-roll one night and rodeo the next.

The Lake County Fair is the oldest fair in northwest Indiana. An aerial view shows the fair laid out around a lake (top); there are smiles for miles every minute of the fair's 10-day run.

Oregionality

Zbigniew Bzdak

Zbigniew Bzdak

Kirk John Mitchell

Zbigniew Bzdak

Munster's Winter Magic Festival lures some of the nation's top talents in ice carving (top). In Kouts, kiddies take a break from pigging out at Pork Fest to spin their wheels (bottom left). Actor Clarence Swenson, who played a Munchkin in The Wizard of Oz, and his wife Myra (bottom right) are honored guests at Chesterton's Oz Fest.

A smorgasbord of music is
served up with style at festivals and fairs. The region was
settled by a variety of ethnic groups
who add distinctive sounds to the mix.
In addition to rock, blues, gospel, and
folk, residents are accustomed to hearing Peruvian pipes, Mariachi music,
the Serbian tamboritza, Greek dances—
and even the occasional accordian.

Natalie Battaglia ▼

Michael Gard ▲

Oregionality

Brett Reierson

Kirk John Mitchell

Ed Collier

Michael Gard

These feet are made for dancing, and that's just what they'll do. Traditional dances are performed at ethnic celebrations throughout northwest Indiana.

Oregionality

The way to a festival-goer's heart is through the tummy. Whether it's pierogi or baklava, or traditional favorites like ice cream and cotton candy, each fest is ultimately judged by the food.

Kirk John Mitchell

Tasos Katopodis

Jon L. Hendricks

Jon L. Hendricks

A long the shores of Lake Michigan, in the land of the dunes, what festival would be complete without a sand art booth? Ignacio Urbina (facing page top) waves the flag of his ancestral home during the Mexican Day parade in East Chicago. Attractions include equestrians in sombreros and señoras in traditional garb.

Oregionality

▼ Natalie Bataglia

▼ Natalie Bataglia

▼ Tom Hocker

D aytime balloon launches
and evening glows sponsored
by the Kiwanis Club have
become must-see events during
Valparaiso's Popcorn Festival.

Carol Duncan ▼

Wayne Wodrich ▼

Oregionality

A lone balloonist casts a reflection on Flint Lake in Valparaiso.

Ed Collier ▶

Kirk John Mitchell ▶

Jon L. Hendricks ▶

A sprawling 30-foot Santa is prepared to stand in downtown Valparaiso (top). The giant Santa Claus makes his appearance every December. Holiday lights make a Hammond home magical (bottom left). Southlake Mall is the place for holiday shopping—and for exacting a promise from good ole St. Nick (bottom right).

Oregionality

The holidays are ablaze with light in northwest Indiana. Michigan City (top left) and Merrillville (bottom) both sponsor a Festival of Lights. Crown Point citizens gather around a bonfire of burning Christmas trees during the city's Twelfth Night Celebration.

Martin Luther King, Jr. is remembered with a morning candlelight vigil in Hammond. The annual vigil includes a march from City Hall to Zion Baptist Church.

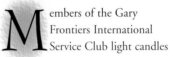

Members of the Gary Frontiers International Service Club light candles during award ceremonies at its annual Martin Luther King, Jr. breakfast at the Genesis Center.

Tears for a Clown: when Donald "Ski the Clown" Berkoski of Valparaiso died in January, 2001, mourners respected his wish to clown around to the end. Berkoski, beloved by many, clowned free of charge for thousands at nursing homes, hospitals, and prisons. Friends Dolli, LuLaBell, and Flossie (left) shed tears at the funeral; pallbearers don clown noses (facing page) to carry Berkoski to his final resting place.

NOTICE!

DO NOT PAY
ANY ATTENTION TO
THIS SIGN

Dianne Sprehe ▼

Kirk John Mitchell ▼

Kirk John Mitchell ▼

Honor guard cadets bow their heads (top) during a Memorial Day observance in Crown Point (bottom).

Oregionality

Buckley Homestead in Lowell is the site of a once-a-year re-enactment of a World War II battle (top, bottom right). Vintage aircraft shows (bottom left) keep memories of the era alive.

Keith Mitchell of Griffith (top), dressed in camouflage, pays his respects at a Veterans Day ceremony.

Zbigniew Bzdak

Tamara Bell

Oregionality

tars and stripes forever: people of all ages, races, and creeds come together to honor neighbors like Sam George (bottom), a WWII veteran who survived the Battle of the Bulge.

ay to remember: the stunning stained glass of Valparaiso University's Chapel of the Resurrection provides a breathtaking backdrop for the exchange of vows.

After the wedding, one couple says, "I love you, Deere" (facing page, top right). Weddings can make some couples hungry to begin the connubial voyage—others choose a hot dog or jet ski ride on the lake.

Jesse Josleyn

Oregionality

▼ John Luke

▼ Sam Riche

▼ John Luke

I t was sportswriter Grantland Rice who penned the famous words: "For when the One Great Scorer comes, to write against your name, He marks—not that you won or lost—but how you played the game." Through rims on the backs of barns, over garage doors, atop portable poles, in schoolyards, and at gyms, hope springs eternal in young hearts that this dunk, this bankshot, this swoosh will prove we played with the best.

Natalie Bataglia ▼

Brett Reierson ▼

John Watkins ▼

Gregg Gearhart ▼

U p, up, and away: high school hoopsters in the region are known for fighting it out to the last. Julie Mandon of Hobart and Danielle Tovsen of Crown Point (top left) vie for a rebound; Patrick Danley (#50) of West Side (top right) struggles to get a shot off; Andrean High School's Andy Gurnak (bottom left) goes for the lay-up; Rameses Montgomery of Merrillville contests Chesterton's Zack Wellsand for the ball (bottom right).

I n northwest Indiana, some say basketball isn't an important thing—it's everything. Fans in the region have been spoiled, perhaps, by great players and special moments.

Bryce Drew (top right) holds Valparaiso University's scoring record and is remembered for the shot he sunk that won his team a spot in the NCAA's 1998 Sweet Sixteen roster.

After a stint with the Houston Rockets, Drew was signed by the Chicago Bulls. Basketball isn't just for the guys, as the Lady Crusaders of Valparaiso University (bottom right)

make clear. Also this page: Damean Clinton of Crown Point dribbles past LaPorte's Jeff Ballard (top left); Gary Steelheads player Ryan Blackwell (bottom left) works to outwit a defender.

Ellen Skye ▼

A mass of muscle and hustle moves through the water as contestants compete in Leon's Triathlon at Wolf Lake in Hammond.

Runners start lining up at six in the morning for Valparaiso's annual Popcorn Panic, a 5K race held in conjunction with the city's Popcorn Festival. Now a nationally known race, it attracts distance runners from throughout the midwest. In 2000, more than 900 runners completed the course.

There are folks in the region who prefer tackle in their sport—as in fishing, not football. The more experienced teach those new to angling, and so the tradition continues whether in Hobart (top), Valparaiso (bottom left), or Michigan City (bottom right).

Oregionality

While some enthusiasts like to fish in shirtsleeves, others opt for a "Nanook of the North" look suitable for long sits luring fish from deep below the ice.

Fine courses and fierce competitors can always be found in the region. Aberdeen's 18-hole course and club in Valparaiso (top) are a golfer's dream. Highland's Wicker Park is known for great golf and stunning scenery from summer through fall.

Oregionality

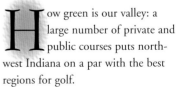

ow green is our valley: a large number of private and public courses puts northwest Indiana on a par with the best regions for golf.

John Luke

At Four Seasons Stables in Crown Point, youngsters become proficient with the ponies, willingly trading blue jeans for jodhpurs.

Brett Reierson

Kate Hodson of Hebron handles a jump with flair atop her horse Copper. Youth in the region learn horsemanship on family farms, at area stables, or by participating in a 4-H club.

Maybe they're too young to dive or dunk, but not to dream. Organized sports leagues and clinics keep kids busy year-round mastering basketball, baseball, football, soccer, and other team sports.

Kim Frizzell ▼

Robert Kauffman ▼

John Watkins ▼

Melisa Goh ▼

Oregionality

Did you say open your mouth and close your eyes, or was it the other way around? It makes no difference to Katie Anderson, who gets a leg up on the competition at a Crown Point clinic. The camp, run by Crown Point High School soccer coach Mike Malaski, has seen attendance grow from 40 kids in 1995 to more than 200.

The boys of summer have a whack at the all-American sport of baseball at fields in Merrillville (top), Schererville (bottom), and East Chicago (facing page).

Ellen Skye ▼

Paul "Maggie" Magurany ▼

Oregionality

▼ Erin Tryon

A ndrean High School goalie
Brianne Sawa (top) watches
the ball roll back into play
after a save. Historically known for
its basketball prowess, the region is
turning out more and more top soccer
teams. Running has experienced a
resurgence in recent years, too.
Cross-country competitors (bottom)
at a sectional meet start the course at
Sunset Hill in Valparaiso.

John Watkins ▲

Michael Gard ▲

O r e g i o n a l i t y

W hose feet are whose? Portage High School's Freddy Joseph wrestles Valparaiso High School's Scott Hinkle.

Northwest Indiana is charged up by fall football and delights in the ups and downs of rival teams. Starting with Pop Warner Football and continuing through high school, many youngsters rack up ten years experience in the game.

The Portage Indians and Valparaiso Vikings (facing page) represent one of the longstanding rivalries in the region. Traffic jams on Friday nights in the fall are not uncommon as fans come in droves to watch the action.

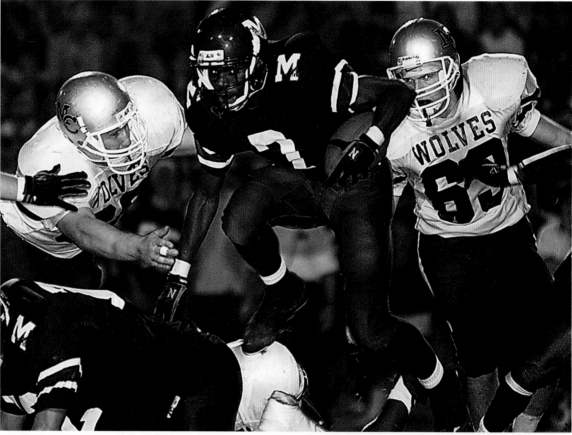

Oregionality

Sam Riche ▾

Zbigniew Bzdak ▾

Everyone in northwest Indiana has a sport—and a distinctive style. Kyle Kwasny of Lake Central High School (left) grimaces through a pole vault. Jeff Lee of Munser (right) shows he's got what it takes to win in the water.

Oregionality

Sam Riche

Natalie Bataglia

The number and quality of sports programs for girls now rival those for boys. Gymnast Brittany Laidlaw of Chesterton High School (left) performs her floor routine; Alexis Glover of Lew Wallace High School (right) competes in the high hurdles.

ave we got fans, or what? Lake Central die-hards (top) fly their colors at a football game, while Chesterton fans go bare-back to root for their favorites. Cheerleaders get a workout whipping the crowds into the spirit, or keeping up with them. The touted Boone Grove squad (bottom) competes annually in the Midwest Cheer and Dance Competition.

Jehan Abuzer ▼

Cheryl Milchak ▼

Sheryl Sue Sidwell ▼

Oregionality

High school athletes routinely prove bodies can defy gravity, exhaustion, or fear to strike poses of stunning beauty and exquisite form.

STATE CHAMPIONS
1. 91. 92. 94. 9

David Wolfe of Chesterton does more than spin his wheels as lead cyclist in the 1999 Outback Trail Mountain Bike Challenge in Portage. Wolfe was defending his 1998 win in the grueling race. What goes up must come down, but not before this skateboarder (facing page) keeps his rendezvous with the clouds.

O r e g i o n a l i t y

S pecial Olympics and wheel-
chair basketball competitions
give everyone an opportunity
to excel. The smiles on the faces of
these athletes are matched by grins just
as broad in the bleachers.

Oregionality

Jon L. Hendricks

I n the end, it's not whether you win or lose, but how you play the game. As the sun sets, a golfer at Lost Marsh in Hammond takes one last swing before calling it a day.

If We Build It

Kirk John Mitchell

Kirk John Mitchell

John Luke

I f we build it, they will come. And come they have, since 1906 when U.S. Steel opened the doors to what was then considered an industrial world wonder. The business of building in northwest Indiana had begun.

Facing page: Ticor Title building in Michigan City; downtown sculpture in Hammond (top); Southlake Mall (bottom left); teen center, Merrillville (bottom right).

O r e g i o n a l i t y

Precision Aerial Photo

Kirk John Mitchell

Magnificent turn of the 20th century courthouses stand as landmarks in the region. Renovated and reigning in downtown districts, the Lake County Courthouse (top) in Crown Point is now home to offices and quaint shops. The LaPorte County Courthouse in LaPorte (bottom) and Porter County Courthouse (facing page) still house courtrooms and judicial offices.

Many streetscapes in the region retain their historic detail and charm, offering a glimpse of the past in the midst of modern commerce.

Oregionality

Kirk John Mitchell

Old and new join in harmony in downtown Hammond (top); vintage public clocks still tick in Michigan City (bottom left) and Hobart (bottom right).

Frank Lloyd Wright ventured from Chicago to work for clients in the region, designing several homes that history buffs hope will soon be restored to their full glory. Christopher Meyers (right) discovered two Wright prairie style buildings in Gary (top and center) and is working to see them rehabilitated. In Ogden Dunes, residents are rightly proud of Wright's design from his Usonian period.

KNIGHTS · OF · COLUMBUS
COUNCIL · 1347

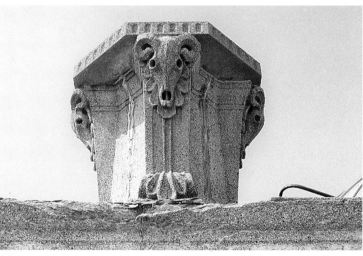

Gary grew from a population of zero in 1900 to nearly 20,000 in a mere decade. Along with residents came religious, commercial, and civic organizations that built with a flourish. The Knights of Columbus Building (top) and Gary's Union Station (bottom right) still stand. Building ornamentation often included columns, statuary, and urns like one from Gary's City Hall (bottom left) that had to be removed due to deterioration.

B uildings of shimmering glass and circular shape herald a new era in northwest Indiana architecture. The Twin Towers office building in Merrillville is recognizable to residents region-wide.

What goes around delights visitors to the Lake County Convention & Visitors Bureau in Hammond (facing page top) and Michigan City Zoo (facing page bottom).

Oregionality

Robert Kauffman ▼

Gregg Gearhart ▶

Kirk John Mitchell ▶

Kirk John Mitchell ▶

Impressive spaces in the region are old and new, large and small. The club house at Sand Creek in Chesterton (top) combines classic detail with cutting edge video conferencing and other technologies. Also pictured: Meyer's Castle in Dyer (bottom left) is now used for receptions and banquets; a circular staircase in a Chesterton residence (bottom right) is both practical and dramatic.

Recent housing developments, like Shorewood in Valparaiso (top), Briar Ridge in Schererville (bottom left), and Sand Creek in Chesterton (bottom right) have provided homes for new residents of the region.

At Tyron Farm in Michigan City, the ecology-conscious developer has used a former farm to construct new housing while preserving most of the fields, meadows, and woods for resident use.

Oregionality

Building in the region goes hand in hand with wise stewardship of resources. Whether learning to appreciate the beauty of a corn field (top) or cleaning prairie parcels, citizens in northwest Indiana lend a hand to care for the land.

▼ Ellen Skye

▼ Robin Perez

▼ Dianne Sprehe

The Calumet River, as well as many other creeks and waterways, necessitated the building of bridges throughout the region, including these in Hammond (facing page), Hobart (top), Gary (bottom left), and at Deep River County Park (bottom right).

Some of the oldest buildings in northwest Indiana have been lovingly preserved and meticulously safeguarded, like the Bailly Homestead in Porter where fur traders in the 1800s set up camp. Now an historic site in the Indiana Dunes National Lakeshore, Bailly Homestead is the venue for annual re-enactments of pioneer life, cooking, and crafts.

Early settlers built with logs, planks, or bricks, but they all created structures that could stand the test of time. Regular stops for visitors to the region include the 1910 farm and schoolhouse at Buckley Homestead (facing page, top left) and Halstead House (facing page, bottom left), both in Lowell, and the round barn (facing page, top right) and early log cabin (facing page, bottom right), both in LaPorte.

Cherie Thyberg

Oregionality

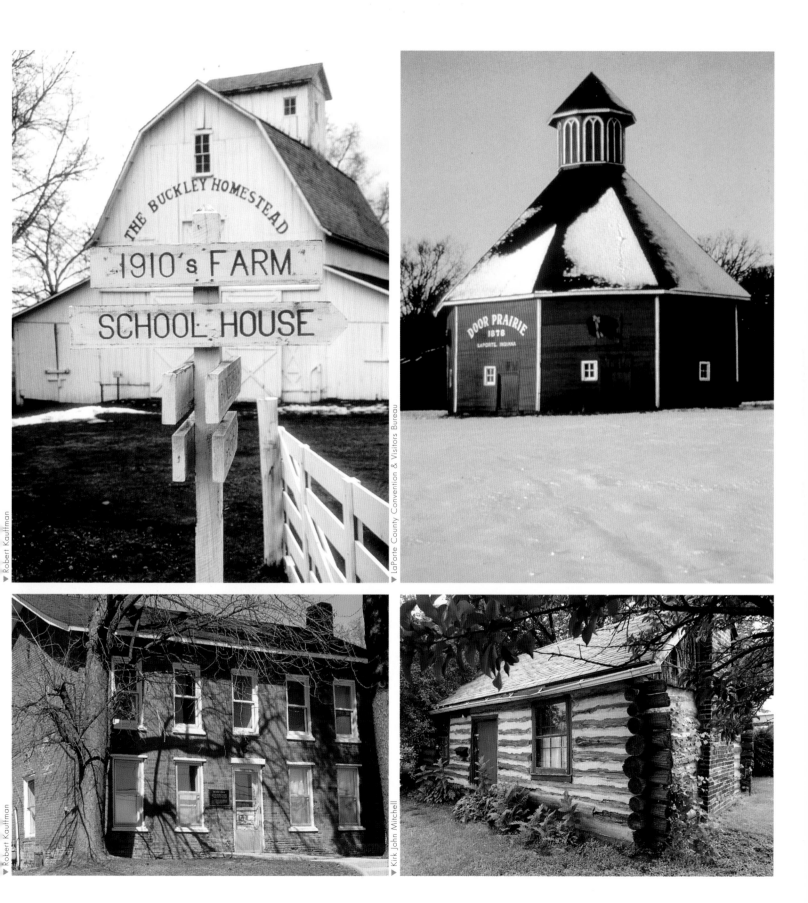

Robert Kauffman

LaPorte County Convention & Visitors Bureau

Robert Kauffman

Kirk John Mitchell

Fur trading and farming were the first occupations in the region. That legacy has left something for future generations to enjoy: rustic maple sugar shacks and historic gristmills.

Oregionality

Tourists find help for over-heating in summer at the region's two water parks: Splash Down Dunes in Porter (top) and Deep River Water Park (bottom and facing page).

▼ Kirk John Mitchell

▼ John Luke

Sam Riche ▸

Sam Riche ▸

I n the 1950s, outdoor drive-in movie theaters sprang up like weeds in an abandoned farm field. The region is lucky it can still enjoy the 49'er in Valparaiso, a holdout against changing tastes that put most of the nation's drive-ins in the path of bulldozers.

Oregionality

Kirk John Mitchell

Jon L. Hendricks

T he built environment isn't limited to offices and stores, but takes in the mythical and magical. Pictured: Hollywood Park in Valparaiso (top); Schererville Golf Center arcade (bottom) in Schererville.

John Niemann ▼

KirkJohn Mitchell ▼

Oregionality

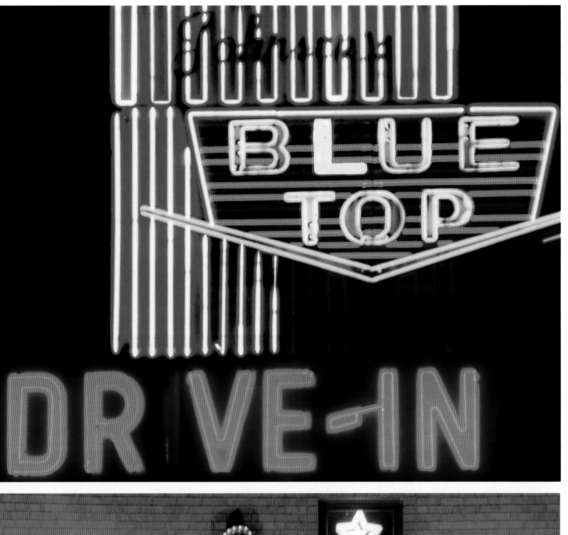

Bright lights at night shine at the Porter County Fair (facing page top), John Dillinger Museum at the Lake County Convention & Visitors Bureau in Hammond (facing page bottom), Blue Top Drive-In in Highland (top), and a Porter County residence all decked out for a southwest-style Christmas (bottom).

Life's a gamble: lakefront gaming provides entertainment for visitors from throughout the midwest.

Oregionality

Kirk John Mitchell

Debbie Steffert

Jon L. Hendricks

Shop 'til you drop: Michigan City's Lighthouse Place offers outlet shopping at its best (top); at the holidays, Southlake Mall in Merrillville (bottom right) is not only Indiana's biggest, but also one of the busiest malls in the region.

An aerial view (following page) taken near I-65 and U.S. 30 in Lake County, with Lake Michigan visible in the background, shows the built environment in the heart of the region saves room for family farms, parks, and open space.

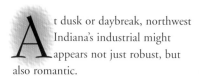t dusk or daybreak, northwest Indiana's industrial might appears not just robust, but also romantic.

Kirk John Mitchell ▼

Gary R. Clark ▼

Oregionality

▼ Michelle Kiem

The region's hearty founders built homes and buildings of wood and brick. Today's equally energetic builders create the houses of commerce from steel and concrete. As always, form follows function.

Michelle Kiem ▼

Oregionality

▼ Tom Hocker

▼ Tom Hocker

Oregionality

▼ Tom Hocker

▼ Kirk John Mitchell

▼ Tom Hocker

▼ Zbigniew Bzdak

The left pipe's connected to the … views from the air (left, Inland Steel) or just inches away show the shape and strength of the region's industrial architecture.

All in a Day's Work

John Watkins

Tasos Katopodis

W̲e have our share of butchers, bakers, and candlestick makers, as well as teachers, steelworkers, ministers, waitresses, bricklayers, painters, and poets. When there's a task to tackle, the region's residents get the job done.

Construction workers straddle beams to build homes and offices. The use of tough, long-lasting steel for structural framing has grown in popularity in the region and worldwide.

Kirk John Mitchell ▾

Zbigniew Bzdak ▾

Kirk John Mitchell ▾

Oregionality

At work, sometimes sparks fly: a Conrail welder performs maintenance on a railroad track line in Portage.

orkers often get a real lift from their jobs. A fueler at Gary/Chicago Airport stands atop a jet to fill its 20,000-gallon tank (top) while painters and welders employ stilts or cherry pickers to reach their targets.

Oregionality

Air and water training is routine for the Lake County Sheriff's Department whose rescuers regularly reach new heights.

Tom Sawyer isn't the only one who has made whitewashing seem like fun. A boom in residential construction in northwest Indiana throughout the 1990s kept painters in overalls overtime.

John Luke ▼

Geoff Black ▼

Kirk John Mitchell ▼

Oregionality

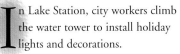

In Lake Station, city workers climb the water tower to install holiday lights and decorations.

For the past century, a large share of the work of northwest Indiana has been steel. Though the economy is today much more diversified, steel production in the region still dwarfs other world smelting centers.

O ur region produces quantities of steel but it's the quality that counts. A journeyman inspects his work at a steel processing plant.

Oregionality

The men and women who toil in the region's steel and industrial plants may look small relative to the equipment they operate, but their output is tremendous.

Oregionality

ay "coils" in northwest Indiana (facing page) and no one will imagine toasters or hair curlers. In this region, coil means steel.

At LTV Steel, employees process millions of tons of rolled and pickled steel for domestic use and global export.

Change is part of life—and work. Engineer Karla Sneed (top left) has seen Amoco's Whiting refinery become part of the international BP (British Petroleum) network.

For Laurie Clark (top right) and others, change has brought new skills and expanded job opportunities. The landscape, too, changes to accommodate our work. From expansion at Indiana's

International Port to new highway and bridge construction (bottom), the region has invested in the infrastructure of economic prosperity.

Oregionality

Kirk John Mitchell

Technological change has created better connections within the region and fueled global conversation and commerce.

Pictured: Internet technician Tim Huffman of Jorsm Internet checks a computer network card.

Indiana's International Port at Burns Harbor is a major asset and will be a force in the region's future economic successes. The conduit for international shipping via the Great Lakes to the St. Lawrence seaway and a designated foreign trade zone, the port handled 2.5 million tons of cargo in 1995 alone. Its annual statewide economic impact is pegged at $409 million.

▼ Gregg Gearhart

▲ Michelle Kiem

▼ Jon L. Hendricks

Food production is a market-place open to entrepreneur as well as corporation. The region is known for its cornfields and dairy farms, but new generations are carving out niches in everything from candy and honey to hand-packed ice cream.

Gregg Gearhart

Natalie Bataglia

Gregg Gearhart

Jon L. Hendricks

Restaurants have grown in number and sophistication in recent years. New favorites like Cafe L'Amour in LaPorte (left) and Miller Bakery Cafe in Gary (top right) have joined popular veterans like Phil Schmidt's in Whiting (bottom right).

There's nothing like steady work, unless it's safe work, something aided by the region's police, fire, and emergency personnel. Every day is different, as firefighter Todd Konradie discovered when he was called upon to rescue an iguana from a burning store in Lowell. For these workers, climbing the ladder of success is fraught with peril—and real ladders.

John Luke ▼

Oregionality

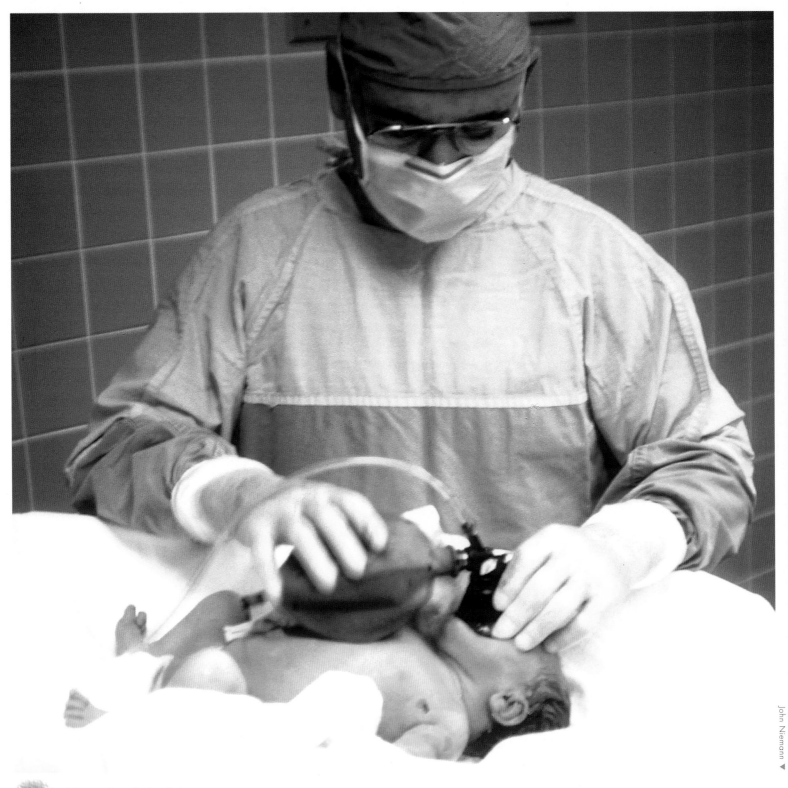

P hysicians and medical technicians of high caliber provide state-of-the-art care to patients from day one.

Kirk John Mitchell

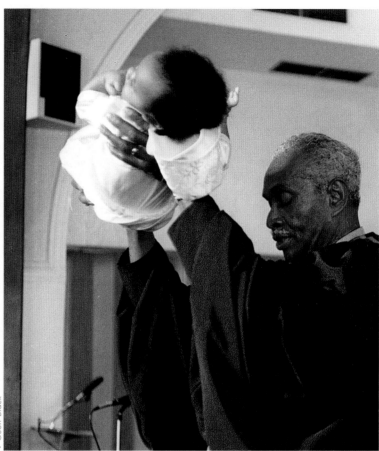

Geoff Black

Melisa Goh

John Watkins

It takes many hands to do much work. Pictured: Calvin Bellamy, CEO of Bank Calumet (top left); Rev. Leo H. Reese, Sr., former assistant pastor of First Baptist Church in Gary (top right); Keviney Woodson, a student at Merrillville Beauty & Barber College (bottom left); and Crown Point police officer Glen Lang.

Teenagers in the region work hard, too, Honing skills for later life, they run the academic gauntlet of the classroom and deftly handle on-the-job challenges.

Pictured: Linda Jonaitis of Pierce Middle School in Merrillville hugs eighth grade essay winner Krista Dora (top) during a celebration of Pierce's designation as a National Blue Ribbon School; some days Nicki Hall needs a break, but most of the time she's all smiles as a McDonald's assistant manager (bottom); teens work at interesting businesses throughout the region, including the Hoosier Bat Company in Valparaiso (facing page).

O r e g i o n a l i t y

C huck Krcilek, owner of Back Road Brewery, has a job many people envy. Krcilek started his beer business in LaPorte in 1996. The microbrewery produces the locally famous Back Road Ale and a host of seasonal beers.

O r e g i o n a l i t y

After a particularly hot day at work, a cold one may just hit the spot.

City & Town Profiles

SAND, STEEL, & SOUL

A LOOK AT SOME OF THE CITIES, TOWNS, AND
ORGANIZATIONS THAT HAVE HELPED BUILD THE REGION
AND MADE THIS BOOK POSSIBLE.

Town of Cedar Lake
City of Crown Point
City of East Chicago
City of Gary
Gary/Chicago Airport
Town of Griffith
City of Hammond
Town of Highland
City of Lake Station
City of LaPorte
Town of Lowell
Town of Merrillville
Schools of Merrillville
Town of Munster
City of Portage
Town of Schererville
Schererville Chamber
Town of St. John
City of Valparaiso
City of Whiting

Cedar Lake is a hidden treasure among northwest Indiana communities. Once a playground of Chicagoans, some quite famous, who vacationed in this tranquil, lakeside community, today Cedar Lake is a relatively young municipality intent on preserving its fascinating past and committed to building a prosperous future. About 10,000

Life in Cedar Lake revolves around the 800-acre lake (top) at its center, the third largest natural lake in Indiana.

Cedar Lake's placid pace and quiet charm earned it a spot as one of *Where to Retire* magazine's top choices for retirees. Amenities include housing in a broad price range, recreational opportunities, and a business community committed to preserving Cedar Lake's best assets.

people call Cedar Lake home, many lured by the 800-acre kidney-shaped lake at its center. Others seek out the small-town, rural atmosphere, which still affords easy access to all of northwest Indiana and is a great place to call home.

For the town's residents, Cedar Lake is just that—home. They relish the neighborly ambience and the friendliness that pervade civic life, and the spirit of mutuality expressed in community events.

Nowhere else in the region is there such a unique blend of people from different socioeconomic classes living together as a community. A $500,000 house on the Cedar Lake shore is balanced by homes in the $70,000 to $90,000 range, making the town an affordable community for just about everyone.

Cedar Lake is a great community. Everyone is very friendly, everybody knows everybody. It's a small-town, family community. The town has a genuine spirit that gives it a distinct personality.

Popular since Potawatomis

Geologists say a melting glacier formed the lake that is the town's namesake. Today Cedar Lake is 2.1 miles long and at its widest point stretches across nine-tenths of a mile. At its deepest, the lake is 16 feet, but averages nine feet. The third largest natural lake in Indiana, Cedar Lake has drawn people to the area since the Potawatomi Indians first discovered its good fishing and bucolic vistas. European hunters also discovered its richness, building a lodge in 1834 near the lake that exists to this day.

By the 1890s, Cedar Lake had become a popular getaway for thousands of people from the Chicago area and elsewhere. The town flourished as a resort with as many as 55 hotels and other attractions that kept people coming back. The winter months were just as busy as local companies worked on the lake, cutting huge slabs of ice to be used by Chicago's meat packing industry. Typical ice-

cutting tools used at the turn of the century have been preserved and are on display at the town's Lake of the Red Cedars Museum.

As people began converting the cottages into year-round homes, the town's tourist image began to fade. Over the years, many of the smaller cottages were torn down and replaced with larger homes. As the area grew and its population stabilized, the need for sanitary sewers became all too evident. But to get federal assistance for the expensive undertaking, Cedar Lake had to incorporate. A local physician, Dr. Robert W. King, and a local mason contractor, Charles L. Kouder Jr., along with others who wanted to better the community, organized a group of residents to get it done, but they met opposition.

In 1965, the courts declared Cedar Lake legally a town, but in 1967 the Indiana Supreme Court declared the town to be non-existent. Not the type of people to give up without a fight, residents again mounted an effort to incorporate later that year. On September 29, 1969, the Indiana Supreme Court upheld the incorporation of October, 1967.

While the lake is one of the town's best assets, its upkeep does require resources. The lake is under the jurisdiction of the state. In earlier times, its water quality suffered due to lack of resources. Town leaders committed to solving the lake's problems created the Cedar Lake Enhancement Association (CLEA) and have been working since 1995 to improve the lake's water quality. Now in progress is a "Pledge to Dredge" campaign that will pool the local, state, and federal funds needed to undertake the multi-million dollar project. CLEA, local leaders, and residents hope the dredging will go a long way toward helping the lake to heal itself. Once its quality improves, there is no doubt that the lake, combined with the community's committed people, will mean only one thing for Cedar Lake: a limitless future.

The Good Life

The lake helps create a quality of life that few communities can match. For nature and recreation lovers, Cedar Lake provides tranquility. The ravines are full of old oak trees and the area teems with wildlife.

Cedar Lake feels rural, but access to everything a person needs is within a 20-minute drive of the town. Because of its proximity to

the Illinois border, the drive to Chicago is just 30 minutes. Cedar Lake's placid lifestyle and convenient location have not been overlooked. Cedar Lake was recently chosen as one of ten great small towns near big cities by the magazine *Where to Retire*.

Several development projects are currently proposed for the community and there is room for additional commercial and industrial expansion. In 1999, planners estimated that less than half of the acreage of the community has been developed to date. Town officials are busy planning the kinds of infrastructure improvements that will attract quality businesses and housing.

Cedar Lake has a lot of growth potential. Land is available for new businesses and opportunities abound for people looking to start new enterprises.

Cedar Lake children attend highly rated schools in the Crown Point and Hanover School Corporations. In both, the focus is on high student achievement. Standardized test scores are some of the best in the state of Indiana.

A Nice Place to Visit; A Nice Place to Live

Cedar Lake's eight parks— including two newly renovated parks, Park of the Red Cedars and Potawatomi Park—delight residents and visitors. The lake and ample parks continue Cedar Lake's tradition as a resort town where

nature is nearby and quiet spaces and places can be easily found. The Town Complex sits along the lakeshore in a peaceful park. One of the newest subdivisions sits across the street from Lake County's very first park, Lemon Lake, a sprawling preserved space with natural beauty affording recreational opportunities. Other local landmarks and amenities include two golf courses, four marinas, the Lake of the Red Cedars Museum, and the Franciscan Friary Grotto.

Many people from out of town visit Cedar Lake during the Summerfest in July when the entire community turns out to celebrate the country's birthday. Residents and visitors alike enjoy the beauty of the sailboat races on Cedar Lake, the most famous of which is the Icebreaker Classic Regatta Race held each May.

For decades, Cedar Lake was a resort town luring visitors from Chicago and elsewhere. Today, residents enjoy the lake year-round for fishing, swimming, boating, and postcard-perfect vistas.

TOWN OF CEDAR LAKE
7408 Constitution Avenue
Cedar Lake, Indiana 46303
(219) 374-7000

THE HISTORIC CITY OF CROWN POINT, INCORPORATED IN 1868, IS A GROWING COMMUNITY OF NEIGHBORHOODS FOCUSED ON A STRONG QUALITY OF LIFE. THE CITY OF 23,000 IS THE SEAT OF GOVERNMENT IN LAKE COUNTY, THE MOST NORTHERN AND WESTERN COUNTY IN THE STATE OF INDIANA, AND IS A 45-MINUTE DRIVE FROM DOWNTOWN CHICAGO. AT THE HEART OF THE

city is the Old County Courthouse, gracing the center of a busy downtown square. The restored Romanesque and Georgian structure was built in 1878 and is listed on the National Register of Historic Places. It now houses quaint retail shops and the Lake County Historical Museum.

Romances and Rogues

The history of the city includes romances and rogues. From 1915 to 1940 the city was well known as a "marriage mill," and more than 175,000 couples flocked to the courthouse in those years to be wed. Couples could be married 24 hours a day, seven days a week. Before a new blood test law was passed in 1940, many tied the knot in Crown Point, including Rudolph Valentino, Ronald Reagan and Jane Wyman, Tom Mix, Red Grange, Muhammed Ali, and two of the Mills Brothers.

The Lake County jail building, still standing across from the Old Courthouse, was the scene of the escape of the notorious John Dillinger in March, 1934. Dillinger took hostages who were later released in Illinois. In July of that year, Dillinger was shot and killed by FBI agents outside the Biograph Theater in Chicago.

Crown Point is known as the birthplace of Indiana's first major car race—the Cobe Cup—which was the forerunner of the Indianapolis 500. The first 25-mile race was held in 1909 and was won by Louis Chevrolet. Now, the Cobe Cup Cruise of vintage cars

Crown Point's quaint downtown (center), built around the historic Lake County Courthouse, is a destination for residents from throughout the region.

Dubbed the "Grand Old Lady," (bottom right) the restored 1878 courthouse is listed on the National Register of Historic Places and houses the Lake County Historical Museum.

Crown Point's historic Crown Theatre on the square offers families fun-filled evenings and bargain prices on hit movies.

follows the same course each summer. In addition to the cruise, the Crown Point Chamber of Commerce and its Downtown Business Merchants Association sponsor other community spirit events, including the annual Corn Roast, Fourth of July Parade, Christmas on the Square, Bastille Days Festival, and Festival Days.

In August of each year, tens of thousands of visitors flock to the city for the annual Lake County Fair, the largest county fair in the state and second only in size to the annual State Fair.

Planned Growth

The city's square is flanked by tree-lined streets of vintage Queen Anne and Victorian homes. With about 16,000 trees located in city parkways, the city has qualified as a Tree City. More than 300 acres of land in 17 parks provide recreation for the city's residents. The city's municipal swimming pool is nestled in Sauerman Woods Park, cradled by more than 25 acres of natural woods. An 80-acre sportsplex features softball, baseball, and soccer fields, as well as an aggressive skate park.

Major businesses in the city include the Lake County Government Complex, which employs 2000, St. Anthony Medical Center, the Crown Point School Corp., and Dawn Foods, a food manufacturer.

Growth of Crown Point's business district has begun to expand toward an Interstate Development Zone. The city annexed six square miles to include the Interstate 65 and State Road 231 interchange, the nearest undeveloped interchange

to metropolitan Chicago. It will be home to regional, national, and international companies.

Investment in infrastructure has included a $6 million Lake Michigan water conversion and projects to deliver sewer and water services to the development zone.

Ground was broken in 2000 for a new $70 million, 465,000 square foot high school to serve 2,600 students. Students in the northern part of the city attend Merrillville School Corp. schools.

"Crown Point is truly a friendly, family-oriented kind of place," says Mayor James D. Metros, who began his third term as mayor in 2000. "We hope Crown Point can be an example of how to balance growth with a respect for history and inevitable change with a focus on how to serve this community."

Crown Point residents love a parade (top left). Annual community celebrations include one of the state's largest Fourth of July events, an annual outdoor Corn Roast, and the week-long Crown Point Festival Days.

Stately Queen Anne and Victorian homes (top right) give Crown Point character. Many of the homes are opened to visitors during historic house tours each year. The city is also home to 17 parks, including Jerry Ross Park (bottom), named for the famed astronaut and Crown Point native.

James D. Metros (center), who began his third term as mayor in 2000, believes Crown Point can grow while retaining its friendly, family-oriented atmosphere.

CITY OF CROWN POINT
**101 North East Street
Crown Point, Indiana 46307
(219) 662-3240
www.cityofcrownpoint.org**

E AST CHICAGO IS A CITY ON THE RISE. LIKE MANY URBAN CENTERS THAT SUFFERED FROM THE FLIGHT TO THE SUBURBS IN THE SIXTIES, EAST CHICAGO IS TODAY TAPPING INTO ITS STRENGTHS. A CITY OF ETHNIC DIVERSITY, INDUSTRY, AND HISTORY, IT IS THE PLACE MANY OF NORTHWEST INDIANA'S SUCCESSFUL CITIZENS CALLED HOME FOR MORE THAN FOUR GENERATIONS.

CITY OF EAST CHICAGO

The City of East Chicago displays its rich mix of culture when its Hispanic dance troupe (top) entertains and when colorful murals (bottom) depicting the history of the city are created.

Now East Chicago is welcoming them—and citizens from throughout the region—back home.

There's much to recommend the trip. Over the last decade, East Chicago has embarked on revitalization and renewal efforts targeted to invest in infrastructure, improve schools and health care, build parks and recreational centers, create housing stock, support the arts, and promote unity among the city's 34,000 residents.

Building Partnerships

Steel and heavy industry built East Chicago, located at the southern tip of Lake Michigan 30 miles southeast of Chicago. Today, companies like Ispat-Inland and LTV Steel have a hand in helping the community to grow and flourish. Newcomer Harrah's East Chicago, the largest casino on Lake Michigan, has become a working partner in development plans for the city. Two foundations—the East Chicago Community Development Foundation and the Twin City Education Foundation—actively promote programs in education for the city's youth.

Innovative new institutions like the Aquatic Research Institute, that affords opportunities for youth from East Chicago and throughout the region to study the ecosystem of the Great Lakes under the direction of scientists and marine biologists, now call East Chicago home. In 1999 Ancilla Systems, one of Indiana's largest health care providers, opened Healthy East Chicago, Inc.

The center offers a panoply of health-related services under one roof and serves as a link with other agencies involved in health care, education, and social services.

Throughout the city, churches, businesses, and organizations work together for the good of East Chicago. "It takes relationships to build the future," says Myrna Maldonado, East Chicago's director of public information. "What we see in this city is a desire on everyone's part to pitch in and help."

East Chicago reaches out to all of its citizens. From educational programs for youngsters to its annual Senior Citizens Ball, the city aims to help each generation of residents pursue success and enjoy life to the fullest.

Touring the City

A tour of East Chicago would not be complete without visits to several attractions. One could start at the lake with Harrah's East Chicago, one of the premier casinos in the region and a draw for visitors from bordering states.

It is near the Robert A. Pastrick Marina with slips accommodating 300 boats as well as dry storage facilities. The East Chicago Public Library, at 2401 East Columbus Drive, features an "East Chicago Room" devoted to photographs, documents, and resources on the city's history.

Walking down Main Street—once the commercial center for shoppers from throughout the region—one sees revitalization efforts on every block. Near the harbor in Marktown, where the Mark Manufacturing Company built worker housing in the early 1900s, an historic district has been established where residents aim to preserve an important part of East Chicago's past.

Colorful large murals depicting East Chicago's diverse history and imagining its bright future are located throughout the city. With the assistance of local artists—and some brushstrokes courtesy of Indiana First Lady Judy O'Bannon, wife of Indiana Governor Frank O'Bannon—the eye-catching murals were created by hundreds of enthusiastic East Chicago schoolchildren.

Forging the Future

While East Chicago is preserving its noble past, it is also forging the future. Among the new initiatives in the city is the construction of a state-of-the-art Public Safety Facility, slated for completion in 2000, to house the municipality's police, fire, emergency services, city court, clerk, public safety, and communications departments.

The Washington Square project, on Columbus Drive, will provide new single family housing in the city. Institutions including National City Bank and Fannie Mae have established assistance and reduced down payment programs to help more of East Chicago's residents become homeowners.

East Chicago has a promise-filled future, according to Robert A. Pastrick, mayor of the city since 1972. "Much of the groundwork we've laid is now paying off," Pastrick says. "Many elements have to come together and they certainly have in this wonderful city."

A Flair for Fun

Much of East Chicago's personality comes from a diverse population representing many different ethnic groups. Eastern European Slavs and Serbians, African-Americans, Poles, Hispanics, and other peoples create one of the country's true melting pots. The fun is everywhere apparent in summer when warm weather provides the climate for ethnic festivals. Some of the largest city-wide celebrations now include the St. Stanislaus Polish Festival, Serbian Fest, the Puerto Rican Festival and Parade, the Mexican Independence Day Celebration, the Umoja (unity) Parade and Festival honoring African-American heritage, and the Greek Festival.

Each August, the flavors truly come together when the city stages "Taste of East Chicago," a culinary tour of cultures held in Veterans Park next door to City Hall.

"Welcome Back to East Chicago" is the city's theme for the new millennium. For longtime residents, it's a reminder of all the city has to offer. For newcomers, it's a hint of great things to discover.

Amenities for citizens, like East Chicago's public swimming pool (bottom), are a top priority at City Hall (center). So are festivals and community celebrations that bring residents together. Each year, East Chicagoans enjoy more than a dozen parades and events including Mexican Independence Day (top), Umoja Festival, St. Stanislaus Polish Festival, and Serbian Fest.

CITY OF EAST CHICAGO
4522 Indianapolis Boulevard
East Chicago, Indiana 46312
(219) 391-8206
www.eastchicago.com

A GARY RENAISSANCE COULD BE A SOURCE OF PRIDE NOT ONLY IN THE REGION, BUT ALSO FOR THE NATION. NOWHERE ELSE DOES ONE SEE SO CLEARLY THE MARKS—BOTH GOOD AND ILL—OF THE MAJOR TRANSFORMATIONS OF THE TWENTIETH CENTURY. ONCE CALLED "THE MAGIC CITY," GARY IS POISED TO RE-INVENT ITSELF AND RISE AGAIN IN THE TWENTY-FIRST.

It is taking more than magic to resurrect this proud city. Determined leaders, citizens, educators, artists, activists, and others are working together to write the next chapter of Gary, Indiana's history. Extolled as a miracle, the world's most modern city, less than two decades after its birth in 1906, Gary gave to the world new ideas about industry and education that informed generations.

The Early Years

Miami and Potawatomi native Americans lived in the area of present-day Gary from the 1600s to the 1800s. Few settled in the area before 1900, as marshes and sand dunes covered the area. On trips back to France from the New World, Father Marquette used the Calumet River portage between the Little Calumet regions. Tradition holds that Marquette camped at the eastern mouth of the Grand Calumet, the present site of Gary's Marquette Park. In the early 1800s, as many as 15 Potawatomi villages were scattered throughout the area, but by mid-century almost all the tribes had been moved to western reservations.

In 1896, on the shores of Lake Michigan, the world's first successful flight in a heavier-than-air machine took place. Octave Chanute, a French native already world famous as a bridge and railroad engineer, first took flight in a glider off the windswept dunes.

The creation of Gary as a major steel center was the dream of Judge Elbert H. Gary, then chairman of United States Steel Corporation. Intent on building the world's largest and most modern steel plant, he chose a lake site midway between the ore mines in

Minnesota and the coal mines in the south. Gary set his sights on 12,000 acres of unoccupied lands at the southern end of Lake Michigan. Work on the mill—to the tune of $100,000, an extraordinary investment at the time—began in March 1906. Three and one-half years later the mill was in operation and pouring ingots of steel. Immediately Gary began to grow, and the new city became a new hometown for thousands of steelworkers and their families. The first subdivision, comprising 4,000 lots, achieved what its corporate planners had envisioned: well-manicured homes along tree-lined,

paved streets in a neighborhood complete with sidewalks and sewers. Seemingly overnight, a busy downtown district sprung up as banks, stores, hotels, and other businesses set up shop to serve the embryonic but bustling metropolis.

The steel industry thrived throughout the next few decades. The city, which had a population of zero in 1900, more than tripled in size from 16,800 people in 1910 to 55,000 people in 1920. Gary became a great ethnic melting pot as jobs in the mills attracted immigrants from Poland, Romania, Serbia, Hungary, Ireland, and other countries.

Gary's stunning vistas include Marquette Park (top) and the downtown area's historic City Hall and turn-of-the-century buildings (center).

Elbert H. Gary, first chairman of United States Steel, created the City of Gary in tandem with his steel mill, considered a wonder of the mechanized world when it opened in 1906. His statue stands in downtown Gary (bottom).

Gary has changed since the 1930s (opposite page) when cable cars and gaslights were downtown fixtures. Today, passengers flying in and out of Gary-Chicago Airport get a bird's eye view of such landmarks as City Hall and the Genesis Convention Center.

Plans for Buffington Harbor include a 25 square mile mixed residential, commercial, recreational, and parkland development (top) expected to attract both new residents and frequent visitors.

Formally dedicated in 1959, Indiana University Northwest (bottom left) in Gary serves students from northwest Indiana and northeastern Illinois. The university offers four-year degrees in more than 30 fields, associates degrees, and certificate programs in a wide variety of professional, occupational, and technical fields.

At Emerson School for the Visual and Performing Arts (bottom right), high school students with talent in music, dance, theater, and the visual arts receive accelerated training.

Revolutionary Concepts

If U.S. Steel's plan for the most mechanized and efficient factory in the world was revolutionary, so were the ideas of William Wirt, who came to Gary in 1907. Wirt was in many ways the father of modern education and he built a system in the city that became a national model. Going beyond the mere basics of "reading, writing, and arithmetic," Wirt believed in the education of the whole child. Into Gary's first classrooms he introduced courses in technical and practical skills from woodworking and bookbinding to cooking and pattern making. Wirt also incorporated playgrounds into the mix, asserting that physical and social development were important attributes of a well-rounded education. Wirt's schools were a beehive of activity where children not only learned mathematics, history, and philosophy, but also tended gardens, fed and learned about animals, and acquired demonstrable skills.

Today educators take it for granted that young minds learn best with visual aids and hands-on tools. It was Wirt who invented the concept. When he decided to teach geology, Wirt made a contour map out of clay and brought it to the classroom. His ideas formed the foundation of educational initiatives—from social development to now extensive programs in vocational education—that continue into the new century.

Growth and Change

Prior to World War I, organized labor failed to gain a foothold among the area's steelworkers, many of whom were immigrants. The postwar period was one of growth for Gary, which by 1920 had become the largest city in the region. A construction boom led to an extensive inventory of impressive architecture, including many apartment buildings and houses, three ten-story buildings, the Hotel Gary, the Gary State Bank, the imposing Knights of Columbus Building, and the massive City Methodist Church. Public structures included Gary City Hall, a courthouse, a 10-acre esplanade as well as Marquette Park and Gleason Park.

Large numbers of African-Americans were drawn to the city in search of labor jobs, although a quota system kept the black workforce at a level no greater than 15 percent. Most of the region's public accommodations, as elsewhere in the country, were racially segregated. Blacks took residence in an area called "The Patch," a neighborhood with the most undesirable housing and primitive infrastructure in the city.

Steel Sets the Stage

As steel went, so went the region. The Great Depression of the 1930s had a devastating effect on Gary's economy, with U.S. Steel dropping from 100 percent production output in 1929 to 15 percent of capacity in 1932. The depression also brought the unionization of Gary's workers and industries. U.S. Steel was one of the first companies to recognize the Steelworkers Organizing Committee as the bargaining agent for its workers. Between 1935 and 1939, steelworker wages rose nationally some 27 percent, and Gary's workers also benefited.

During World War II, steel production soared and the tide of prosperity returned. For the next two decades Gary and the region flourished as a manufacturing powerhouse with the technology and manpower to serve the nation's needs. After the war, an insatiable American appetite for cars, refrigerators, and other products kept Gary mills on perpetual overtime. However, a recessionary economic cycle and the growth of foreign competition led to a manufacturing decline. Between 1979 and 1986, northwest Indiana's loss in manufacturing totaled 42.5 percent, led largely by cutbacks and slowdowns in steel production and petroleum processing. Changes in the world market made U.S.-made steel more economical by the late 1980s, and the steel industry rebounded to a substantial degree through the early 1990s.

Changing Demographics

Beginning in the 1960s, like other large U.S. metropolitan areas, Gary suffered the population decrease caused by many families' "flight to the suburbs." Within

three decades, the population was 80 percent African-American. Voters elected Gary's first black mayor, Richard G. Hatcher, in 1967 and he was subsequently elected to four more terms. Hatcher's administration worked to improve housing conditions in the city and garner federal job training programs for displaced workers and the unemployed. In 1982, the Genesis Convention Center was built in the heart of Gary's downtown, a first stab at revitalization of the business district.

Gary made great progress during the 1960s and 1970s in reducing air pollution emitted from factory and mill smokestacks. Airborne impurities were reduced by nearly 60 percent from 1966 to 1975, with the city as a committed partner that allocated $180 million in revenue bonds to help local facilities like U.S. Steel reduce pollution at local facilities.

Steel may be the daily bread for thousands in the region, but sports reign during off-hours. Gary residents are proud to host the Steelheads (top right), Gary's International Basketball League team, and the touted Roosevelt High School Panthers (bottom right), a perennial powerhouse that has nurtured players like the NBA's Glenn Robinson.

Tourists turn to Gary for a host of unique offerings including shopping and dining in the Miller Beach community. A day in Miller might include browsing for one-of-a-kind finds at the Lake Street Gallery (top) and dinner at the award-winning Miller Baker Café (right). Gaming at local casinos (bottom left), and events like the annual City of Gary Gospel Fest (bottom right) are among other popular tourist draws.

New Century, New Vision

Those who have been patient as Gary served as the brunt of jokes may have the last laugh. More than a few now see that the city is positioned for a comeback—like many cities in the U.S. that suffered bad times—and will again demonstrate its unique ability to literally invent itself.

According to Scott L. King, a former lawyer elected mayor in 1995, it's not one individual thing that changes a city's destiny, but a multitude of efforts made in concert.

"The critical component is commitment, because it does take time," King says. "A new housing development here leads to business growth there; a new basketball team brings visitors and economic development; good housing stock serves residents and lures new ones; lakefront parks boost amenities for citizens and show visitors who we are."

Top Priorities

There's a lot going on in Gary today. City officials and corporate leaders are working to diversify Gary's economy, adding service industries and high-tech jobs to a business mix that will include but not be limited to steel. Businesses like Trump Casino and Majestic Star Casino have brought more jobs and their contributions to municipal coffers are helping to finance vital infrastructure improvements across the city. The construction of new housing and refurbishment of existing residential neighborhoods is a top priority for the mayor and his staff, who have put into place several local, county, and federal programs to help underwrite some of the costs of this valuable effort. Projects like the Glen Park community development at 33rd and Virginia will provide new single family housing for residents.

"Gary is a very diverse community primed for many types of development," says Gary deputy mayor Suzette Raggs. "Now is a great time for citizens of Gary as well as private sector investments. It's a perfect time to take advantage of the resurgence in housing development, business ventures, and entrepreneurship."

Expectations are high among business and industry honchos, who see developments like the one proposed for Buffington Harbor as a step in the right direction. Now in the final planning stages, the 25 square mile development will feature housing, shops, parks, museums, theaters, designated open space, marinas, and other amenities along the picturesque Lake Michigan shoreline in Gary.

Gary is more and more becoming the place to go. The city's annual independence Day Celebration, featuring a festival of nationally known blues, rap, funk, rock, and other music acts as well as a parade on Broadway, has tripled its attendance since 1996. Summers in downtown Gary feature a Gospel Fest in August and a Blues Fest in September, as well

as an Air Show. Up and running the court–literally–is the Gary Steelheads basketball squad, a Continental Basketball Association team introduced to the region in 2000. The Steelheads play home games downtown at the Genesis Convention Center, attracting crowds from Gary and throughout the greater metropolitan area. Plans are also on the drawing board to establish a professional baseball team with headquarters in Gary.

While Gary is working to become "pretty as a picture," it has already lured many who are—like the Miss USA pageant contestants who will compete in Gary beginning in 2001. Gary, Indiana won the coveted three-year contract from contest organizers, who believe the city's attractions and proposed developments will create the perfect backdrop for the nationally televised event.

Pieces of the Puzzle

The city's efforts are designed to trigger private investment, a partner in the plan for a new Gary. It's destined to be a win-win situation. Gary's location at the heart of the country, situated along the lakeshore, with its own airport and access to major highways and the Indiana's International Port at Burns Harbor, is ideal. Location led to Gary being selected by U.S. Steel at the turn of the last century, and is a big reason why investors and developers want to be involved in this one.

"We have both natural and manmade assets," explains Ben Clement, director of economic development for the city. "If you put them together right, it's unbeatable. Gary has every potential to again be a major hub of the nation."

Public information director LaLosa Dent Burns agrees. "It's like a puzzle where the pieces have to come together just right," she says. "When I close my eyes I can see the whole picture. What's amazing is how many pieces have come together already—we can see that with our eyes wide open."

New Age City

Gary has given the nation a great deal, but its glory days are not past. In many ways, the hopes of the region rise and fall with Gary, a city that grew from swampy marshland to become the symbol of industrial progress and might. In a new century, Gary will make the transformation from the industrial age to the information age, from factories to fiber optics. Because so many of the problems that bedeviled metropolitan centers hit Gary especially hard, the renaissance will be all the sweeter.

The city's leaders, like Mayor Scott King (top left) and Deputy Mayor Suzette Raggs (above), are enthusiastic promoters of a Gary renaissance. The City of Gary recently scored national attention when it signed a three-year contract to host the Miss USA pageant beginning with the 2001 contest. Contestants visited with Drew Elementary school children (bottom) during their tour of the city.

CITY OF GARY
401 Broadway
Gary, Indiana 46402
(219) 881-1301
www.gary.in.us

Strategically positioned 25 miles (just 35 minutes) from downtown Chicago, Gary/Chicago Airport represents an economic engine for the northwest Indiana region as it takes its place as Chicago's third airport. The Gary/Chicago Airport is an asset to travelers in a marketplace that extends east from Chicago to South Bend, Indiana.

Strategically located in the heartland of the country and just 35 minutes from Chicago's Loop, the Gary/Chicago Airport (right) serves the greater metropolitan area with passenger and cargo flights. A convenient choice for regional customers, the airport offers amenities like free parking and is a less congested, hassle-free option for both business and leisure travelers.

Strategic Alliance

The Gary/Chicago Airport became the focus of attention in 1995 when an unprecedented strategic alliance between the City of Gary and the City of Chicago paved the way for substantial aviation resources and capital improvements for the facility. With the support of Gary Mayor Scott L. King and Chicago Mayor Richard M. Daley, a bi-state compact for the strategic positioning of the Gary/Chicago Airport initiated a series of expansions and upgrades. Now in Phase II, the Gary/Chicago Airport master plan lays the foundation for development over the next 20 years to prepare the airport for anticipated growth in both passenger and cargo service.

Gary/Chicago Airport has launched a comprehensive program communicating the benefits of convenient, hassle-free, and time-saving travel through print ads, business publications, billboards, radio, cable television, direct mail, and strong regional promotions. Its Web site (www.garychicagoairport.com) provides round-the-clock information to the general public on flights and services.

Popular Destinations

Owned by the Gary/Chicago Airport Authority, the airport is bustling. Daily flights to Orlando/Sanford, Florida and St. Louis, Missouri (Belville, Illinois) have opened up direct travel channels for thousands of metro area business and recreational travelers. Pan Am currently operates from Gary/ Chicago Airport and plans are underway for additional airlines, offering more and more popular destinations. In addition, Casino Express Airlines provides gaming charter service to Elko, Nevada.

As the gateway to the Midwest, Gary/Chicago Airport is the convenient choice for regional customers. Gary/Chicago Airport offers convenient access to popular destinations in Chicagoland, northwest Indiana, and key business centers in North America. Major highway access includes I-90, I-80/94, I-65, US-12, and US-20 with commuter rail connections to Chicago. Situated at the center of the country and in the middle of the midwest, the Gary/Chicago Airport is the most stress-free of the metro area's airports.

New Renovations

Upgraded passenger servicing facilities are underway including new ticket counters, baggage retrieval area, concessions, and other facilities. In addition to free secured parking for 800 vehicles, on-site car rental agencies and public transportation service provide convenient connections for airport travelers.

Located within a federal economic empowerment zone and airport development zone, Gary/Chicago Airport will benefit from an infusion of funds to help it grow over the next decade. Planned improvements include completion of a 30,000 square foot maintenance hangar complex including a heavy aircraft bay, an 18,000 square foot support facility, and a 19,200 square foot Aviation Technology Training Center.

Gary/Chicago Airport is ready to attract quality air carriers with a longer runway than Midway's and operating investment and tax incentives, as well as foreign trade zone opportunities.

Airport upgrades to date have focused on runway and systems improvements to serve both passenger and cargo flights. In the air traffic control tower, a Rapid Deployment Voice Switch provides a computerized control system for land and radio communications. An IDS-4 Chicago Approach Control computer system integrates weather satellite, Doppler radar map, ground condition, and other reports. Its Automated Weather Observation system provides continuous reporting of weather information. Recently constructed was a 4,800 square foot de-icing facility near the terminal with its own infrastructure for the capture

and treatment of de-icing fluid. Full-length, parallel taxiway and runway accommodates heavy jet aircraft including the Boeing 727, 737, 757, DC9, and MD80 aircraft. New fuel tanks, constructed at a cost of $2 million, have increased fueling capacity, and installation of systems like an FAA DBRITE radar repeater and CBI training computer have made Gary/Chicago Airport fully equipped to serve passenger and cargo planes 24 hours a day.

Gary/Chicago Airport offers top quality, convenient service to millions of metro travelers who can now—as the Gary/Chicago advertisements proclaim—"Take the easy way out." With easy access, less wait time, fewer highway hassles, free parking, and its other selling points, the facility has grown immeasurably in stature across the region.

Partnership Support

Business and industry in the region represent a major sector joining in partnership to support the airport. A "Stakeholder's Club" cooperative advertising incentive program motivates a "Who's Who" list of regional corporations, institutions, small businesses, and social/civic organizations to contribute financially and via co-sponsored promotional initiatives to the success of the Gary/Chicago Airport.

Gary/Chicago Airport has also created opportunities for new levels of regional and bi-state cooperation most fitting for the 21st century. Focused on the people and businesses of the greater metropolitan area rather than boundaries, government officials and airport management believe Gary/Chicago Airport is one facility with benefits for all.

Daily flights to to popular destinations have opened up direct routes for thousands of regional customers (top and bottom right).

Gary/Chicago Airport enjoys wide support among government officials including Gary Mayor Scott L. King and Representative Pete Visclosky photographed at the airport in 2000 (center).

Currently under construction (bottom right) is an aircraft maintenance hangar and cutting edge Aviation Technology Training Center.

GARY/CHICAGO AIRPORT
6001 West Industrial Highway
Gary, Indiana 46406
(219) 949-9722
www.garychicagoairport.com

F ROM THE ANCIENT OAK TREES LINING ITS QUIET STREETS TO ITS RICH HISTORY AS THE CROSS-ROADS OF THE MIDWEST, GRIFFITH FEELS LIKE HOME. TODAY, THE TOWN OF GRIFFITH RETAINS ITS COMMITMENT TO CITIZENS OF ALL AGES, AND PRESERVES A TRADITION OF SERENITY AND SECURITY. FOR GENERATIONS, RESIDENTS HAVE MADE IT A TRUE HOME BY DEDICATING THEMSELVES

to preservation of the town's heritage, using their energies to decorate downtown every Christmas, and hosting special events to bring the community together.

Griffith is not just another seven square miles along Ridge Road on the way to someplace else. Griffith is proud of its sense of place.

"I feel there is a real sense of closeness," says clerk-treasurer Ronald Szafarczyk, who has made Griffith his home for more than 35 years. "I think the people themselves are the reason so many of us love Griffith. Residents here are willing to pitch in and help one another."

Railroad Brought People

In 1852, the Erie and Kalamazoo railroad and the Michigan Southern railroad connected the northern portion of Lake County to Chicago and Michigan. Soon other rail lines laid trunk lines through Griffith, according to the town's official history. By the end of the 1880s, four railroads crossed at what would become the center of town, bringing people and progress. Among the people who arrived were brothers Jay and Elmer Dwiggins, real estate developers who had the grand

vision of creating "Chicago's Best Factory Suburb."

Jay and Elmer Dwiggins bought 140 acres of land for $8,400 and laid out a plat of blocks, lots, and streets to lure businesses and residents to a town they wanted to name "Dwiggins Junction."

In advertisements, the brothers offered residential lots for $120 or more and business lots for $300 and up, with monthly payments ranging from $4 to $12. But they didn't have enough cash and by the time the Panic of 1893 hit, the brothers went broke and left town forever, according to town historical society records.

Those who stayed helped the town thrive. Griffith and its approximately 18,000 residents will celebrate the town's 100th birthday in 2004.

A Town Built Around Community

The tradition of the railroad still carries on today, say Szafarczyk and town councilman Stan Dobosz. Though traffic has

lessened over the years, the EJ&E and Grand Trunk railroads still cross the town's center about 30 times a day.

For train buffs, Griffith is certainly a destination not to miss. Every fall, the Historical Society hosts the Griffith Railroad Fair to celebrate the town's history, sponsored in conjunction with the Boy Scouts annual Fall Harvest Festival.

Thousands of people make their way to Griffith for its cultural offerings as well. Every July, Central Park plays host to A Park Full of Art, a 26-year-old art fair and one of the most popular in the state. The juried show attracts artists from all over the country.

In August, the park again fills with thousands of people for A Park Full of Music, an all-volunteer effort that brings the community together for a day of neighborliness and music. It is the work of the Griffith Special Events Committee, a group of volunteers that make the event successful every year.

Griffith, settled after the railroads were built in northwest Indiana, will celebrate its Centennial in 2004. Several rail lines built track through the community, and each year the town recognizes its history at the Griffith Railroad Fair.

Good Place to Settle Down

The community is proud of its low crime rate and its status as a good, safe community in which to raise active children. Its six parks, the largest of which is Central Park, host girls softball, Little League, Babe Ruth, and Pop Warner teams. Some residents jokingly say the cheers can be heard in adjacent towns when the high school's teams take the fields. The community rallies around its young people who play sports. In 1997, the football team won the state championship and came home to a heroes' welcome as community residents stood in a cold rain to cheer them.

For its children, Griffith offers a top-notch education through its schools and extracurricular programs.

Dobosz says Griffith also is a community that works for its senior citizens. Responding to the needs of the community's large senior population, the town built a senior center now used for daily meals and activities.

The town fathers know well that when people choose Griffith, they stay to raise their families and grow old here. "We want to make that a good experience," Dobosz says. "We focus on services and events that serve every age group in our town."

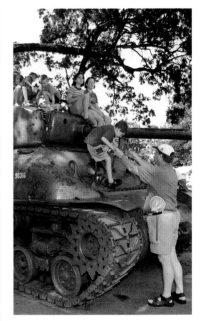

A Park Full of Art (top) brings thousands to Griffith for the town's annual art exhibition and sale in Central Park.

Good schools (bottom), attractive homes, and a location close to major attractions but in its own quiet corner rate high with Griffith's 18,000 residents.

Cozy and Convenient

Griffith finds itself in a unique position because of all that surrounds it. The town is poised minutes from top universities, near excellent medical facilities, and with access to entertainment corridors and some of northwest Indiana's most beautiful places.

Griffith is located just 30 miles from Chicago and 160 miles from Indianapolis and is so close to the Indiana Toll Road, Interstate 80/94, and other major highways that it appeals to commuters searching for not only a cozy, but also a convenient hometown. About 700 businesses, including Pactiv (originally known as Mapes Packaging Corp.) and LaSalle Steel, call Griffith home and provide local residents with jobs "in their own backyards."

For Szafarczyk, the small-town atmosphere of this caring community has kept him working to make it even better. Now his children are choosing to make their homes in Griffith to raise their own families, something he sees time and again in this community of generations where it seems everybody is either relative or friend.

"It's a good place to raise a family," says Szafarczyk. "It's close enough to the big cities to go there when necessary and we're far enough away to have our own little private areas. Griffith is a hard place to beat."

Town of Griffith
111 North Broad Street
Griffith, Indiana 46319
(219) 924-7500

"LET ME PRESENT YOU WITH THIS PIN," MAYOR DUANE DEDELOW SAYS, OPENING A SMALL PACKAGE, THEN HELPING THE VISITOR ATTACH THE PIN TO HIS LAPEL. "IT EXPRESSES OUR HOPES FOR HAMMOND. YOU SEE THAT SUN? IT'S RISING, YOU KNOW." DEDELOW SMILES, SITTING DOWN BEHIND HIS DESK, ACROSS WHICH A DAILY BARRAGE OF PAPER FLOWS. EACH PAGE IS EXAMINED BY THE MAYOR

with an eye to one essential question he poses of every policy or project: "How will this help Hammond?"

A few decades ago, Hammond was a hard place to beat. Its downtown streets were filled with shoppers, its neighborhoods were lovingly maintained, its industrial areas hummed with the sound of productivity. As in many urban areas, however, the late 1970s and early 1980s took their toll. The era socked cities throughout the nation with inflation, recession, flight to the suburbs, company failures, and public programs that grew in expense while the federal dollars to support them shrunk.

That was yesterday. Today, Hammond is up off the mat—and Mayor Duane Dedelow, Jr., its indefatigable and optimistic leader—is pinning everyone in sight.

"We have terrific strengths and we're building anew," Dedelow says. "There isn't anyone who's counting us out now."

Strength through Diversity

One of the city's strengths, according to Dedelow, is its diversity. Hammond draws vitality and uniqueness from the economic, racial, and religious

diversity of its people. Once a solidly "blue-collar town," now African Americans, Eastern Europeans, Hispanics, and others have joined forces to create a city in which there are responsibilities and opportunities for all.

The changing business landscape also offers opportunity. The City of Hammond has spent the last decade delicately directing efforts to the burgeoning service economy with its growth prognosis and job creation potential. Many longtime Hammond companies and major employers—Mercantile

Bank, Bank Calumet, and St. Margaret Mercy Hospital, among many others—never left the city. Today, they are being joined by businesses that recognize Hammond's future looms bright. The city itself spurred economic development through construction of industrial facilities like the Columbia Avenue Business Park and the West Point Industrial Plaza, as well as investments in infrastructure. An urban enterprise zone (UEA) covering three miles in the city has also helped spur economic development.

Downtown Revitalization

Hammond got a boost in 2000 when the federal government consolidated its agencies and courts at a new $50 million courthouse downtown. The project has made Hammond a daily destination for thousands of regional residents. Now attorneys, office supply companies, restaurants, print shops, and other retail stores and businesses have ample reason to hang out a shingle in Hammond.

Those business owners like what they see in downtown Hammond. A massive, targeted effort toward downtown revitalization is paying

Hammond is experiencing citywide revitalization from the lakefront to downtown to the neighborhoods. Assets like the Hammond Marina (bottom left) and Harrison Park (bottom right) provide recreational opportunities for residents and visitors.

big dividends. The new Hammond Rotunda—a much-talked about 27 foot tall public sculpture—has become a gathering spot for shoppers and workers on lunch break. The city has doubled its efforts to demolish outdated structures while saving historic buildings that could help form the fabric of a reborn downtown. A fiber optic network to support business with high-tech communications was installed by the city to attract business.

The Hammond Marina and development of lakefront parks and recreation will increase the number of tourists and provide amenities for residents. Wisely, the city uses revenues paid by local Lake Michigan casinos to invest in infrastructure, parks, and facilities that will serve citizens for generations.

"All these things have a domino effect," explains Phil Merhalski, Hammond's director of economic development. "When enough of the right pieces are put together, it encourages more investment."

From Arts to Education

The city's "Arts Inside Out" project—spearheaded through the Mayor's Hammond Commission for the Arts & Humanities and supported with grants from the National Endowment for the Arts—has brought live music and dance downtown. Simultaneous offerings on three stages make Hammond a top choice for family outings in summer.

Education is a priority in Hammond. Exciting new projects, such as the Challenger Center, which teaches children science in a NASA-inspired environment, and Substation Number 9, which provides art education, prove Hammond is in many ways ahead of the pack when it comes to innovation. These projects were pursued in partnership with Purdue University Calumet and the City of Hammond Schools, both assets in building the intellectual capital of the city and offering educational opportunities for youth.

The neighborhoods are benefiting, too, from all that is happening. The carryover effect of downtown development translates into investment in community areas. In 2000, a new Wal-Mart opened in the Woodmar neighborhood, bringing with it not only retail goods but also more jobs for citizens. Plans in other neighborhoods, from Hessville to Harrison Park, call for housing, infrastructure, landscaping, and related improvements. Neighborhoods, Inc., a new community organization, has become a major force in home buyer training, loan and credit counseling, and first time buyer programs.

Building a Wave

Hammond is a proud city with a long history. Incorporated in 1884, it grew with the industrial boom in the region that brought steel-making, petroleum processing,

and other heavy industry to northwest Indiana in the twentieth century. At the dawn of the 21st century, Hammond is embarking upon a new journey, as fraught with growth pains—but as full of possibilities—as its first one was.

"What are we trying to do?" Dedelow asks, then answers. "We want Hammond to be the place people want to live, work, and play."

That's the reason for the pin. Part of the City of Hammond's marketing program for the new millennium, the enamel pin portrays a home ("where all good things begin"), a giant "H" (which stands for Hammond), a wave (representing the lakefront), and a bold yellow sun ("rising to a prosperous future"). Taken together, the symbols portray a horizon: bright, beautiful, and obtainable.

Mayor Dedelow gives the pin to the visitor—who doesn't even live in Hammond—because he knows the big march into the future is composed of a million human-scaled steps. He makes a partner of everyone he meets—university administrators, business experts, artists and poets, federal government representatives, parents, neighborhood organizers, schoolchildren, and leaders in neighboring cities.

Dedelow knows the visitor will turn to at least one other person and say, "Hey, have you heard what's happening in Hammond?"

Enough ripples like that, Dedelow believes, could generate one heck of a wave.

Mayor Duane Dedelow (top) pursues an economic development strategy that focuses on commercial development, education, and the arts. Community facilities like the Ophelia Steen Family and Health Services Center (center) provide valuable resources for residents.

While a summer arts festival, "Arts Inside Out," brings residents and visitors downtown, the new Challenger Center (bottom) is a must-see.

CITY OF HAMMOND

5925 Calumet Avenue
Hammond, Indiana 46320
219-853-6301
www.hammondindiana.com

LIKE THE TREES RESIDENTS HELPED PLANT AROUND THE PICTURESQUE MAIN SQUARE PARK, HIGHLAND IS BLOOMING AND THRIVING. WHILE IT IS CHANGING TO MEET THE DEMANDS OF TODAY'S BUSINESSES, THE TOWN IS CONSIDERED BY CITIZENS A CLOSE-KNIT, SAFE, AND INDUSTRIOUS PLACE TO SPEND THE BEST TIMES OF THEIR LIVES. A LOT OF HARD WORK AND VISION WERE INVESTED

Highland's Main Square Park (top) is the scene of many community events throughout the year including the annual Twelfth Night Celebration.

"The Spirit of Highland," a steel sculpture paying homage to the region, was erected in front of the fire station in 1999.

into the seven square miles that comprise Highland today. According to clerk treasurer Michael Griffin, who has resided in Highland his entire life, the town affords residents all the virtues of small town living and also the conveniences of easy access to nearby urban areas and events. "It's a wonderful place to live," Griffin says with a smile. "And I'm just one of the 24,000 people who says so."

Location, Location

Just 21 miles from Chicago and minutes from Lake Michigan's shores, Highland is perfectly situated to take advantage of the area's cultural and recreational offerings—from concerts by the Northwest Indiana Symphony to the stunning vistas of the Indiana Dunes National Lakeshore. The town's own 20 parks, totaling 198 acres, are unrivaled in the region. The community also comes together at the Lincoln Community Center. The Center offers year-round programs for every age group from school-children to senior citizens, and now houses a 36,000-square-foot athletic field house.

Highland is a community that rallies together, say locals. "There's a tendency for people to know each other here, more so than in other places," explains Mark Herak, vice president of the town council. It's a quality, he says, that has historically given Highland an ambience of village-like intimacy, where residents take time to chat and inquire after one another's families and activities.

"In Highland, we look after each other," Herak notes. "We're close to Chicago, we have access to the big cities. But we appreciate coming to Highland, a slice of Small Town USA."

Though land-locked and bordered by Griffith and Munster, Highland simply cannot be considered just one of the communities along the ridge that runs east to west through northwest Indiana. A progressive community with a stable tax base, Highland has benefited over the years from sound fiscal stewardship, always with an eye to the future and always with a focus on the town's most important asset: its people.

"It's a safe, clean, welcoming community—a town of working-class people who are interested in what's going on around them, but who know their hearts are at home," says Kathy DeGuilio-Fox, a Highland resident and president of the town's Redevelopment Commission.

Revitalizing Downtown

Incorporated on April 4, 1910, Highland, like many communities in northwest Indiana, is booming. The downtown area, carefully guided through a transition from a solidly retail corridor to a splendid mix of shops, offices, entertainment, and eateries, is highly successful.

Thanks to a progressive Redevelopment Commission, attention to aesthetics and planning has allowed Highland to nurture its downtown as a vital destination in the community. The second phase of a three-stage improvement program aimed at upgrading infrastructure and retrofitting downtown for more commercial development is underway. The commission also plans to provide incubator space downtown for new business ventures.

Already, DeGuilio-Fox says, more people are spending time downtown, and the corridor's economic viability looks secure for the future. As part of the downtown revitalization effort, residents and people who do business in the community were surveyed to see what kind of new businesses are needed downtown and to open up a forum for ideas. One suggestion town leaders will pursue is to market downtown Highland beyond the municipality's borders, promoting it as a destination for visitors from throughout the region.

Businesses that move to Highland appreciate the strong local

demographics. The median household income in 2000 was pegged at $39,437, and its educated workforce numbers about 18,772.

Meanwhile, Jewel Foods/Osco, Target, Borders Books, and other national retailers are attracting shoppers from throughout the region to the town's 60-acre shopping center, Highland Grove. The center offers 566,540 square feet of retail and commercial space. The adjacent Meijer store itself represents 237,000 square feet of commercial retail space.

DeGuilio-Fox believes the Redevelopment Commission and Plan Commission will continue to work together closely to seek wise improvements for Highland and to attract more businesses and industries.

"Like many communities in the new millennium, we're rebuilding for the 21st century," she says. "We want to ensure that the community will remain economically strong."

While about ten percent of Highland's land area remains to be developed, town officials believe there's a great future in redevelopment, capitalizing on the new trends in retailing and shopping.

Highland also continues to see residential development.

Many Parks, More Promise

There's a lot of positives about this community," says Griffin, who quickly ticks off a laundry list of just a few. "There are a lot of opportunities that are family fortifying." Griffin cites Highland schools, some of the best in the region. Here graduation rates are high, and a significant number of students head off to colleges and universities or attend the many technical schools in the area. Parks and recreation facilities, which cater to young and old alike, are designed with families in mind, and located within walking distances of every neighborhood. The town also meticulously maintains its 3.1 mile section of the popular Cross-Town Bike Trail.

Highland's parks are where residents come together as neighbors for summer block parties, community musicals, and blockbuster events like the town's annual Twelfth Night Celebration, held every year in Main Square Park.

The future looks bright in Highland. Property values, always stable, are now rising. Town officials work diligently to keep taxes low by finding creative ways to pay for amenities. Downtown is on the move. All in all, says Griffin, these are good days to live in Highland.

Revitalization of the downtown commercial corridor (top) has been a high priority in Highland. Downtown Highland is now promoted as a destination to residents throughout the region.

Good schools, attractive parks, and affordable housing make Highland a great place for families (bottom).

TOWN OF HIGHLAND
3333 Ridge Road
Highland, Indiana 46322
(219) 838-1080

T ODAY IT COULD STILL BE KNOWN AS EAST GARY—AS IT WAS FROM 1908 TO 1977—OR AS INDEPENDENCE, A NAME SOME FAVORED IN 1976. BUT LAKE STATION HARKENED BACK TO ITS ROOTS WHEN IT OFFICIALLY CHANGED ITS NAME IN 1977. AN EARLY DEPOT STOP ON THE MICHIGAN CENTRAL RAILROAD'S DETROIT TO CHICAGO LINE THROUGH THE CALUMET REGION, THE VILLAGE

CITY OF
LAKE STATION

3705 Fairview Avenue
Lake Station, Indiana 46405
(219) 962-2081

Marketed as "East Gary" at the turn of the century, Lake Station was home to executives and management of U.S. Steel who desired residences in the suburbs. Today, Lake Station is embarking on a new millennium strategy to increase development and restore infrastructure.

was first named when George Earle mapped out a town of about 6,500 acres in 1852, dubbing it Lake Station.

The City of Lake Station, like many northwest Indiana communities that sprung up along either Sauk Trail, the Indian route through the region, or railroad lines, had other brushes with history. A transportation hub for more than three decades beginning in the 1850s, the prosperous community took a hit when the railroad post office moved its operations in the 1880s further west to Joliet, Illinois.

The outlook brightened at the turn of the century when U.S. Steel set up its "million dollar factory" in bordering Gary. Lake Station, marketed as "East Gary" to attract executives and management who might want to live in a suburban enclave, functioned as a bedroom community. Twists of fate have their effect to this day. Being a bedroom community, Lake Station did welcome Abraham Lincoln to its Audubon Hotel— perhaps on more than one occasion according to oral history. But George Pullman, who tried to negotiate for land in Lake Station for his proposed railcar company, never struck a deal and set up shop on the south side of Chicago instead.

Steps to the Future

T oday, Lake Station remains a mostly residential community. According to Mayor Shirley Wadding, the city is now focused on accenting its positives and building the future. Selected a Millennium Community by the Governor of the State of Indiana in 2000, Lake Station initiated projects to celebrate and preserve its local history and prepare its

children for the new millennium. With its share of monies collected in taxes from regional casinos, Lake Station is making the kinds of infrastructure and revitalization investments that will help it in 2000 and beyond. Water and sewer line upgrades are in the works and many road projects are coming to fruition. New residential housing, including a 400-unit apartment community, will provide homes for residents and newcomers as well as help spread out the local property tax burden among a greater number of citizens.

"It's tough for smaller communities like ours that have more housing but less commercial development," says Wadding, who nonetheless feels that undeveloped land within the city's boundaries could prove conveniently located space for new or relocating companies. "We're playing to our strengths, though, and expect growth and improvements will come surely, if sometimes more slowly than we'd like."

The youngsters in Lake Station will depend upon their elders to grow the city. In the meantime, they grow strong in a close-knit community where Little League baseball games, good schools, and family outings to beautiful Riverview Park are all a kid could ask for.

"The new millennium has brought a new partnership between leaders and citizens," Wadding smiles. "If Lake Station once was changed by fate, today it's being improved through careful planning and a positive outlook."

LaPorte is one of northwest Indiana's destination cities. An historic city and the county seat, LaPorte has amenities that endear it to residents and also draw an increasing number of tourists. LaPorte, French for "the door," is truly the doorway to a number of delights. Visitors may first walk the streets of its historic downtown

now undergoing restoration. A downtown beautification project is restoring brick sidewalks, benches and planters, landscaping, and historically inspired light posts on LaPorte's most famous thoroughfares. Turn-of-the-century mansions along tree-lined boulevards like Michigan Avenue and Indiana Avenue provide a glimpse of LaPorte's past. Many are designated landmark homes featured at Christmas time during a candlelight tour highlighted by horse and buggy rides.

City with History

Incorporated in 1835, LaPorte has many architectural and historic gems. Must-visit buildings include the massive LaPorte County Courthouse on Lincoln-way, designed by Chicago architect Daniel Burnham and completed in 1894, and the historic City Hall on Michigan Avenue. Across the street from City Hall sits the Rumely Hotel, a former inn that has been renovated to serve seniors with independent living apartments. In its foyer is a faithfully restored curved stained glass dome in delicate shades of green and gold. The turn-of-the-century Civic Auditorium on Ridge Street, revered as a local landmark, once welcomed big stars like Bob Hope to its stage.

LaPorte has become a draw in the region for antique collectors and artifact fanciers. A trip to LaPorte is not complete without visits to some of the fifteen-plus antique stores with more than 300 dealers in and around the downtown area.

Attractions also include the landmark nine-sided Door Prairie Barn; the LaPorte County Historical

Society Museum, housing more than 80,000 city and county artifacts, documents, and exhibits; and the Door Prairie Auto Museum, with its collection of cars spanning 100 years of automotive history.

Residents enjoy LaPorte's family-friendly atmosphere, bustling economy, excellent schools, and recreational opportunities. Citizens here also enjoy their sports, supporting a system that offers training and league play for tots to teenagers. LaPorte has earned its recognition as "Baseball Capitol of Indiana." The city's dynamic Slicers baseball team captured its eighth state championship in 2000, making it one of the winningest teams in the country. In football, basketball, and baseball, LaPorte teams routinely have the largest fan base. In 2000, the City of LaPorte was the host city for the Indiana All Star Basketball exhibition.

If no local team is playing, there are ample other opportunities for family fun. The LaPorte Symphony Orchestra enjoys wide

support, as does the city's Little Theater where local actors stage several plays each year. In the summer, citizens enjoy LaPorte City Band concerts in Fox Park near Clear Lake. LaPorte boasts an enviable inventory of parks and five lakes accessible to the public. In fact, the lakes of LaPorte—Clear, Fishtrap, Lily, Pine, and Stone—provided the city with one of its first industries as ice company workers cut ice from the lakes and shipped it to Chicago. Each July, citizens celebrate with one of the largest Fourth of July parades in the state. In September, the turnout is large for the annual Sunflower Festival.

In LaPorte, industry is strong and the job base is growing. Over the decades, city businesses have produced everything from baby carriages to jet engines. Today, LaPorte's largest employers include LaPorte Hospital and Health Services, Inc., Howmet Corp., New York Blower, Teledyne, and Whirlpool.

Life is good in LaPorte, according to Mayor Kathy Chroback. "This is a terrific place to raise a family, to live, to do business," she says. "We have a proud history and a future full of promise."

**801 Michigan Avenue
LaPorte, Indiana 46350
(219) 362-8220**

Door Prairie Barn (left), is a LaPorte landmark and one of the few remaining "round barns" in the U.S. Built in 1878 and recently placed on the National Register of Historic Places, the barn may be the only one of its type in   existence. The LaPorte County Courthouse (below) on Lincolnway is the city's best known building. Also historic—but young—are the LaPorte Slicers. The touted baseball team has won eight state championship titles.

LOWELL SEEMS UNTOUCHED BY TIME, THOUGH ALL AROUND IT PEOPLE ARE RUSHING BY. HERE, RESIDENTS STILL SMILE AND WAVE TO EACH OTHER. THEY TAKE CARE OF EACH OTHER AND WATCH OVER THE CHILDREN. IT IS THE KIND OF TOWN PEOPLE IMAGINE WHEN THEY DREAM OF ESCAPING THE RAT RACE OF URBAN LIFE. MOST IMPORTANTLY, DAY IN AND DAY OUT, LOWELL LIVES UP

Antique and specialty shops make Lowell's downtown (top) a destination for visitors.

Lowell's Labor Day Parade (center) is one of the largest and oldest in the State of Indiana.

A new public library (bottom) was generously supported by Lowell businesses and townspeople.

to its long-time town motto: "The friendly town with friendly people."

For Amy Taylor, past president of the Lowell Chamber of Commerce, Lowell represents the best of both worlds.

"It's a great place for me to raise my children," Taylor explains. "Lowell is a small town with a clean environment, but close to opportunities available in the Chicago area, which is just 45 miles away."

Donald Gustafson, administrator of the Lowell Loyal Order of the Moose Lodge 2437, is another one of the 7,200 people who have found their true place in Lowell.

"It's a quiet, peaceful, and friendly town away from the city life," he says.

Just a drive through its historic downtown, past its immaculate parks and older homes, is enough to convince a person that Lowell feels exactly like home should feel.

Primed for Development

"Lowell is a pretty town," says Donald Yeoman, superintendent of the Tri-Creek School Corporation which serves Lowell. "There is a community spirit that pervades all that we do. Here we

really believe that by working together we can make the future better for coming generations."

Indeed, that's exactly what town officials, residents, business owners, and civic leaders have been doing for years. Together, they are making an investment in Lowell they hope will pay off in big dividends as developers discover the community's vast potential.

With Interstate 65 at its backdoor, U.S. 41 at its front door, and freight rail service through its center, Lowell is prime territory for commercial and industrial development. It is only a matter of time, many say, until major development moves to southern Lake County.

In 2000, townspeople rallied behind a proposal that would bring commuter rail service linking Lowell to Chicago, a move that would open even more doors to growth. Already Lowell boasts several new residential subdivisions, including the Oaks of Cedar Creek, Meadowbrook, Gwen's Cove, Brookwood, Deere Acres, Indian Meadows, and Carriage Crossing.

In pursuit of economic development initiatives, town planners are methodically updating Lowell's infrastructure. More than two

years of work and $2.6 million in funds recently expanded the capacity of Lowell's sewage treatment plant, an improvement that will help get 25 proposed developments off hold as well as open the door to a number of newly proposed projects.

Rick Dal Corobbo, Lowell's director of administration, believes the town could eventually expand its borders all the way to Interstate 65 and U.S. 41. In five years, he expects Lowell will become a more metropolitan community, yet still retain its small, hometown flavor because of local leaders who scrutinize projects with an eye to maintaining quality of life.

Lowell is also investing in its unique and thriving downtown. Antique and specialty shops in the downtown area now attract thousands of residents and visitors each year. But it wasn't always that way. As in many small downtowns across the nation, traditional businesses struggled and often failed in the 1980s, leaving empty storefronts. In Lowell, town officials, the Chamber of Commerce, and downtown business owners never accepted that fate. They put their heads together to save downtown, Dal Corobbo says.

Today, the downtown is packed. An active chamber, the Lowell Downtown Merchants Association, and the Lowell Main Street Association jointly promote local businesses by sponsoring a number of activities, including the annual four-day Oktoberfest celebration, Cobe Cup Cruise, Hometown Heroes Day, an antique car show, Lil' Britches Day, Tunes in Town, and the annual Festival of Lights Christmas Parade.

A $500,000 grant from the Indiana Department of Transportation in 2000 spurred enhancements downtown, from sidewalk restoration to replacement of outmoded light fixtures with decorative period lighting. A second phase will improve downtown's Old Towne Square Park and fund development of a walking path linking the downtown area with Evergreen Park. At Evergreen Park, one of Lowell's six community parks, the basketball courts have been expanded and new playground equipment has been installed.

Dal Corobbo and town leaders are seeking additional funds to beautify downtown Lowell. When completed, he says, downtown Lowell will be a show place. Marcia Carlson, who served as the town's clerk-treasurer for 25 years and retired in 1996, agrees.

"Lowell refuses to accept the premise that small towns are dying," she says. "We've got quite an asset here, and we fully intend to protect it and preserve it."

Hometown and Heart

Lowell was founded in 1852 by Melvin A. Halsted, who brought to the community a paper mill, church, school, and railroad. His own house, the Halsted House, still stands today. Halsted's investment in Lowell, along with his family's desire to build a friendly community, lead to its early prosperity and growth.

The same community-mindedness typifies the people who live in Lowell today. Valuing a sense of neighborliness, they look forward to Friday nights in the fall when

there's not a free seat left in the stadium as residents cheer on the Red Devils high school football team. It's standing room only at events from all-town spaghetti suppers to the historic Lowell Labor Day parade. The parade, the oldest continuous Labor Day observance in the state, was started in 1919 as a homecoming welcome for returning World War I veterans.

Dal Corobbo says residents are rightly proud of Lowell for all the town has done, and also because of its future promise.

"It's the idyllic hometown: a nice place to raise a family, with good schools and sense of community," Dal Corobbo says. "People here work hard to preserve all that is best about Lowell, for the present and also for future generations."

Parks are an important part of life in Lowell. At Evergreen Park (top), recent renovations include new basketball courts and equipment for the community's youth.

Excellence in education is the goal in Lowell where investment in local schools like Three Creeks Elementary School (center) is substantial and on-going.

Agriculture is still an important part of life in Lowell (bottom), though land for development is available for new light industrial businesses and residential neighborhoods.

Town of Lowell

501 East Main Street
Lowell, Indiana 46356
(219) 696-7794
www.lowell.net

MERRILLVILLE IS THE CROSSROADS OF NORTHWEST INDIANA. LIKE THE GREAT ANCIENT CITIES OF CONSTANTINOPLE OR ALEXANDRIA, THE TOWN OF MERRILLVILLE IS A PLACE WHERE A DELIGHTFUL AND ECLECTIC ASSORTMENT OF OFFERINGS LURES VISITORS FROM SURROUNDING COMMUNITIES AND BEYOND. MERRILLVILLE IS HARDLY ANCIENT, HOWEVER. A YOUNG

Merrillville is a crossroads, but it also boasts quiet corners, like the historic Deep River County Park (left).

Ethnic festivals, parades, and celebrations are a hallmark of the Town of Merrillville. The town's young people enjoy events like the annual Independence Day Parade and Celebration (right).

municipality, incorporated in 1971, the town is in the enviable position of having many current amenities as well as land for future growth.

Nearly everyone in the region passes through Merrillville at least once a week. No wonder. Here one can find Las Vegas style entertainment at the Star Plaza Theater, an array of ethnic dining opportunities, the largest shopping mall in the state of Indiana, three golf courses, the region's most touted water park, 14 town and two township parks.

Everyone Is Welcome

The people of Merrillville are the town's greatest asset. Representing a wide variety of cultures including Slavic, Greek, Hispanic, African-American, and Polish, the residents work together to create a community where "everyone is welcome." In fact, that idea—everyone is welcome—is the theme of the town where billboards honor and celebrate Merrillville's ethnic diversity.

Residents come together at a spate of ethnic festivals each year like the Greek and Serbian celebrations. They also celebrate their shared identity at the annual Independence Day Parade, one of the most spectacular in the region.

Great Place To Visit, Great Place To Live

Merrillville is a great place to visit. The town boasts diverse shopping, entertainment galore, and eateries that offer everything from Polish pierogis to French fondue. Its Deep River County Park, featuring a nineteenth century mill and grounds, provides a glimpse of history in a quiet corner away from the hustle and bustle.

For its approximately 35,000 residents, Merrillville is a great place to live. While it has one of the lowest tax rates among incorporated municipalities in the region, the town offers its citizens excellent public and parochial schools, affordable housing, and public safety services that rank as some of the best in northwest Indiana. Its convenient location—with access to all major highways that criss-cross the region—make it the preferred choice of residence for people who work within a 50-mile radius of the town.

Encompassing 38.5 square miles in central Lake County, Merrillville is 40 miles east of Chicago, 70 miles west of South Bend, 145 miles northwest of the state capitol in Indianapolis, and has immediate access to U.S. Hwy. 30 and Interstate 65.

Growth and Renewal

Youthful and energetic, Merrillville is embarking on a period of growth and renewal. Shepherded by Merrillville's town council, two tax increment financing (TIF) districts were implemented in 2000 and earmarked for public infrastructure.

Oregionality

The active Redevelopment Commission is focused on road improvements that will keep this crossroads community one with modern, convenient, and safe transportation corridors. A pending election will determine if Merrillville will soon adopt city status. Key to the municipality's growth is the available land town leaders say can accommodate housing, commercial and retail development, and light industry.

Merrillville demonstrates great community spirit, as evidenced by the large number of civic organizations that serve the town. They include the Merrillville Chamber of Commerce, Business and Professional Women, Civitan Club, Exchange Club, Inter-Club Council, Jaycees, Kiwanis, Lions Club, Optimists Club, Rotary, and Partners in Contracting Corporation.

Rich History

Merrillville boasts a long and rich history. In 1834, the entire area that was to become Merrillville was a province of the Potawatomi Indians known as McGwinn Village. In approximately 1835, a frontiersman named Jeremiah Wiggins, along with other frontiersman, camped and traded in the area later known as Wiggins Point. It became a popular stop for wagon trains bound for Chicago and points west. One of the most popular trails that traversed this area was the Sauk Trail (along what is now 73rd Avenue), the main stage route between Chicago and Crown Point. When Wiggins died in 1838, local settlers decided upon a more dignified moniker for the thriving development. The settlers decided upon the name of Centreville. In the 1850s, brothers William and Dudley Merrill settled in Centreville. Because of the Merrill brothers' great impact on the area's early growth, Centreville was renamed Merrillville. Until the town incorporated, the communities of Merrillville, Rexville, Lottaville, Ainsworth, Turkey Creek, Ross, and Deep River were governed as Ross Township.

The town that was once Centreville is still the center of the region. A great place to live, to dine, to shop, to hear the symphony or take in a play, to go to school, to play, to work. The town may be young, but it's a definite destination. And in Merrillville, everyone is welcome.

"Everyone is Welcome" is the motto in Merrillville. With citizens representing a panoply of cultures, the town honors its ethnic diversity at every opportunity (top).

Country phenomenon Tim McGraw (bottom) wows the audience at Merrillville's Star Plaza Theatre. The theatre presents more than 110 world class performances each year.

TOWN OF
MERRILLVILLE
7820 Broadway
Merrillville, Indiana 46410
(219) 769-5711
www.townofmerrillville.com

T HE MERRILLVILLE COMMUNITY SCHOOL CORPORATION IS A MICROCOSM OF THE OPPORTU-
NITIES, RESOURCES, AND ADVANTAGES OF NORTHWEST INDIANA. MCSC DEVELOPS IN STUDENTS
SKILLS FOR INDEPENDENT LEARNING, RESPONSIBLE CITIZENSHIP, AND PRODUCTIVE EMPLOYMENT,
AND IT PROVIDES THE COMMUNITY WITH EDUCATIONAL, VOCATIONAL, AND RECREATIONAL RESOURCES.

MERRILLVILLE COMMUNITY SCHOOL CORPORATION

This mission statement reflects the commitment of the corporation to development of the whole person throughout a journey that begins with kindergarten and continues through high school graduation.

Diversity and Excellence

The Merrillville Community School Corporation (MCSC) begins its work early in the lives of the community's children. Even before babies have gone home from the hospital, their parents have received a newborn parenting packet with valuable information about childhood development, daycare options, and the local school system from the MCSC.

Decades later, as adults and senior citizens, residents find the doors of the school still open to them for extensive adult education offerings, recreation, and social events at the Senior Citizen Center at Merrill-ville High School.

With about 6,000 students, 325 teachers, and 400 support personnel, the MCSC is at the heart of the Merrillville community. The school system has won kudos for its focus on diversity. With students from a wide variety of ethnic, racial, and religious backgrounds, the school system helps students appreciate the richness inherent in diversity. Positive social interaction, through programs like STAND (Socially Together and Naturally Diverse), provides a framework within which students learn about themselves and each other, and build bonds focused on mutual respect and responsibility.

It has also earned accolades for a focus on excellence that encourages all students to achieve their great potential, whatever their occupational or career choices might be. MCSC has received the "What Parents Want" Award seven years

in a row. The award recognizes schools that meet parents' criteria for top-notch schools.

Individual schools, like Pierce Middle School, have also won awards and brought positive attention to the community. Recipient of the year 2000 Blue Ribbon Award from the U.S. Department of Education, Pierce Middle School was one of only 198 schools nationwide to receive the country's highest education honor. MCSC students are routinely state level contenders each year in academic competitions ranging from math and science to music and art.

Strong Foundation

The MCSC supports learning and achievement with a devotion to staff excellence and a commitment to cutting edge facilities and programs. Merrillville teachers regularly participate in professional development programs that provide them an opportunity to increase their skills. Every year, many are recipients of grant awards that allow them time and resources to study a variety of subject areas and technologies.

A technology rich curriculum in Merrillville schools ensures students are prepared for the challenges of the modern workplace. Recent renovations at the high school and middle schools included construction of state-of-the-art computer laboratories (right). Merrillville students get year-round attention. In summer months, the school corporation's traveling book bus (bottom left) helps youngsters "read and succeed."

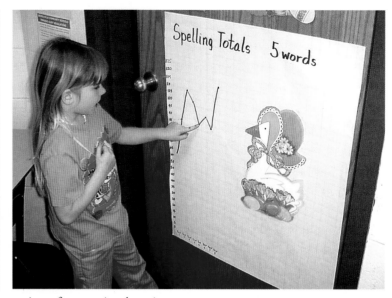

The technology-rich curriculum is supported by computer labs and Internet access, all networked into a state-of-the-art fiber optic system. Every student in the school corporation is learning word processing, data base, spreadsheet, keyboarding, multi-media, and information systems skills.

A $53 million renovation of the high school in 1995 was aimed at ensuring the institution would continue to offer the finest classrooms, laboratories, computer centers, media center, and athletic and social facilities in the region. This was followed by $28 million and $20 million renovations of Pierce and Harrison Middle Schools.

Known for Innovation

The MCSC is also lauded for continuous improvement efforts. Innovative programs—whether social, academic, or vocational—provide opportunities for students to learn and grow. For instance, a unique aspect of the MCSC's current program involves use of Malcolm Baldrige principles to guide the school system's improvement efforts. Originating in the non-educational environment, the Baldrige principles applied to education help students understand key ideas such as taking personal responsibility for quality, data driven decision making, and commitment to improvement. The system is driven by the pursuit of quality as defined by Dr. W.

Edwards Deming. The school corporation was also the first in the region to consider a unique Intermediate School specifically designed for the pre-adolescent 5th and 6th grader. The school system's required reading program is enhanced by a summer "Book Bus" that brings books to the students' neighborhoods.

MCSC's Gifted & Talented program provides accelerated classroom work for students who need it. In a Merrillville school today, it is not uncommon to find fourth and fifth graders logging on to the Internet to check out the stock market or learning to balance a checkbook, in addition to their academic studies. Life skills are integrated into classroom activities whenever possible, another component in the education of well-rounded citizens.

Working with the business community, the MCSC strives to not only expand the minds of its charges, but also to ensure they will find meaningful employment in the community after graduation. Training and mentoring programs build links between businesses in the region and the young people who constitute the workforce of the future. While a great percentage of MCSC students matriculate at colleges and universities nationwide, others find valuable training is available to them while they're still in high school. The vocational education program boasts a wide

variety of occupational curriculums, from welding and mechanics to childcare and cosmetology.

Career Days, job shadowing, and the school system's annual "Reality Store" for eighth graders ensure young people make informed career decisions.

For social and athletic involvement, the MCSC boasts a large number of athletic teams and sports activities housed in excellent facilities. Clubs and extracurricular activities for students allow youngsters to further develop interests and hone skills.

Changes for Future

Schools, like all other social institutions, are not immune to change. That doesn't frighten Dr. Tony Lux, superintendent of the MCSC, who believes community schools have changed and grown to meet the demands of the modern world and workplace. The key, Lux says, is to balance academic learning with development of the vocational, social, and citizenship skills that form the recipe for student success in later life.

"The years a person spends in school are some of the most formative," Lux says. "Our job is to present a well-rounded and balanced curriculum that prepares students for life and for work—and that nourishes a desire to be lifelong learners and responsible contributors to society. Graduation isn't an ending, it's just the beginning."

Talented teachers in Merrillville help students make sense of swirls of information. At Pierce Middle School— a national Blue Ribbon Schools honoree—planetarium director Greg Williams (top left) rightly tells students that "the sky's the limit."

In the Merrillville schools, even youngsters in the primary grades have access to cutting edge concepts. Elementary students (top right) learn how to make decisions, process information, and take responsibility for decisions using principles developed by Malcolm Baldridge and W. Edwards Deming.

MERRILLVILLE COMMUNITY SCHOOL CORPORATION

6701 Delaware Street
Merrillville, Indiana 46410
(219) 650-5300
www.mvsc.k12.in.us

I F MUNSTER WERE DESCRIBED IN JUST TWO WORDS, THOSE WORDS WOULD BE PRIDE AND INTEGRITY. THIS TOWN ON THE RIDGE PRIDES ITSELF ON ITS BEAUTIFUL PARKS AND WELL-MAIN- TAINED HOMES WHILE ALWAYS KEEPING ITS RESIDENTS FIRST AND FOREMOST IN EVERY DECISION IT MAKES. IN MUNSTER, IT IS QUALITY OF LIFE THAT MATTERS. CAREFUL PLANNING BRED AN EXCELLENT

school system; safe, comfortable neighborhoods; and a solid commercial base.

The largest industrial business is Pepsi-Cola General Bottlers with 1,500 employees. Other major employers include The Hammond Clinic, the Times Newspaper, and School Town of Munster. Outside its borders, Munster may be best known for its excellent medical facilities. The Community Hospital is nationally recognized and employs 2,200. Its growth has helped spur development of a multi-million dollar medical corridor that includes a medical fitness center and senior living community. Excellent medical facilities are a key component of the quality of life not only in Munster, but also in the region.

Planning in the town has produced an enviable balance of residential and commercial development. That balance, combined with excellent housing, schools, and public facilities, makes Munster one of the region's top draw cities.

In fact, when planners sat down to create the 1938 master plan, they envisioned the Munster of the future. Today it is clear the town did not stray far from that plan for a safe, stable community on the leading edge.

"I find Munster to be a very comfortable place to live," says town councilwoman Helen Brown. "Most of the people here have made their housing decisions based on educational goals for their children. Munster's schools have an excellent reputation that is well deserved." If people pay a premium to locate in Munster, adds Brown, it's because of their emphasis on education. Once the children are grown and gone, Munster is comfortable for empty nesters and seniors, with fine homes and city services.

"Our town government is professional and fiscally responsible," Brown notes. "Our tax rates have remained stable for five years."

Taming the Swamp

In the 1800s, early settlers found wet, woody land in the Calumet region. Not to be deterred, immigrant Netherlanders who knew how to cultivate the damp, fertile soil grew food to feed the burgeoning Chicago population. Town records indicate the first to arrive in the territory that would become Munster was Peter Jabaay. By 1870, there were 23 Netherlander families living in the area, including Eldert Monster, his wife,

Nieltje, and three sons from a previous marriage. As years passed, Jacob Monster (later anglicized to Munster), the couple's oldest son, was a store clerk, farmer, shopkeeper, school board member, and road supervisor. The contract post office he ran in his Munster store gave the town its name.

Incorporated in July 1907, Munster began as a community of 500, a number that has grown steadily to today's 20,000 residents. People are attracted by the town's beauty, its culture, and its easy access to Interstate 80/94, giving residents almost immediate entry into Chicago and to all points in the nation.

One doesn't see smokestacks in Munster. When it comes to economic development, the town has sought only businesses that are a good fit with the community.

"We're not out looking for any kind of business just to get some business in here," says clerk-treasurer David Shafer. "The community's values dictate clean industry, high-tech, and service industries."

Within the next seven to 10 years, Munster is expected to be fully developed. Then town planners will turn their eye toward

Munster is widely known for its excellent quality of life. Officials at the town hall (top) are committed to maintaining the town's record for excellent housing, top schools, superior parks, and well-managed city services.

Twenty parks grace Munster, offering recreational opportunities for citizens (bottom).

redevelopment to capitalize on older neighborhoods.

"Munster has been a wonderful place to live and also a great place to raise children," says John Mybeck, assistant to the president of the Community Foundation and the Ridgewood Arts Foundation. He has lived in Munster for 30 years. He says it is a selling point that Munster's elected officials, municipal employees, volunteer firefighters, and civic leaders are committed to doing the very best job they can.

Vision Pays Off

"What I always like to hear people say about Munster is that it has always looked farther out than the next year or two—it always looked way beyond that," says Tom DeGiulio, who has been town manager since 1984. Vision has helped the town make the kinds of long term decisions that strengthen quality of life in Munster.

One example is Lakewood Park. Currently a landfill in use since 1908 and purchased by the town in 1968 from the now defunct National Brick Company, the land will be transformed into a recreation zone with soccer fields and a fishing and nature area after the landfill is completed in 2003. The area is surrounded with high-end residential development.

Another example is the town's 20-plus mile network of bike paths, many of them along tree-lined

streets. Many parts of the path have been in place for two decades; ultimately, town leaders plan to link the trails with paths in surrounding towns.

Quality recreation is important in Munster. A drive by the town's 40-acre Community Park on a summer night reveals it is filled with the sounds of families cheering a child's first home run, the whoops and hollers of youngsters on baseball and softball teams. The 25-acre Bieker Woods, the site of the town's fall Heritage Festival, offers serenity and a refuge for birds and wildlife. In all, Munster boasts 20 parks, many of them conveniently situated for residents adjacent to quiet neighborhoods.

Every July, people from all over come to Munster for the annual Blues, Jazz and Arts on the Ridge Festival, the second largest free jazz festival in the Chicago metropolitan area. In the winter, Community Park is home to world-class ice

sculpting, having twice served as host for the annual National Ice Carving Competition. "The Community Hospital Winter Magic Festival is an incredible extravaganza of winter fun for the whole family," says councilman David Nellans. "The ice carving and the summer music festivals exemplify the commitment of the town, its businesses, and civic organizations to support activities that enrich the life of this community."

Munster also has become a cultural center thanks to its Center for the Visual and Performing Arts, which houses two art galleries, a theater, classrooms, a television studio, and banquet facilities. The center is home to the Northern Indiana Arts Association and the Northwest Indiana Symphony Orchestra.

"Community programs and amenities offer rich resources for residents," Mybeck says, "and opportunities to meet other people. Munster is a very friendly community blessed with a host of first-class facilities."

In Munster, residents credit generations of people—from founders to present day leaders—for the town's top amenities and high quality of life. According to town council president John Hluska, he and other members of the Munster Town Council—Helen Brown, David Nellans, and Steve Pestikas—pledge to maintain Munster as a community all can be proud of in years to come.

Visitors from throughout the region enjoy arts performances, events, and conferences at the Center for Visual and Performing Arts (top left) on Ridge Road.

Schools are a high priority for Munster families. Educational achievement records and state-of-the-art facilities (top right) attract families to the town. Cutting edge medical care is provided for Munster residents and people throughout Northwest Indiana at The Community Hospital (center).

Festivals are a mainstay of community life in Munster. One of the town's most touted annual events is Blues, Jazz and Arts on the Ridge (bottom), the second largest free jazz festival in the greater metropolitan area.

TOWN OF MUNSTER

1005 Ridge Road
Munster, IN 46321
(219) 836-8810
www.ci.munster.in.us

RAVELING THE INTERSTATE FROM WEST TO EAST AROUND LAKE MICHIGAN, THE CITY OF PORTAGE IS THE FIRST PORTER COUNTY MUNICIPALITY ONE ENCOUNTERS. PORTAGE IS A BUSTLING, ENERGETIC, VISIONARY INTRODUCTION TO THE COUNTY AND A KEY PLAYER IN THE GROWTH OF NORTHWEST INDIANA. ONCE THE QUIET HOME TO MANY OF THE REGION'S STEELWORKERS AND

tradespeople, today Portage is experiencing residential and commercial growth and is ranked as the largest city in the county. Younger than most of its neighbors, Portage is in many ways "the new kid on the block"—albeit the kind with the talent and enthusiasm to clear the bases. With a youthful city administration and demographics tilted toward the young, Portage has exuberance in ample supply. It also has the wisdom of its senior citizens, some of the most active residents in the city.

Attractive Location

The geographical location of Portage on the southern tip of Lake Michigan makes the city an attractive place to live. Portage is the only city in Porter County with a public marina and is home to West Beach, the largest public beach on the Indiana shoreline and a gem in the crown of the Indiana Dunes National Lakeshore. Amid growth and change, city planners have kept an eye on the kinds of amenities important to Portage's future. The city is now a destination, drawing visitors to its

A nationally ranked BMX bicycle track in Portage draws racing enthusiasts from throughout the region (top).

Portage is home to Porter County's only public marina on Lake Michigan (bottom).

300-acre Imagination Glen Park, the six-mile long Prairie-Duneland Trail, and the brand new, nationally ranked BMX bicycle race track.

New housing stock has created a real estate market that attracts a wide demographic and that together with educational, recreational, and cultural offerings is luring many homebuyers to Portage. A 50-bed hospital with emergency facilities was opened in 1995 and regional medical centers like St. Mary's Hospital have established medical offices and therapeutic clinics in the city. Investments in infrastructure, such as widening of roadways along the U.S. Hwy. 6 and Willowcreek Road commercial corridors, have supported the growth of shopping, service, and entertainment businesses in the city of Portage.

Committed to the future of its young people, Portage is serious about its schools. The city emphasizes education and opportunities for youth. Portage has received

state and national recognition for its middle school initiatives. Its high school earned a Special First Class Commission, the highest honor awarded by the State of Indiana. Amenities for children range from a bevy of sports leagues to concerts sponsored by the Community Concert Association. A brand new Boys & Girls Club was christened in 1997.

Economic Boom

Business is booming in Portage. The city is currently home to 25 industries, mainly steel manufacturing and processing. National Steel is the largest employer in this city of 34,000 with 1,600 workers. Other national corporations include DaimlerChrysler/Indiana Logistics, Coca-Cola, and Cargill.

Within the city limits is the International Port of Indiana. Built to handle St. Lawrence Seaway traffic, the tonnage handled by the port in 1999 was 30 percent greater than at the Port of Chicago, making it the largest and busiest port on the Great Lakes. The relatively young port, opened in 1970, has become a linchpin in expanding the economy of Portage and the entire northwest Indiana region. More than two million tons of goods—mostly steel and agricultural products such as corn and soybeans—were shipped in 1999. An Indiana University study found the port's economic impact is more than $409 million annually, much of it benefiting local companies. Today the International Port of Indiana employs about 600 workers from Portage and the region.

A new development bodes future good fortune for the City of Portage. Ameriplex, the first Class A industrial park in the region, is being built on 400 acres of land adjacent to the Port of Indiana to house light industrial, warehouse, distribution, and other businesses. New hotels are slated to occupy land along the park's frontage. Constituting thousands of square feet of commercial space, Ameriplex will be built in phases throughout the next eight to ten years.

Building a Future

Because of its youth, Portage is "building the city it wants to be," according to Mayor Douglas Olson, who at the age of 43 is the youngest leader in the municipality's history.

"We have energetic residents, committed business leaders, available land, and natural amenities like the lake and parks," Olson said. "Our vision is to pursue the best ideas and plans and to grow Portage in smart and thoughtful ways. We're thinking not just about tomorrow's housing, jobs, and parks, but also what Portage will be 20 or 30 years down the road."

So many resources combined with a rational plan for the city's future is making Portage the place to watch in northwest Indiana.

An excellent education for every student is the goal of Portage schools. At Kyle Elementary School, students learn from talented teachers.

The International Port (center) has brought economic benefit to Portage, the county, and the region. An adjacent development, a new Ameriplex industrial park, will be built in phases through 2010.

Quiet, safe neighborhoods make Portage an excellent choice for housing and raising a family (bottom).

CITY OF PORTAGE

6070 Central Avenue
Portage, Indiana 46368
(219) 762-5425
(219) 762-7784
www.ci.portage.in.us

R ICHARD KRAME REMEMBERS BACK TO A TIME WHEN, STANDING AT THE "CROSSROADS OF THE NATION" AT U.S. 30 AND U.S. 41, A PERSON COULD SEE OTHER COMMUNITIES SURROUNDING THE YET UNDISCOVERED RURAL COMMUNITY OF SCHERERVILLE. NO LONGER. SCHERERVILLE HAS BECOME A THRIVING COMMUNITY FULL OF LIFE AND OPPORTUNITY.

Schererville is at the crossroads of the northwest Indiana community (top). Railroads brought the first settlers in 1865.

Affordable homes in quiet neighborhoods (center) lure many to Schererville.

Town manager Richard Krame (bottom), in front of Schererville's new Police & Court Building, believes quality, orderly growth has helped the municipality thrive.

In the past two decades, the 900 souls inhabiting the community swelled to nearly 20,000 as developers saw the town's potential and began building in those wide open spaces.

"I believe we are doing something right," says Krame simply. Krame, the town manager, credits the town councils that have served the community with wise foresight and good planning. They not only ushered in orderly, quality growth for Schererville, but also steadfastly maintained the kind of small-town, rural atmosphere that has historically endeared residents to Schererville. "It's a great town," Krame says. "I'm very proud to be a part of Schererville."

Long History of Hard Work

The town's beginnings were anything but spectacular. Pioneers, many of whom were German Catholic, arrived to find land almost surrounded by marsh, according to History of the Crossroads, a publication produced for the town's 125th anniversary in 1991.

Tenacity was something the pioneers had in ample supply. They committed themselves to the new town. In 1865, the

railroad arrived, bringing with it new promise. One newcomer was Nicholas Scherer, who would become the official founder of the town.

According to the record, Nicholas Scherer was a determined and industrious man who sometimes gambled on ideas his neighbors thought sheer folly. A resolute planner who displayed the sturdy German industriousness that had enabled others to persevere the swampy terrain, Scherer planned out his village on 40 acres of land. He divided the town into 400 lots, and gave it his family's name. The town was recorded in the county's books on April 10, 1866.

Townspeople nurtured their community first by building a school and churches. Soon businesses began to flourish, starting a trend that continues to this day. Schererville became home to some nationally recognized names: Hoosiers Boys' Town; Teibel's Restaurant; and the Old Lincoln Highway, the nation's first transcontinental route.

"I've seen the town grow from horse and buggy streets to the roads we've got today," Krame reflects. "I've seen it grow because nice people—community-oriented people—moved to this town."

A Quiet Life

Denise Sulek grew up in Schererville and has no plans to leave. She stays for the top-rated elementary schools and the sense of community togetherness that defines the town.

"It's not like you are in the middle of the city," says Sulek, assistant director of the town's Building and Planning Department. Schererville is an easy commute to Chicago and elsewhere, she says, but about as distant from that lifestyle as a place can be.

Now the secret is out. "We're booming," Sulek says. With about 40 percent of its land still available for development, growth could easily get out of hand in Schererville. But town leaders only pursue development that is good

for the long term future of the town, Krame says. Local leaders, according to Krame, take a "brighter, bigger outlook of the town, what we need, what's the best way to go and what will keep people here."

A Town with Character

One selling point is the distinctive character developers have lent to subdivisions in Schererville, which offer housing ranging from $125,000-$275,000. Another is its park system, an achievement that engenders much pride. In 1987, there were two parks comprising a mere 15 acres. Today, Schererville boasts eight parks accounting for more than 100 acres in the community.

The town is investing in economic development as well. Currently underway is a $3.5 million three-phase rejuvenation of the downtown district along Joliet Street expected to entice new businesses to an area that hadn't seen change in nearly four decades.

One can shop in Schererville where 52 restaurants, a host of retail stores, and growing service industries offer everything citizens need. Still a crossroads community, it is close enough to Chicago to make an outing to the "Windy City" convenient, and near all of the region's major highways. The town is also less than 30 minutes from the beauty of the Indiana Dunes National Lakeshore.

"Schererville grew rapidly in the 1990s and I see a great future for Schererville in economic development," says Dana Vozar, executive director of the Schererville Chamber of Commerce. "We must provide the necessary businesses so that Schererville can thrive."

Despite all the talk of growth, however, Krame often focuses on the town's tradition as a place where people are committed to making Schererville a better place than when they arrived. The same cheerful industriousness displayed by early pioneers, he says, applies to the town's residents today. Groups like the Lion's Club are extremely active, lending support to a multitude of community projects. The Chamber of Commerce—a 50-member organization in 1963—now boasts a roster of more than

250. And a volunteer organization, Schererville Civic Funds Inc., established in 1956, has dedicated itself to helping those in need.

"The town has been very successful because of the people who have been involved in it," Krame stresses. To celebrate everything good about the town, the community has come together the last Friday of every July since 1963 for the Schererville Corn Roast—an event described by townspeople as "not to be missed."

Krame knows new faces make it difficult to "know everybody in town" as residents once did. Now bigger and busier than its sleepy predecessor, Schererville has grown steadily and thoughtfully from a small enclave of settlers to a bustling community of caring and concerned neighbors.

Community parks and family entertainment offerings (top) make Schererville a great place to raise a family.

Schererville may be a crossroads, but residents can still enjoy a quiet afternoon at places like the Scherwood Golf Course (center).

TOWN OF SCHERERVILLE
833 West Lincoln Highway
Schererville, Indiana 46375
(219) 322-2211

PROMOTING THE BEST INTERESTS OF BUSINESS AND COMMUNITY IS THE HEART OF THE MISSION FOR THE SCHERERVILLE CHAMBER OF COMMERCE. AN ACTIVE ORGANIZATION WITH 290 MEMBERS, THE CHAMBER IS INVOLVED IN A HOST OF EVENTS THAT SERVE BUSINESS MEMBERS, COMMUNITY RESIDENTS, AND STUDENTS. THE SCHERERVILLE CHAMBER OF COMMERCE WAS ORGANIZED

SCHERERVILLE CHAMBER OF COMMERCE

105 East Joliet Street
Schererville, Indiana 46375
(219) 322-5412
www.jorsm.com/scc

Schererville chamber board members include (l to r) secretary, Margie Schwartz; executive director, Dana Vozar; past president, Donald Schlyer; director, Barb Gulden; president, Bob Pesavento; director, Mary Watson; vice president, Marti Golas; director, Kathleen Willman; president-elect, Paulette Young; and treasurer, Janice Malinowski. Not pictured are directors Michael Troxell and Richard Krame.

in 1963. Like thousands of chambers of commerce nationwide, it solicits participation from leaders in local business and industry who know that working together is the key to success. In Schererville, the chamber has had a critical role in projects ranging from beautification of the town to consultation on legislative matters affecting its members. It also takes an active interest in the community's young people, hosting a number of events that support education and the arts.

Vision and Effort

Lead by a board of 11 directors voted into office by the general membership, the chamber seeks to get everyone involved, according to executive director Dana Vozar.

"We have an excellent group of intelligent and committed members," Vozar says. "Our ability to get things done is directly attributable to their vision and efforts."

The list of "things to get done" is long every year. With 21 distinct committees, the chamber has carved out a substantial number of

initiatives. Each fall, the chamber hosts a popular Consumer Show—now in its tenth year—which brings Schererville businesses and consumers together. Displays and demonstrations of the latest products and services help customers learn more about local stores and industries, and allow business owners to develop relationships with area shoppers.

The beautification committee can be credited for sharing the cost with the town of attractive "Welcome to the Town of Schererville" signs visible today at the major approaches to the municipality. Now visitors have visible landmarks to tell them when they have arrived, courtesy of the Schererville business community.

Chamber members help each other through committees that organize everything from seminars on important business topics and technologies to "business after hours" events that provide time for local networking and relationship-building.

Enjoyment is a part of the chamber's agenda, too. For more than three decades, it has sponsored an annual corn roast celebration that brings out the town for an evening of food, entertainment, and merriment. Proceeds support numerous chamber programs for members and the community.

Supporting Community's Youth

The Schererville Chamber of Commerce does as much as it can to support education and youth in the community, Vozar notes.

"Our young people are the future and the business community here feels strongly that part of our

focus should be directed to programs for youth," she explains.

It is the reason why the chamber annually organizes a Career Day for eighth graders that helps youngsters understand how the choices they make early about education, careers, and training will affect their success in later life. It also gives local business people a chance to interact one-on-one with Schererville's young people, taking time to explain different careers and occupations. Another event, the chamber's annual Mardi Gras Madness Fashion Show, raises money for Parent-Teacher Organizations for each public school in Schererville to support special programs.

The chamber also hosts programs that benefit young and old alike. The organization was instrumental in bringing the Indiana Symphony Orchestra to Schererville for a concert especially for townspeople.

Members help each other by doing business locally and willingly sharing their expertise. Whether the question is about product lines, advertising methods, inventory, employee incentives, or some other issue, a chamber member is likely to obtain assistance from another chamber member. Members stay in touch through committee meetings, general meetings, and the organization's bi-monthly newsletter.

The Schererville Chamber of Commerce is distinguished for its care for members, spirit of volunteerism, and concern for community. Its track record of accomplishments, say community members, has strengthened not only business in Schererville, but the entire town.

THE TOWN OF ST. JOHN TRACES ITS BIRTH TO THE ARRIVAL OF JOHN HACK, A GERMAN IMMIGRANT AND FARMER WHO SETTLED IN SOUTHWEST LAKE COUNTY IN 1837. IT WAS ONLY 21 YEARS AFTER THE "INDIANA TERRITORY" HAD BEEN ADMITTED TO THE UNION AS A STATE. HACK DISCOVERED AN UNTRAMMELED WILDERNESS. HE BUILT A HOMESTEAD, AND BEGAN TO FARM, SOON

joined by other German families who put down roots, tamed the new frontier, and created a new life in America.

Prior to the arrival of the railroad in 1881, the townspeople depended on their own resources for sustenance. The earliest trades and businesses were agricultural. Plowing was done with oxen with plows often made of hedge limbs. Pioneer settlers delivered wheat to Chicago in oxen-driven wagons. In 1846, the town—now known as St. Johns—built its first post office. By 1881, an official plat of the town had been drawn. In 1911, the town was incorporated and its name reduced by one letter to become St. John.

Hardworking Character

St. John still has that earnest and hardworking character. The quiet that Hack and his family found—miles from the nearest settler and many more from anything that could be called a metropolis—is still cherished by the community. Here residents relish the opportunity to escape the "hustle and bustle" of more crowded places, to fashion lives focused on family and simplicity.

Still, the town has grown. The population has nearly doubled since 1989, now estimated at 8,000 residents. A number of new and attractive housing developments, ranging from moderately priced homes to more upscale single family residences, have lured more citizens to this quiet corner of northwest Indiana.

The St. John town government delivers outstanding municipal services, carefully preserves a stable tax rate, and exercises foresight in its commitment to long-term

Visitors to St. John routinely visit Pioneer Church (top), a log cabin church built in 1839. Many of the town's early settlers are buried nearby on the grounds of what is now St. John the Evangelist Catholic Church (bottom).

New residential housing (center) has made room for more people in St. John, a quiet community where family comes first.

planning. As a result, business, light industry, and residents prosper in a community carefully prepared not only for the present, but also for a future of continued economic expansion. The town participates with other neighboring communities to curb costs of municipal

purchases through the Quad-Town Interlocal Cooperation Agreement.

Excellent medical facilities, including the Hammond Clinic, serve the town. Also, Community Hospital of Munster recently broke ground in St. John for a 70,000 square foot multi-million dollar outpatient center slated for completion in 2001.

Treasure Trove of Landmarks

St. John has kept close watch on its treasure trove of historical landmarks. In fact, visitors to the town come explicitly for the history lesson instead of a shopping spree (the town does not, for instance, have a shopping mall). A must-see is always the Pioneer Church, located on Route 41, the town's main arterial. Built in 1839, the historic log church is known as the first Catholic church in Lake County, though some records indicate an earlier frame building preceded it. Today, the small cabin church sits surrounded by the gravestones of early settlers on the grounds of the present St. John the Evangelist Catholic Church.

Historic homes—those of early citizens such as Francis P. Keilman and Bernard Scheidt—are still standing. The history of St. John was recorded in a book by town resident William Tuley in 1987 and contains fascinating early records and photographs. The St. John Historical Society keeps a sense of history alive, sponsoring local history programs and publishing items like a series of note cards featuring photographs of first settlers, homesteads, and businesses.

Quiet and Quaint

Life remains calm in St. John. The local economy is built on service businesses. One of the town's largest employers is Schilling Lumber. The longstanding community business was born when twin brothers Frank and Louis Schilling opened a gas station in 1932, selling a little lumber on the side. After a stint at the shipyards during World War II, the brothers established Schilling Brothers Lumber & Supply. The Schillings and their heirs have been responsible for much of the commercial development in St. John, businesses that are family-owned and designed to meet the needs of townspeople.

Others work at Lake Central High School, located in St. John and serving students from St. John, Schererville, Dyer, and the unincorporated areas of St. John Township. On Friday nights in the fall, students take a break from studies to cheer for the Lake Central Indians football team.

The majority of St. John residents live in the community but work elsewhere in Lake County and the Chicagoland area. While the town is not averse to economic development, St. John welcomes only clean, light industry compatible with the character of the community. Plans on the drawing board now will give St. John something it wants: a bicycle trail through the town covering roughly eight miles and connecting the two parts of the town that are bisected by Route 41.

Not Your Typical Town

St. John is not your typical town. That, say those who love it, is a part of its charm. Change comes slowly and methodically. There are no annual festivals that urge citizens into the streets. St. John residents enjoy their quiet weekends, spent with family and friends, in a place where people come before pomp and circumstance. Its government shares qualities of the early settlers: earnest, open, frugal. Consider that when St. John built its new town hall in 1995—a pleasant but unprepossessing structure—it plunked down $650,000, all in cash.

In many ways, residents of St. John today share the sentiments of founder Hack. They, like Hack, could have forged their futures in the big cities. In St. John, the priorities are different. People here happily forge their own frontier, trading hustle and bustle for calm and quiet.

St. John offers a slice of small-town life that the town's residents enjoy. On Fridays in the the fall, the stadium is full when the high school football team (top) takes the field. The St. John Ice Arena (center) provides opportunities for local youth to learn skating and hockey.

There is no major mall in St. John, but a host of local businesses (bottom)—mostly owned and operated by town residents—provide the goods and services people need.

TOWN OF ST. JOHN
10955 W. 93rd Avenue
St. John, Indiana 46373
(219) 365-4800

A VISIT TO VALPARAISO'S WEB SITE OFFERS THE READER A "PICTURE POSTCARD HISTORY" OF THE CITY. THE IMAGE IS APT, FOR VALPARAISO TRULY IS ONE OF THE REGION'S PICTURE POSTCARD PLACES: PRETTY, CHARMING, NEIGHBORLY, HISTORIC. WITH A "CAN DO" SPIRIT AND UNRIVALED QUALITY OF LIFE, VALPARAISO HAS BECOME KNOWN AS A CITY WHERE RESIDENTS, LEADERS,

businesses, and civic organizations work together for the good of all.

Vale of Paradise

Valparaiso was a teeming expanse of rich farmland when first platted out in 1836. After the State of Indiana separated LaPorte and Porter counties just after the War of 1812, commissioners searched for a site suitable to be the Porter County seat. They selected land on a glacial moraine and along the ancient Sauk Indian Trail from Rock Island, Illinois to Detroit, Michigan in a tiny village that had seen its first log cabin settler in 1834. They named the city "Portersville" after Commodore David Porter of the U.S. Navy whose frigate Essex joined the 1812 battle in Valparaiso, Chile.

The city would not remain Portersville for long. Old sailors who stopped at Hall's Saloon retold the tale of Porter's courage in the Chilean harbor of Valparaiso, capturing the imaginations of local residents. In 1837, the town was renamed Valparaiso which in Spanish means "vale of paradise."

Quality of Life

To the city's 27,000 residents and visitors, Valparaiso does seem a paradise. Valparaiso grew around an historic downtown where the Porter County Courthouse, built with Second Empire and Neoclassical architectural elements in 1885, reigns as Valparaiso's much-loved landmark. A fire destroyed its clock tower in 1934 and the building was subsequently restored.

The quaint and commercially bustling downtown, a participant in the National Trust for Historic Preservation's Main Street program

since 1986, is a shopper's haven with many restaurants; gift, clothing, sports, candy, and other stores; and professional business offices, many located on the upper floors of the restored historic buildings.

"Meet me at the courthouse" is a common refrain. The grand building serves as ground zero for many city-wide events like the annual Popcorn Festival, held the first Saturday after Labor Day since 1979, and the annual winter holiday celebration featuring caroling, hot chocolate, and horse and carriage rides. The Popcorn Festival, honoring the city's most famous resident ever— Orville Redenbacher—now attracts about 70,000 people from throughout the midwest for its parade of popcorn floats, the Popcorn Panic race, music, food, and merriment.

Valparaiso has successfully balanced a pro-business environment with attractive quality of life amenities. The city has devoted more than 650 acres to parks where residents enjoy swimming, fishing, golf, jogging, soccer, baseball, picnicking, and more. At

Rogers-Lakewood Park, residents can enjoy nature, catch a fish, and even go snow sledding down the city's most exciting hill in winter. Fairgrounds Park, the former site of the Porter County Fair until new quarters were built in Washington Township, is a beehive of activity with baseball diamonds and running tracks. At Ogden Gardens, Valparaiso's expertly landscaped and tended public garden, couples book the gazebo for outdoor weddings.

Newcomers to Valparaiso often report they moved to the city because of its excellent schools. Valparaiso Community Schools enjoys a longstanding reputation as one of the top-performing districts in the region. With several blue ribbon schools and a host of extracurricular and cultural activities designed to hone young minds, Valparaiso is a perennial contender in academic and sports competitions and is renowned for the high number of students it sends off to top-ranked universities and technical schools each year.

Downtown Valparaiso (top) has charm and historical flavor. It's the venue for Valparaiso's annual Popcorn Festival (below) which draws up to 70,000 visitors from throughout the region.

Can Do Spirit

Valparaiso is a volunteer city. An extraordinarily high percentage of citizens and businesses, together with Valparaiso University, the Greater Valparaiso Chamber of Commerce, and local churches work to make the city and the region a better place to live and work.

Every year, the city sponsors one of the most successful "Christmas in April" programs that repairs and maintains homes for low income elderly and the needy. Chamber of Commerce members annually volunteer to present "Reality Store," a day-long educational program for eighth graders that shows how career choices and other decisions will affect the youths' futures. Thousands throughout the city volunteer at senior centers, as scout troop leaders, in charitable organizations, and more.

VU a Local Asset

Valparaiso University is one of the community's best assets. Its history stretches from the founding in 1859 of the Valparaiso Male and Female College that later became the Northern Indiana Normal School and Business Institute. It grew in educational offerings and numbers of students, and offered training in such subjects as law, engineering, and pharmacy. By 1903, it had purchased medical and dental schools in Chicago. The university's reputation rivaled top eastern

schools but its prices were more modest, which earned it the moniker "poor man's Harvard." In 1906, the college officially changed its name to Valparaiso University and in 1925 it was purchased by the Lutheran University Association. Today, Valparaiso University continues to be recognized as one of the outstanding institutions of higher education in the country. A four-year, private university with nearly 4,000 students from throughout the U.S. and more than 40 countries, it is regularly ranked as one of the nation's best comprehensive universities and a "best buy." Valparaiso University offers more than 65 undergraduate majors in its College of Arts and Sciences, College of Business Administration, College of Engineering, College of Nursing, and Christ College, which is one of the most distinguished honors colleges in the United States, as well as programs in the graduate division and the School of Law.

Strong Business Climate

Residents work in cities throughout the region and in the Chicago metropolitan area, but many have jobs in Valparaiso. That's because the city is home to a host of national, regional, and local businesses and enterprises. The largest employers are Porter Memorial Hospital, Valparaiso University, Valparaiso Community

Schools, Emerson Power Transmission, Jet Corr, Opportunity Enterprises, Urschel Laboratories, Magnequench U.G., McDaniels Fire Systems, First National Bank, UGN, Rexam Beverage Can, and Task Force Tips. Most engage in international trade. Several, like Urschel Laboratories which makes high-precision food processing and size reduction machines, and Task Force Tips, which fabricates cutting edge commercial fire fighting hose nozzles and equipment, export their products worldwide.

The Greater Valparaiso Chamber of Commerce, with nearly 600 members, works with city leaders and businesses to help companies thrive and to attract new firms to Valparaiso. It also is a key player in promoting amenities, supporting schools and education, and building partnerships that honor the city's past and help fashion its future.

Picture Postcard City

Valparaiso is the kind of city that can sound too good to be true, say residents. In the new millennium, this vale of paradise continues to charm with its beautiful old buildings and homes, quality schools, volunteer spirit, good government, healthy economy, community-minded businesses, and fun-filled city events. It's a picture postcard kind of place where what you see is exactly what you get.

Valparaiso boasts more than 650 acres of parks and recreation areas. Popular for swimming, fishing, and bicycling—and snow-sledding in winter—is Rogers-Lakewood Park (top).

The Porter County Courthouse (center), built in 1885, is a beloved local landmark and ground zero for many community festivals and events.

A four-year, private university, Valparaiso University is one of *U.S. News & World Report's* top-ranked midwest colleges. Chapel of the Resurrection, one of the largest collegiate chapels in the world, is at the campus center and is the site of daily worship services and activities.

CITY OF VALPARAISO
166 Lincolnway Avenue
Valparaiso, Indiana 46383
(219) 462-1161
www.ci.valparaiso.in.us

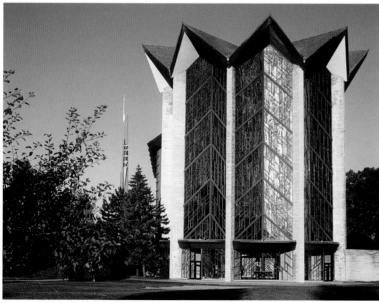

CITY OF WHITING

I F SMALL TOWN CHARM COULD BE BOXED OR BOTTLED AND SOLD AT MARKET, WHITING WOULD BE RICH BEYOND ITS DREAMS. IN AN ERA WHEN DEVELOPERS STRIVE TO CREATE NEIGHBORHOOD INTIMACY AND MAIN STREET-STYLE BUSINESS CENTERS IN PLANNED SUBDIVISIONS, THIS VILLAGE-LIKE CITY OF 1,100 ACRES AND 5,200 RESIDENTS STANDS OUT AS A ROLE MODEL IN THE REGION.

Rich in Amenities

Dubbed "The Little City on the Lake" many decades ago, Whiting is already rich in the kinds of amenities and values that money alone can't buy. In Whiting, citizens still wave to one another on the street; schoolchildren saunter along the bustling 119th Street commercial business district with dimes and nickels in their pockets for ice cream or a donut; and families walk to the city's beautiful lakefront park, Andrew Carnegie Library, or the historic Whiting Memorial Community Center.

It was "Pop" Whiting who set down roots in 1869. An engineer who derailed his freight train so that a passenger line could pass, he was immortalized when the locals named the derailment site "Pop Whiting's Siding." The railroads had brought settlers to the swampy dune land along Lake Michigan. Natural bounty encouraged habitation. The area boasted

strawberries, huckleberries, cranberries, wild turkey, geese, ducks—but most of all, wide-open land ripe for development. In 1851, when the Michigan Southern Railroad was built across what was then considered "the wilderness," settlers multiplied. German and Irish workers and their families came first, often laboring for the railroad for one dollar a day, followed by immigrants from central and eastern Europe. The melting pot city flourished.

Refinery Part of History

Like the Pullman neighborhood in Chicago, Whiting soon became a company town when the Standard Oil Company and the Rockefeller family in 1889 chose this shoreline town as the site of its Midwestern industrial facility. From the moment the first shipment of 125 tank cars of kerosene arrived at the refinery that next year, Whiting and Standard Oil would share an intertwined history that continues to this day.

A tour of Whiting is not complete without glimpses of "The Village," where stately houses were built for Standard Oil managers and supervisors along Ohio, Pennsylvania, and New York Avenues. On the south side of town, worker cottages were constructed to house the increasing number of eastern European immigrants hired by the company. Ethnic and religious ties were strong among the residents and immigrants who built its magnificent churches. The turn-of-the-century homes and churches are architectural gems that have been meticulously cared for by the community. They now count for a great measure of Whiting's indisputable hometown charm.

Small town America thrives in Whiting (bottom) where historic homes and preserved traditions survive only moments from the big city of Chicago (top, as viewed from Whiting's lakefront).

Whiting is a living history lesson. Because many of the city's residents are second and third generation residents, stories are still told on the street of the massive explosion at the Standard Oil plant in 1955 that rocked residents from their beds and destroyed most of the homes in the small Stiglitz Park section of the city, but that surprisingly killed only two. Tales are also passed on about the city's rich heritage. Here the community gathered at the Hoosier Theatre in the 1920s and 1930s to watch touted vaudeville performers and catch glimpses of famous movie stars like W.C. Fields and James Cagney. The still open Hoosier, listed on the National Register of Historic Places and painstakingly restored in recent years, is the only "movie palace" that remains in the region.

Small Town Charm

People in Whiting have a terrific respect for the heritage of the city and its architectural and cultural assets," says Gayle Faulkner-Kosalko, Executive Director of the Whiting-Robertsdale Chamber of Commerce. The charm and small-town feel she says, are safeguarded by everyone from residents to businesses to the city's planning department.

Today, Whiting attracts tourists and residents of the region with its annual Pierogi Fest, a tribute to Eastern European food, culture, and song. Its "Summer with the Symphony" lures hundreds to the Whiting Lakefront Park Pavilion to hear the Northwest Indiana Symphony perform under the stars. At Christmas time, residents celebrate with "Home for the Holidays," featuring an illuminated parade, decorated homes tour, hand bell concert, and ethnic cookie-bake.

Though land-locked, the City of Whiting does have some new plans on the drawing board. Currently slated is the Whiting Park Shoreline Improvement Project that will enlarge the city's lakefront park, add walkways, bike paths, and landscaping, and provide a 30 to 50 boat slip marina. Additional improvements under study include reconstruction or redevelopment work along many of Whiting's historic and picturesque streets.

Change comes carefully and cautiously in Whiting. That, too, is part of its charm. In a world where landscapes are transformed overnight and hometowns lose their familiarity, Whiting is fortunately a city that time sometimes forgot. Today, both residents and visitors say that's an asset and a blessing.

Plans now on the drawing board could expand Whiting's much-visited lakefront park (top).

To honor the Eastern European heritage of many of its residents, the City of Whiting hosts an annual Pierogi Fest. A popular event, the fest gives the locals an opportunity to display their sense of humor with such parade participants as the Babushka Ladies Broom & Mop Battalion, and Mr. Pierogi (bottom).

City of Whiting
1443 119th Street
Whiting, Indiana 46394
(219) 659-7700

Corporate Profiles

Oregionality

SAND, STEEL, & SOUL

A LOOK AT SOME OF THE ELITE CORPORATIONS THAT HAVE HELPED
BUILD THE REGION AND MADE THIS BOOK POSSIBLE.

Airtek, Inc.

Kenneth J. Allen & Associates, P.C.

Alternative Distribution Systems, Inc.

Amarillo Roadhouse

American Renolit Corporation

American Savings FSB

American Trust & Savings Bank

Ancilla Systems

AT&T Broadband

Avery Dennison

The Bachman Partnership, P.C.

Bethlehem Steel Corporation

BP Amoco

The Brant Companies

Bulk Transport Corporation

C & C Iron, Inc.

Calumet Abrasives Company, Inc.

Calumet College of St. Joseph

Calumet Flexicore Corporation

Chicago SouthShore & South Bend Railroad

Chicago Steel

Cicco's Menswear, Inc.

L.I. Combs & Sons, Inc.

Dawn Food Products, Inc.

Edgewater Systems for Balanced Living

Empress/Horseshoe Casino Hammond

Family Care Centers of Indiana, LLC

Five Star Hydraulics, Inc.

Green Light Creative

Hammond Group, Inc.

Hardings Inc.

Hessville Cable & Sling

HFS Bank

Hoosier Boys' Town, Inc./Campagna Academy

Hospice of the Calumet Area, Inc.

Hyles-Anderson College

Indiana University Northwest

Indiana's International Port

International Longshoremen's Association

Isakson Motor Sales

Ivy Tech State College

Lake Area United Way

Lake County Commissioner Frances DuPey

Lake County Commissioner Gerry Scheub

Lake County Community Economic Dev. Dept.

Lake County Convention & Visitors Bureau

Lake County Parks and Recreation Department

Lamar Advertising Company

Lincoln 'Way Animal Complex

Mercantile Bank

The Methodist Hospitals

R.L. Millies & Associates, Inc.

Miner Electronics Corporation

National Metal Services Corp.

National Steel Midwest Operations

NiSource Inc.

Northwest Indiana Forum

Pollution Control Industries

Purdue University Calumet

Radio One Communications

Rieth-Riley Construction Co., Inc.

Roman Catholic Diocese of Gary

Southlake Mall

State Line Energy

Sullair Corporation

The Times

Union Tank Car Company

University of Chicago Hospitals

U. S. Steel Gary Works

Varied Products of Indiana, Inc.

Villa Cesare

Wagner Homes

Weil-McLain

WYIN Channel 56

MILLIONS OF PEOPLE BREATHE EASIER BECAUSE OF THE WORK OF A HOBART, INDIANA HEAD-QUARTERED COMPANY. AIRTEK, INC., A MANUFACTURER AND WORLDWIDE DISTRIBUTOR OF CATALYTIC CONVERTERS, IS AN AMERICAN SUCCESS STORY, TOO. FOUNDED BY THE PROIMOS FAMILY IN 1990, AIRTEK ORIGINALLY EMPLOYED 15 AND MANUFACTURED THREE TYPES OF CONVERTERS.

Today it has a staff of more than 120 and markets 1,000 types of converters and emissions components. And its growth chart for the future features an arrow pointed straight up.

At the head of the company is Andreas Proimos, president of AirTek and recipient of a nomination as Entrepreneur of the Year in 2000. Proimos arrived in the United States from Greece at the age of 16, shepherded to a new shore by a father who believed America was the land of opportunity.

American Dream

By 1975, Andreas and his brother Evangelos, who both saved much of their earnings from U.S. Steel, had put together the money needed to purchase a Texaco gas station in Hobart. But times—and air quality standards—were changing, and the Proimos brothers kept a close eye on the marketplace. By 1990, it was clear to the Proimoses that the more stringent federal clean air laws being enacted in the 1980s offered opportunities for a new company.

After selling the service station, the brothers incorporated AirTek in 1990 to manufacture the catalytic converters automobiles would require to meet stricter air standards. The new business wasn't an overnight success. Lengthy government approval processes and start-up glitches plagued the new company, but the Proimos brothers were patient. Within five years, the company employed 20 workers who fabricated the company's converters. Within a decade, AirTek would earn a reputation as a quality manufacturer of CATCO catalytic converters and other emission-inhibiting components and its

More than 120 workers manufacture the CATCO catalytic converters (top) and emissions inhibiting components for which AirTek has become recognized worldwide. Trained employees now fabricate 1000 types of converters (bottom).

payroll roster would mushroom to more than 120.

Cleaner Air Technology

Today, AirTek is one of the world's most competitive suppliers of catalytic converters. A catalytic converter is the primary component of the pollution control system for automobiles with gasoline-powered internal combustion engines. The converter, incorporated into the exhaust system of a vehicle downstream from the manifold and before the muffler, is composed of a metal or ceramic substrate (called a "biscuit" in the industry). This substrate material is wrapped in heat resistant matting and encased (or "canned") in

a stainless steel shell. The substrate is "loaded" with precious, heat-reactive metals (palladium, platinum, or rhodium, for instance) by means of a chemical washcoat process that binds the metals to the substrate. The heat of the engine's exhaust sets off a reaction in the converter—a catalytic conversion—that reduces harmful pollutants in emissions to innocuous gases and benign by-products such as oxygen, nitrogen, hydrogen, and water.

The nature of chemical conversions is a matter of common knowledge to scientists and manufacturers. Turning noxious emissions into harmless exhaust, however, is a technology now widely appreciated by the public, even if many find the chemistry difficult to understand. First developed in the late 1960s, catalytic converters can be credited for a massive reduction in the number and kinds of pollutants released into the atmosphere.

"We're extremely pleased that the work we do has improved air quality," Andreas Proimos says. "The marketplace for products of this type is growing, and we intend to grow with it."

Expanding Marketplace

AirTek produces some of the most effective and cost-efficient catalytic converters on the market. In compliance with United States Environmental Protection Agency guidelines, AirTek's converters also meet the more stringent standards of the California Air Resource Board (CARB). While the company entered the marketplace in the 1990s with three versions of its converter, now it fabricates, markets, and ships more than 1,000 models suitable for use on most of the vehicles operated worldwide. It also manufactures a complete line of products installers use to bring auto emissions systems into compliance with regulatory standards, such as air tubes, carbon dioxide sensors, and air injection manifolds. AirTek intends to remain a global leader in product development and marketing of state-of-the-art catalytic

converters and automotive anti-pollution devices. AirTek's market has expanded to serve not only the United States and Canada, but also South America, Europe, Australia, and the Far East. Company engineers and technicians have also become valuable experts in demand for consulting and training services.

It's a growth market, indeed. AirTek sits poised at the intersection of booming worldwide auto production and ever-stricter air quality standards. The need

for reliable products that convert noxious chemicals into more harmless emissions is obvious to government leaders and environmental experts around the globe.

A Future Full of Promise

After years of diligent work, the Proimoses built a business of which its family—and the entire region—can be proud. Andreas and Gus Proimos manage the AirTek operation in Hobart, while brother Evangelos now heads Goldsboro, North Carolina-based Goerlichs, Inc., a manufacturer of auto exhaust systems the family acquired in 1998.

The Proimoses give credit for their success to a crew of dedicated employees focused on quality. "We couldn't do this without their contributions," Andreas says. "We believe in a team effort at AirTek."

The Proimoses believe in solid teamwork. They believe in the value of their contribution to continuous reduction of air pollutants. And they also—of course—can't help but believe in the American Dream.

Tough quality standards and routine testing (top) ensure AirTek's products are some of the best in the marketplace.

From its Hobart headquarters, AirTek ships its catalytic converters, anti-pollution components, and accessories to automobile and vehicle manufacturers around the globe (bottom).

AirTek, Inc.
4410 West 37th Avenue
Hobart, Indiana 46342
(219) 947-1664

ASK ANYONE ON THE STREET WHAT PROFESSION TRAFFICS IN PASSION AND THE ANSWER COULD LIKELY BE "POET." ASK WHAT PROFESSION DEPENDS UPON THE THOROUGH EXECUTION OF LOGIC AND A COMMON ANSWER WOULD BE "LAWYER." WHAT IS LESS KNOWN PERHAPS IS THAT THE BEST ATTORNEYS COMBINE KNOWLEDGE OF LAW WITH A PASSION FOR ITS PURPOSE,

imbuing the pursuit of justice with compassion.

Passion is one of the first words Kenneth J. Allen uses to describe the profession he has practiced for twenty years. Principal attorney in Kenneth J. Allen & Associates, P.C., the articulate and energetic Allen is passionate about his firm's representation of accident and injury victims. Licensed to practice in both Indiana and Illinois, he has obtained more than $40 million in trial verdicts on behalf of

clients, and millions more in out-of-court settlements.

Passion for People

No one needs Allen and the services his firm provides more than the injured, disabled, and despondent who walk through his doors. Kenneth J. Allen & Associates represents the victims of accidents and injury only—persons whose lives have often been seriously dislocated by physical or psychological trauma.

"People come to us at a difficult time in their lives, having sustained tremendous physical, emotional, and financial losses," Allen explains. "I can't think of many higher callings than the representation of people whose lives have literally been turned upside down—often in the blink of an eye—by incidents that shouldn't have happened."

Even attorneys across the aisle respect Allen's unrelenting pursuit of justice for clients. He has been called everything from "ruthless" to "remarkable." But to Allen, it simply boils down to quality representation for human beings who have been hurt.

"Yes, I'm passionate about what I do," Allen says. "Our system of justice has protections for the people who turn to us. We're here to make sure the system works for them."

From Literature to Law

Kenneth J. Allen had loves before he found law. A lifelong resident of northwest Indiana, he received a B.A. from Valparaiso University where he studied English and Literature. He then studied at Cambridge University in England. There he spent time not

only in classrooms, but also in the ring as a member of the university's boxing team. No longer pulling his punches, Allen returned to the U.S. to attend Indiana University at Bloomington as a Stephenson Fellow. He graduated with honors and received his J.D. in 1981.

There were other experiences that molded the young man who would become an indefatigable fighter for justice, fairness, and safety. Allen held jobs while still in high school, worked with and learned from men who toiled in the building trades, and served a stint as a railroad track laborer. A member of the Carpenter's Union (UBC) to this day, and a former member of the Teamsters Union (IBT), Allen developed a respect for the working lives of ordinary people that fuels his passion as an attorney.

As a lawyer, Allen looked to people of courage—the Ralph Naders of the world—who were not afraid to stand up for what they believed was right, who had the gumption to fight the good fight against giant companies and entrenched interests. Allen learned that to practice law in such areas as products liability, safety regulations, and workmen's compensation, one needed to have a heart for the war, and thick skin to brave the battle.

A sustaining member of the Association of Trial Lawyers of America, Allen is a member of the bar of the U.S. Supreme Court, the Seventh Circuit Court of Appeals, and the Indiana and Illinois Supreme Courts. He holds membership in the Indiana Trial Lawyers Association, the Illinois Trial Lawyers Association, the Indiana State Bar Association, the Illinois State Bar Association, the Lake County

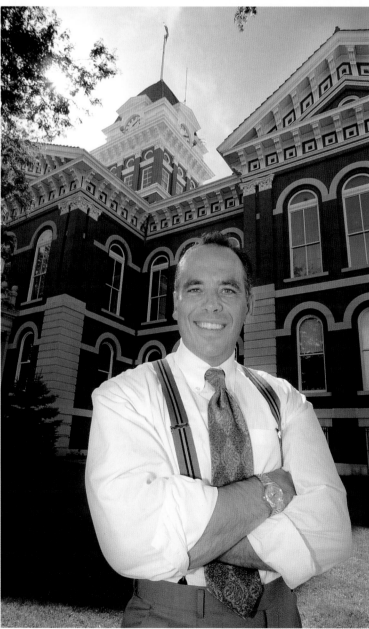

Attorney Kenneth J. Allen, whose firm represents accident and injury victims only, has won more than $40 million in trial verdicts for clients and millions more in out-of-court settlements.

(Indiana) Bar Association, the Porter County (Indiana) Bar Association, and the American Bar Association. A former Superior Court Judge pro tempore, Allen is the author of numerous publications including *Arguing the Tough Issues* (2000), *Achieving Success in the Practice of Personal Injury and Wrongful Death Law* (1998), *Insurance Bad Faith Law* (1997), *Tort Reform, Auto Cases and Premises Liability* (1996), *Crashworthiness and Products Liability* (1992), and *Trying Auto Injury Cases* (1991).

In addition to $40 million in trial verdicts for clients, and millions in out-of-court settlements on behalf of plaintiffs, Allen has been appointed as Class Counsel in several important class action lawsuits including In Re: South Shore Train Crash at Gary, Indiana on January 18, 1993; In Re: Nurseryland Bus Crash at Gary, Indiana on June 25, 1998; and In Re: Truck/Train Collision at Portage, Indiana on June 18, 1998. Allen also participated as a member of the plaintiffs' discovery committee for In Re: Air Crash Disaster at Sioux City, Iowa on July 19, 1989.

Respected Practice

Today, Kenneth J. Allen & Associates is a respected legal firm with offices in Valparaiso and Merrillville. Practicing exclusively in the fields of personal injury and wrongful death, the firm of attorneys, consultants, and support personnel has a concentrated practice in Indiana and Illinois, but has represented clients throughout the country. The law firm is both proud and humbled, Allen says, by the fact that it has never lost a jury trial.

Kenneth J. Allen & Associates represents people involved in a broad range of cases involving negligence that leads to bodily injury or death as a result of situations ranging from auto accidents to defective products to medical malpractice. Work-related injuries, semi-tractor/trailer collisions, and insurance claim suits are a specialty. The firm has represented people from all walks of life: priests, politicians, physicians, laborers, housewives, journalists. It does not accept opportunities to represent corporations.

Many of the legal cases pursued by the firm bring compensation

and closure not only to the individuals, families, or classes of citizens who are clients, but a measure of protection for the general public as well. Many of the cases with which Allen has been involved have resulted in changes in law and modifications to products, occupational health and safety standards, and workplace procedures that have helped to protect thousands of Americans from potential injury.

Making a Difference for Its Clients

At the beginning of a new century, Kenneth J. Allen & Associates continues to invest in the people and technology required to represent its clients. The firm's track record in skillful litigation, based on meticulous understanding of the legal issues involved, will continue to restore some measure of wholeness to damaged personal lives.

"Our work has a precise impact on the specific cases of individuals," Allen stated. "At its very best, it also has the potential of safeguarding many lives when laws are obeyed, standards are raised, and products are made safer."

The young man who once stepped into the boxing ring now packs a more powerful punch. In applying that same passion to the practice of law, Allen discovered he could deliver a wallop when the win would benefit everyone.

The firm's attorneys put in long hours reviewing medical histories, accident diagrams, and other information critical to cases (top).

Competency and compassion define the firm's attorneys and staff: (bottom l to r) Bryan L. Bradley, trial attorney and Captain, USAR (J.D. Valparaiso University); Brock P. Alvarado, trial attorney and former deputy prosecutor (J.D. Valparaiso University); James E. Brammer, appellate attorney and treasurer, Emmanuel Baptist Church (J.D. Notre Dame University); Nina Allen, office administrator (B.A. Indiana University); John A. Walter, III, case administrator (J.D. Indiana University); and Kenneth Allen (seated). Not pictured: George Cullen, Of Counsel (J.D. Loyola University); and Patrick Nicholson, Of Counsel (J.D. Loyola University).

KENNETH J. ALLEN & ASSOCIATES, P.C.

Kenneth J. Allen & Associates, P.C.
Allen Law Building
1109 Glendale Boulevard
Valparaiso, Indiana 46383
(219) 465-6292

Bank One Center
8585 Broadway, 8th floor
Merrillville, Indiana 46410
(219) 736-6292
www.kenallenlaw.com

A MERICAN RENOLIT CORPORATION IS A LEADING NORTH AMERICAN MANUFACTURER OF A PRODUCT THAT—FRANKLY—ANYONE CAN SEE THROUGH. THAT'S A GOOD THING FOR THE COMPANY'S CUSTOMERS. FROM A GLEAMING FACILITY IN LAPORTE, INDIANA, AMERICAN RENOLIT TURNS OUT MILLIONS OF POUNDS OF PLASTIC, THE KIND USED TO MAKE SPORTSCARD HOLDER

pages, sheet protectors, book-binders, video cassette covers, and photo albums. The high-tech plant also manufactures self-adhesive label stock, signage films, and membrane press furniture laminates.

American Renolit is a subsidiary of Renolit-Werke GmbH, which purchased the LaPorte facility in 1998. Renolit-Werke, headquartered in Worms, Germany, employs 4,000 globally. One of the largest producers of precision cast Polypropylene and PVC films in the world, Renolit-Werke also operates 14 facilities in Europe.

More than one hundred people work at the LaPorte plant. In 2000, the company announced several expansions, including a 30,000 square-foot addition to the existing warehouse and office facility and the addition of a second PVC calender line. The plant is operational 24 hours a day, seven days a week to fulfill the ever growing needs of its customers.

Wide Application

The marketplace for American Renolit films is wide, indeed. Plastics produced through extrusion or calender processes are ubiquitous, used for a broad variety of products to be found in every home, office, and school.

Customers for the top-quality, precision-made films manufactured in LaPorte include end-producers of sheet protectors, album pages, and videocassette boxes used the world over. Among American Renolit's customers are internationally recognized companies in the stationery, office products, furniture, outdoor signage and fleet graphics, and other industries.

American Renolit is highly regarded for its production

abilities, not only in the manufacture of films to exacting specification, but also in the service of particular customer needs. Polypropylene and PVC films in any thickness, from heavyweight to razor thin, are produced by the company, as are plastics with special opaque or color tint qualities.

"We work with each customer to devise the exact formula that's right," says Dave Mittiga, president of American Renolit. "Our ability to produce both kinds of films, and to tailor specifications with precision, allows us to come up with the plastic to suit any purpose." This customer-focused service, Mittiga believes, is the driving force behind American Renolit's growth.

Quality Counts

One way American Renolit focuses on customers is to maintain an unrelenting quest for quality. The company—from upper management to the newest workers—works to achieve the industry's highest standards. That, Mittiga says, is a benefit to both the end producers of products manufactured with American Renolit films and to the customers at large.

The corporation is willing to make the investment required for quality. American Renolit's equipment—like $14 million German-designed polymer processing machines—are strictly state-of-the-art. Understanding the complexity of these machines, the company developed a comprehensive program for the LaPorte workers to train with seasoned veterans in Germany. Quality control processes and checks are in place at every step in the manufacturing process—from initial order through final shipment.

"We're very keen on training at American Renolit," Mittiga notes. "Our programs run the gamut from higher level math skills to quality control processes to

American Renolit senior managers (top) review the new product introduction schedule for top quality polypropylene and PVC films.

American Renolit films in any thickness—from heavyweight to razor thin—are used by the company's customers to produce sportscard holders, photo albums, CD/DVD pages, label stock, and furniture laminates, among other popular products (bottom).

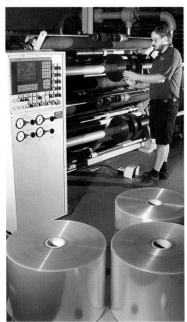

training with equipment experts and manufacturers. There isn't an employee here that hasn't been the beneficiary of on-going education in plastic films production."

Company concern for quality is even exemplified in the spotless manufacturing facility. Workers at American Renolit take pride in a plant kept immaculate at all times.

Cutting-Edge Technology

American Renolit equipment is the best available for the production of plastic films. Cutting edge technology is employed, including computerized monitoring of various stages in the process. Specially designed monitoring cameras, which track production at each phase, give immediate visual read-outs of all manufacturing information required by operators.

The films are produced by the cast extrusion method or the calender method. For both methods, raw materials—resins, additives, color tint granules, and other ingredients—are received by rail at the 70,000 square foot plant.

Processing Plastic

In extrusion, the exact "recipe" of ingredients for a specific grade, thickness, and color of plastic required by a customer is mixed

according to specification. After the dry chemicals are combined, the mixture is heated to its melting point, extruded to a specific thickness onto a casting drum, and then delivered to a high-speed continuous roller system. Rolls of plastic film as wide as 80 inches are manufactured at the plant, which operates three cast extrusion machines.

The calendering method features the same initial process of mixing together the right raw materials in specified quantities. The mixture is then sent through computerized rollers that press out film to specifications and uniform consistency. The art, as any cook can tell, is in precise replication of the recipe and final product—each and every time. American Renolit has equipped its lines with computerized controls that remove any impediments to consistency. The internally developed, proprietary software has turned the original art of plastic production into a science. American Renolit's cutting edge production tools take care of waste material, too. Precise

controls limit the amount of scrap produced, and excess plastic is automatically recycled by specially designed equipment.

The final product is plastic film of an exact thickness, width, strength, and color. Embossing machines can also cater to customers by creating custom effects in the texture of the plastic.

Company on a Roll

Not only is the plastic on a roll, so is the corporation. American Renolit has enjoyed dramatic growth in market share in recent years, growth that Mittiga attributes to the company's focus on customers' needs. Today, plastic films produced in LaPorte are shipped to clients nationwide and exported to customers around the globe. Mittiga anticipates future expansion.

"We're committed to our customers and aim for the highest quality in the industry," Mittiga says. "The market for our products is growing, and we expect to grow with it."

Quality is the focus at American Renolit. Highly trained employees conduct product inspections at every stage of the manufacturing process (top).

American Renolit's LaPorte plant is a model of high-tech efficiency. Cutting-edge equipment (bottom) and proprietary software have helped the company to expand its global customer base.

AMERICAN RENOLIT CORPORATION

1207 East Lincolnway
LaPorte, Indiana 46350
(219) 324-6886
www.americanrenolit.com

AMARILLO ROADHOUSE

1924 U.S. Route 41
Schererville, Indiana 46375
(219) 322-1142
www.amarilloroadhouse.com

Amarillo Roadhouse has high appeal for parties (top) with its relaxed, southwest-flavored atmosphere and Texas-sized portions of expertly prepared food.

There's fun for cowboys and cowgirls of all ages at Amarillo Roadhouse, where the décor includes everything from silver pails of peanuts on tables to painted murals (bottom).

FROM SILVER PAILS OF ROASTED PEANUTS TO THE CACTUS IN THE CORNER, FROM THE COWBOY-SIZED MASON DRINKING JARS TO THE MURALS OF BRONCOBUSTERS ON THE WALL, AMARILLO ROADHOUSE IS AN ATMOSPHERE-PACKED SLICE OF THE SOUTHWEST. LOCATED ON U.S. 41 IN SCHERERVILLE, THIS TOTAL EXPERIENCE RESTAURANT MAY SERVE CUSTOMERS IN NORTHWEST

Indiana, but its tact is strictly Texas.

Restaurants making it in the market today are targeting not just with food, but also with environments that pack entertainment value into the experience. It's a big concept that requires meticulous planning and coordination of every aspect of the business from menu to music to mood. At Amarillo Roadhouse—which takes its themes from the biggest state in the union—no small amount of thought went into creating a four star venue.

Plenty of Food, Plenty of Fun

One of a growing number of Western steakhouse restaurants managed by Chicago Road-house Concepts, LLC, Amarillo Roadhouse has become a popular destination for a wide demographic. A distinctly different and fun watering hole for young professionals after hours, the restaurant offers comfortable service for business lunches during the day. With special rooms for parties and banquets, Amarillo Roadhouse is a hit for large gatherings throughout the year. Live enter-

tainment on weekends—featuring bands that play pop hits or country classics—is another draw.

Families flock to Amarillo Roadhouse. No wonder. The freedom a youngster feels dropping peanut shells on the floor, visiting the kid-friendly arcade, or counting the Texas license plates on the walls makes for a liberating dining experience. By providing a little room to roam, the restaurant makes both adults and children feel at home.

As for food, Amarillo Roadhouse—recipient of top scores from northwest Indiana and Chicago area restaurant critics—knows how to unpack the saddlebag and create entrees that are sumptuous. Popular entrees include the restaurant's

thick, juicy steaks and chops; ribs and burgers; and southwest-inspired specials. Signature items include hefty baked sweet potatoes and soups and salads made fresh by restaurant chefs each day. Generous Texas-sized portions can be counted on.

Little Things Count

"Our aim is quality food served in an atmosphere that is entertaining and fun," explains Paul Switzer, a partner in the corporation. "Today's sophisticated diners value a restaurant that offers a total experience."

Amarillo Roadhouse is a big concept restaurant. But it's the little things that count. The corporation's designers and decorators thought of everything when they decked out the restaurant. Customers are delighted by perfect touches: the breathtaking buffalo head over the entrance doorway; salt and pepper shakers fashioned from Tecate bottles; the murals depicting cowboys unwinding at a saloon; the rustic wood throughout the restaurant.

Amarillo Roadhouse is in northwest Indiana, but it definitely feels like Texas. And that, Switzer says, is what will spur continued success.

IN A WORLD OF MEGABANKS AND FREQUENT MERGERS, AMERICAN SAVINGS FSB REMAINS A LOCALLY OWNED HIGH TECH ALTERNATIVE. HEADQUARTERED IN MUNSTER, THE FINANCIAL INSTITUTION IS SMALLER THAN THE CONGLOMERATES, BUT PROVIDES WHAT TODAY'S CUSTOMERS WANT: PERSONAL SERVICE, EFFICIENCY, AND TECHNOLOGY. IN A HIGHLY COMPETITIVE FINANCIAL

AMERICAN SAVINGS FSB

marketplace, American Savings proves at least one time-honored economic maxim: bigger doesn't mean better.

First in Financial Technology

American Savings FSB was one of the first community banks to integrate state-of-the-art financial technologies. It offered debit cards to northwest Indiana customers long before most institutions adopted the technology. On-line, real-time banking via the Internet was a service American Savings investigated and made available to its customers early on. American Savings was one of the first to establish a local area network (LAN), now being converted to frame relay for faster processing. The bank has also earned kudos from customers and the banking industry for its award-winning "Kid Safe" Web site (www.amb financial.com).

Balancing its cutting edge technology, though, is an absolute commitment to personalized service. In the pursuit of any technology, management always asks first: "What's in it for our customers?" Today, American Savings is still the bank where human beings answer the phone and customers receive friendly and efficient service.

"Customer service is our main business," confirms Clement B. "Skip" Knapp, Jr., president of American Savings. "We switch gears quickly, we refuse to get bogged down in committee, we pursue every tact and technology that helps our customers."

Originally chartered as the first Polish Building, Loan & Savings Association in 1910, the bank has always stayed close to its customer

base in northwest Indiana. The bank later became a federally insured institution, changing its name to the American Savings & Loan Association. On March 19, 1987, the bank converted to status as a federally chartered institution and was renamed American Savings FSB.

Built on Customer Service

With its home office in Munster, Indiana and branches in nearby Hammond (4521 Hohman Avenue) and Dyer (1001 Main Street), American Savings serves the financial needs of families and local businesses in its primary market area of northwest Lake County and southeastern Illinois. End of year assets in 1999 totaled $125 million and assets on deposit reached $89.5 million.

Traded on the NASDAQ (AMFC), American Savings seeks safe and profitable investments, mainly residential mortgages, non-residential real estate, land, commercial business, and consumer loans in its defined marketplace. The bank also invests in mortgage-backed securities and investment securities consisting largely of U.S. government bonds and various types of short-term liquid assets.

The strategy at American Savings is working. The bank's assets have doubled in the past four years. Accomplished through unrelenting focus on the customer, growth has come from the marketplace of families and businesses that appreciate a friendly, helpful voice and personal response to financial requests. In an era renowned for voice mail, it has made all the difference.

"We've never been interested in change for change's sake, just change that will benefit the customer," Knapp stresses.

American Savings FSB is happy to remain with its winning strategy, a strategy aimed at servicing customers' needs first.

8230 Hohman Avenue
Munster, Indiana 46321
(219) 836-5870
www.amfinancial.com

Personalized service is the watchword at American Savings FSB (top) where help is available 24 hours a day.

Clement B. "Skip" Knapp, Jr. (below) serves as president of American Savings which is headquartered in Munster (bottom) and has offices in Hammond and Dyer.

A MERICAN TRUST & SAVINGS BANK IS A BANK BUILT TO STAND THE TESTS OF TIME. IN BANKING AND FINANCE, THERE HAVE BEEN MANY TESTS. CONSIDER THAT AMERICAN TRUST & SAVINGS HAD JUST MOVED INTO A NEW OFFICE BUILDING AT THE CORNER OF LaPORTE AVENUE AND 119TH STREET IN WHITING WHEN THE GREAT DEPRESSION HIT. YEARS LATER, BIG BANKS WITH

national muscle proliferated and threatened smaller, hometown banks. Acquisitions and mergers have all but gobbled up the banks of the golden era with their gilded doors, hometown financial institutions that stood proudly on the main streets of every town in America.

Today, American Trust & Savings is as strong as ever. It is a feat, according to president Philip J. Grenchik, that proves hometown banking and personalized service have never gone out of style.

"Our focus has always been in this community," Grenchik observed. "Over 80 years the bank and the people here have built a partnership significant to all of us."

American Trust & Savings Bank, opened in 1920, was established as a hometown financial institution and has retained its community-oriented focus for more than 80 years.

In many ways, the City of Whiting and American Trust & Savings grew up together. Nurtured by the growth of the northwest Indiana region and home to one of the largest U.S. refineries, the city—and the bank—enjoyed plentiful employment, booming industry, and longstanding prosperity.

Proud Beginnings

On August 20, 1920, President Michael Kozacik, Sr. pulled out his key, unlocked the door, and welcomed the first customers of the American Trust & Savings Bank. The bank was open for business and two employees processed the transactions of the day. First

deposits amounted to $54,737.45. By September 28, 1925, deposits had increased to $467,372.

The first location of American Trust & Savings Bank was the building now occupied by the American Slovak Club at 1324 119th Street. Business grew so rapidly that soon a new, larger building was needed. Operations were moved to a new facility at 119th Street and LaPorte Avenue in 1925. The two-story edifice, built for $100,000, housed the bank on the main floor while business offices and apartments occupied the upper floor.

After years in the grocery business—Grenchik's Goldmine Gro-cery—Mr. Joseph Grenchik, Sr. came to American Trust & Savings Bank as its new president in 1940. The banking business proved to be much like the grocery business: buy at wholesale, sell at retail, and take care of the customer. Skilled management, sales, and marketing combined with a tenacious staff helped the community-oriented bank flourish.

By 1948, American Trust & Sav-ings Bank employed a full-time staff of 12. The upper story was converted into bank offices. In addition to an insurance department established in the early years, the bank purchased its own travel agency in 1967.

Branching Out

On August 14, 1991, American Trust & Savings Bank opened its Lake Front Branch at 1349 Calumet Avenue in the Whiting-Robertsdale area. Keeping up with the times, the new branch featured a four-lane drive-up facility and a drive-up ATM in addition to traditional

lobby banking. The modern, three-story branch is located on one of the corners of the historic "Five Points Intersection" near the entrance to the Hammond Marina and the Empress Riverboat Casino.

The bank acquired Peerson & Co. Investment Services on September 1, 1995. Located on the third floor of the Lake Front Branch, the new subsidiary of American Trust & Savings Bank has been an established brokerage firm in the region since 1957 and offers a wide variety of financial investment products to customers.

The Travel and Insurance departments, growing divisions of the bank, were relocated to a new building on 119th Street in Whiting in 1996. The insurance division provides a complete line of personal and commercial insurance products as well as life, health, and financial services. The travel division helps northwest Indiana residents with tours, honeymoon packages, cruises, air/rail tickets, hotel reservations, and other services for business and personal travel.

The Crown Point Branch represents another level of growth for American Trust & Savings Bank. Located at 1300 North Main Street in Crown Point's Market Place Mall, the branch opened in 1996 with fully staffed lobby service, three drive-up lanes, and a drive-up ATM.

For as many years as residents can remember, American Trust & Savings Bank has been a steadfast partner in the community. Home loans, business loans and lines of credit, car loans, home improvement loans, and education loans have enriched the lives of citizens

who were able to make dreams come true.

The bank that Michael Kozacik opened in 1920 with $50,000 in capital, a state charter, and two employees still knows the majority of its customers by name. At the dawn of the new century, American Trust & Savings could claim $115 million assets on deposit and an abiding foothold in the community unchanged over time.

A Number of Firsts

Customer-oriented service has been a hallmark of American Trust's business methodology. Disinclined to favor growth over service, the bank nabbed a number of firsts that rank as important to customers. In its community, American Trust was the first to offer off-premises computerized checking and savings accounts and the first to offer 44 hours weekly

of complete banking services. It is one of the few banks that can boast of having had a female Chairman of the Board. It is one of fewer still whose Board of Directors is made up completely of residents and former residents who know and appreciate the needs and concerns of the community.

"The bank on the corner" is still the place youngsters open their first passbook savings accounts to deposit their newspaper route earnings. Later, they return to borrow money for college tuition, to buy a first home, to finance the opening of a new business in the region.

We've made it a pledge to stay in touch with our customers," Grenchik stated. "Quality service is something they've come to appreciate and expect. American Trust & Savings Bank is keeping that pledge into the next millennium."

AMERICAN TRUST & SAVINGS BANK

**1321 119th Street
Whiting, Indiana 46394
(219) 659-0850**

ANCILLA SYSTEMS

ᴀNCILLA SYSTEMS INCORPORATED, A REGIONALLY ORGANIZED NON-PROFIT HEALTH CARE CORPORATION SPONSORED BY THE CONGREGATION OF THE POOR HANDMAIDS OF JESUS CHRIST, IS DEDICATED TO PROVIDING QUALITY HEALTH SERVICES THAT MEET THE NEEDS OF THE COMMUNITY. HEADQUARTERED IN HOBART, ANCILLA SYSTEMS OPERATES FOUR AFFILIATE HOSPITALS

1000 South Lake Park Avenue
Hobart, Indiana 46342
(219) 947-8500
www.ancilla.org

Community health is a core concern for Ancilla Systems. In addition to its work through affiliate hospitals, St. Mary Medical Center (bottom) and St. Catherine Hospital, it was a partner in the opening of Healthy East Chicago, a cutting edge clinic offering medical and social services expected to help more than 50,000 residents each year.

St. Catherine Hospital

including two in northwest Indiana: St. Mary Medical Center in Hobart and St. Catherine Hospital in East Chicago.

A Catholic health care provider, Ancilla Systems is a contemporary cousin in a long line of predecessors. Ecclesiastical medicine, originating in the monastic infirmary, was the first organized effort to document conditions and treatments and to care for the sick. The first hospitals were separate Catholic charitable institutions designed to care for the many sufferers of leprosy and other disorders.

Compassion for the Needy

Today, Ancilla Systems carries on the tradition of state-of-the-art medical practice combined with compassion for the sick and the poor.

In this region, St. Mary Medical Center and St. Catherine Hospital are thriving. St. Mary has become a national role model, having been recently recognized by the American College of Health Care Executives and the American Hospital Association as one of only six hospitals nationwide chosen as a demonstration site. This designation was based on the hospital's extensive community health work the hospital has done.

Also, the development of a "medical city" on 40 acres adjacent to the hospital, offering everything from dining and child care services to assisted and independent living quarters for the elderly, will set the hospital apart from others. The comprehensive development will provide a full range of personal and health care services for patients, families, physicians, employees, and community members.

The 183-bed hospital received a score of 98 out of 100 from the Joint Commission on the Accreditation of Hospital Organizations in 1998, a feat achieved by only 10 to 12 percent of medical facilities nationwide. St. Mary has also completed a 9,000-square-foot Family Health Center in Merrillville and a 14,000-square-foot center to serve residents in the fast-growing Winfield Township-Lakes of the Four Seasons community.

St. Catherine Hospital is a continuing success story. Once suffering from decline in a classically under-served community, St. Catherine Hospital recently opened a new 23-bed telemetry unit. The Cardiovascular Center has expanded its services to include Millennium, a health and wellness center and the Advanced Lipid Clinic offering new, state-of-the-art technology and testing that identifies the genetic traits most often linked to heart disease. For women, the St. Catherine Hospital Diagnostic Imaging Women's Center provides the latest mammography and core biopsy mammography

technology and bone density analysis. As part of its effort to reach out to the community, St. Catherine Hospital was a partner in the opening of Healthy East Chicago Center, a state-of-the-art comprehensive medical and social service facility expected to serve more than 50,000 area residents annually.

Building Partnerships

Building partnerships has been a hallmark of Ancilla Systems' service to northwest Indiana. According to Sister Jolise May, Provincial of the Poor Handmaids of Jesus Christ, this Catholic organization will continue to look to faith partners to help it provide medical care and compassionate service in this region and throughout the midwest.

"We are called to work in the neighborhoods and show how Catholic organizations and others can work together to create healthy communities," Sister Jolise says. "The future, we hope, will mean more covenants with those who believe as we do in service to the poor and under-served."

Northwest Indiana is the crossroads of the U.S. The most urbanized and industrialized sector of Indiana, the region has been at the heart of the country's major transportation corridors since the 1800s. Rivers were the chief means of travel for early settlers until railroads superseded waterways as the principal form of

transportation. The nation's first intercontinental route from New York to California—the Lincoln Highway (now known as U.S. 30)—passed through northwest Indiana. In fact, Indiana's state motto is "Crossroads of America."

Today, the proliferation of the northwest Indiana network continues albeit in 21st century high-technology fashion. Thousands of miles of new network—fiber optic lines, digital paths, and high-speed cable—connect people to others in the region or halfway around the globe. Now information, entertainment, and news are traveling—and at unprecedented speed.

Vision for the Future

AT&T, one of the world's largest telecommunications companies, is at the forefront of this new network. In northwest Indiana the company provides state-of-the-art video programming, digital cable, high-speed internet access, long distance phone service—and soon, local telephone services—to customers in communities large and small.

According to Mike Tanck, Government Relations Manager with AT&T Broadband, the company is intent on building a "huge pipeline that serves people now but also has a vision for the future."

More than 300 employees work for AT&T's northwest Indiana offices managing the growth of both customer base and new technology. More than 5,000 miles of new fiber optic cable have been installed in the region, providing state-of-the-art service for residential and commercial clients.

"We're making the investment now that will help the region continue to prosper," Tanck comments.

Top Technology

That investment has led to an amazing growth in both choice and speed for consumers. In a competitive marketplace, AT&T is capturing an audience with its cable video programming services, phone services and internet access— all of which have vastly expanded the options for individual consumers and business customers. In the telecommunications age, AT&T has pledged top-notch technology and services in delivery of entertainment, video, voice,

cable, internet, local, long distance, and cellular phone service. Research and development initiatives ensure AT&T offers maximum choice and greatest ease of use for customers.

While AT&T is helping its customers reach for the future, it also takes seriously its impact in the present. Through its locally-based channels, its sponsorships of area festivals and events, and its involvement in chambers of commerce and other organizations, AT&T seeks to strengthen communities throughout the region.

"Being a good corporate citizen is a role we take very seriously," Tanck says.

AT&T Broadband provides telephone, cable, internet, and other services to thousands of northwest Indiana residents. More than 5,000 miles of new fiber optic cable have been installed in the region by AT&T to provide top-notch technology to residential and commercial customers.

PERFORMANCE FILMS DIVISION IS AN OPERATING UNIT OF AVERY DENNISON CORPORATION, A WORLDWIDE, LEADING PRODUCER OF PRESSURE SENSITIVE ADHESIVE MATERIALS, OFFICE PRODUCTS, AND VARIOUS CONVERTED AND SPECIALTY PRODUCTS. AVERY DENNISON IS TRADED ON THE NEW YORK STOCK EXCHANGE AND IS HEADQUARTERED IN PASADENA, CALIFORNIA.

AVERY DENNISON PERFORMANCE FILMS DIVISION

650 W. 67th Avenue
Schererville, Indiana 46375
(219) 322-5030
www.pfd.averydennison.com

Avery Dennison manufactures functional and decorative films for the automotive, construction, and office products industries from its facility in Schererville. The company's trademark films are used in the production of a host of goods—from automobiles to adhesive labels—used by consumers everyday.

Local Entrepreneurs Pioneers in Technology

Performance Films was originally founded by local entrepreneurs as Thermark, a pioneer in hot-stamp foil technology, and located in Hammond, Indiana. Thermark quickly outgrew its modest beginnings and was relocated to a brand new facility in Schererville, Indiana in the early 1970s. Shortly thereafter, the company was acquired by Avery Dennison. With the support and resources available through its new parent, Performance Films developed into a major supplier of decorative and functional plastic films to the automotive, construction, office products, and other targeted markets.

Key products produced at Performance Films' facility in Schererville include: **Avery Dennison Avloy® Dry Paint Films,** which are exterior, durable products designed to replace wet paint and provide a high gloss, class "A" finish to plastic exterior automotive trim parts; **Avery Dennison GraphiColor® Architectural Films,** which provide a realistic, stained cedar look to premium vinyl house siding, as well as impart the outstanding weathering properties necessary for today's maintenance-free living; and **Avery Dennison Thermark® Decorative Finishes,** which provide a printed pattern, such as woodgrain, for interior automotive trim parts.

Exciting New Markets

Growth through new product development and the penetration of new markets is a key strategy of Performance Films Division. Exciting work is going forward in commercial aviation, industrial fabrics, and heavy trucks, to name a few of the markets. New technologies include a line of very low gloss, tactile films for interior trim applications and an extensive new offering of functional films for office products applications and labels.

Performance Films develops and produces truly innovative products that serve the needs of many markets. Its continuing growth and prosperity are a testament to the high quality of its fine employees and surrounding communities.

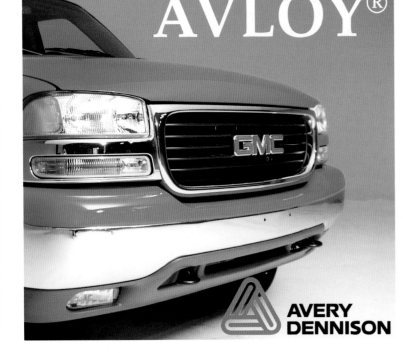

AVLOY®

AVERY DENNISON

THE BACHMAN PARTNERSHIP, P.C.

Reputation for Design Excellence

The firm, managed by president Philip L. Bachman, AIA, has built a reputation for design excellence with many projects well known to the public: Fitness Pointe, constructed in 1998; Community Hospital building projects spanning more than 30 years; the Powers Computer Education Building at Purdue University Calumet in Hammond; a host of medical facilities and schools throughout the region; and—a regional asset—the Center for Visual & Performing Arts in Munster.

An aesthetically pleasing building whose form compliments its function—as Thomas Jefferson once postulated it should—is the end result of a relationship with The Bachman Partnership. Consider Fitness Pointe in Munster, a 74,000 square foot cardiac rehabilitation complex featuring physical therapy facilities, a basketball court, exercise rooms, offices, and swimming pools. When Philip Bachman approached the design of the lap pool used by cardiac patients, he did his homework. After carefully considering the design parameters, he researched how such a pool would serve its clientele. As a result, the firm created a plan for the tile work that included images of fish, in abstract form but clearly distinguishable by swimmers. In this way, users of the pool would be able to mark their progress through each lap—a matter of importance, and often encouragement, to cardiac rehabilitation patients.

It is a matter of importance to Bachman and his staff of architects, engineers, designers, and support personnel that aesthetics melded with workability-beauty blended with benefits—be the ultimate goal. On every design project, the firm aims to achieve a perfect pairing of form and function.

The Bachman Partnership offers basic services in architecture, from initial analysis and budget studies to architectural design, specifications, construction documents, bidding, and construction observation. Additional services include impact studies, graphics, color and material selection, remodeling, and historic restoration.

Services in engineering include plans and specifications for structural design, mechanical systems, wastewater treatment, electrical systems, lighting, and special acoustical design. Planning services are provided to clients who would like assistance in site selection, master planning, site development, and landscape.

Distinguished History

The company has a long history in northwest Indiana. Established as Bachman and

Dawn breaks at Community Hospital in Munster (top). Over the years, the Bachman Partnership has designed the original building and several new additions and renovations for the medical institution.

Fitness Pointe, a 74,000 square foot cardiac rehabilitation complex in Munster designed by the firm (bottom right), features cutting edge equipment and a stunning lap pool (bottom left).

Bertram and Associates in 1939, the firm was started by William J. "Bill" Bachman, an architect and engineer who was born and raised in Hammond, and his partner Joseph K. Bertram, an architect who emigrated to the U.S. from Achen, Germany in the early 1930s. Bachman studied both architecture and structural engineering at the College of Fine and Applied Arts at the University of Illinois at Urbana, graduating in 1935. Bachman credited his interest in architecture to the many buildings he saw as a child visiting relatives in Chicago. Riding the streetcar with his family from Hammond to the city, the young man was inspired by sights like Frank Lloyd Wright's Midway Gardens.

After working on World War II design projects to help the war effort, Bachman and Bertram returned to their civilian practice, continuing as partners until Bertram's death in 1971. The firm was reorganized, and became William J. Bachman and Partners, Architects and Engineers.

According to his son Philip, Bill Bachman—like Frank Lloyd Wright—always believed his best building would be "his next one." But he took great pride in many of the firm's achievements in the region: its design for Community Hospital in Munster, for instance, and the preservation of the cast bronze doors of Hammond City Hall which Bachman helped save from the wrecking ball and placed at the entrance to the Purdue University Calumet library. A committed architect and lifelong lover of the arts, Bachman lived to see his last commission—the Center for Visual and Performing Arts in Munster, Indiana—become a reality.

Bachman also took pride in the fact that his son Philip became an architect. Philip Bachman studied architecture at Arizona State University in Tempe and at the University of Illinois at Chicago, from which he received a Bachelor of Architecture degree in 1970. A registered architect in Indiana and Illinois, Bachman received his Master of Architecture degree from the University of Illinois at Urbana in 1973. In 1977, after four years with international architecture firm Helmuth, Obata and Kassabaum of St. Louis, Missouri, he became a partner with his father in the firm. In 1989, after the death of Bill Bachman, the firm was reorganized as The Bachman Partnership, P.C., Architects and Engineers. The company relocated to Highland, Indiana after its original home—the Indiana Hotel building in downtown Hammond—was demolished to make way for the Hohman Avenue overpass.

Grand Design, Small Details

The Bachman Partnership continues to be a pivotal player in northwest Indiana architecture. Applying the same time-honored principle upon which the firm was founded–that each new structure, addition, or renovation should satisfy both practically and aesthetically—the firm has been responsible for a host of touted projects. In addition to projects already cited, The Bachman Partnership can be credited for the 130,000 square foot Medical Office Building constructed for Community Hospital in 1999 and renovation of the west pavilion of the Oncology Diagnostic Center; numerous classroom, computer, and office facilities at Indiana University Northwest in Gary; educational facilities at Purdue University Calumet in Hammond; renovations at Westminster Presbyterian Church in Munster, Our Lady of Grace Church in Highland, Blessed Sacrament Church in Gary, Trinity Lutheran Church in Hammond, and a host of other religious buildings and facilities; and school design, renovations, additions, and facilities at more than 50 public and private elementary, middle, and high schools throughout the region.

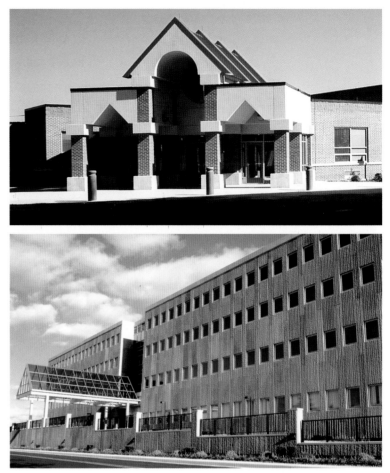

The year 2000 saw a number of the firm's latest projects constructed, including a Humane Society facility in Munster and the Savannah Center academic activities building at Indiana University Northwest in Gary, among others.

Educational, institutional, industrial, and medical facilities figure prominently on the firm's resume. The Bachman Partnership's knowledge of the diverse types of diagnostic, process, and communications equipment required by such facilities has made the company a wise choice for area clients. The ability to synchronize a grand design with the critical engineering, telecommunications, space planning, and other details is a specialty of the firm.

Today, The Bachman Partnership serves a broad range of clients with its experience and skill designing buildings that convey a sense of beauty and pride, and that rate high in functionality and flexibility. The Bachman trademark, as ever, is in putting the pieces of the puzzle together in distinctive and delightful ways.

For Eldon Ready Elementary School in Griffith (top), The Bachman Partnership created facility expansion plans that coordinated architectural detail with the school colors.

Vision and innovation typify the firm's work in northwest Indiana. For Community Hospital's Medical Office Building (bottom), The Bachman Partnership created an outpatient surgery center that separates patients and staff with a circular interior design.

THE BACHMAN
PARTNERSHIP, P.C
8145 Kennedy Avenue
Highland, Indiana 46322
(219) 923-8008
e-mail: bachman@niia.net

BETHLEHEM STEEL CORPORATION

BURNS HARBOR DIVISION

Lake Michigan to build a world-class flat-rolled steelmaking facility, the last "greenfield" integrated steelmaking plant built in this country. The Burns Harbor facility, ideally situated for raw material sourcing and near water, rail, and highway shipping routes, placed Bethlehem Steel in the heart of America's largest market for steel sheet and plate products.

Designed to Be a Leader

From the beginning, the Burns Harbor plant was designed to be a leader in every way. It would not only raise the bar for quality and efficiency, but also would train its employees in the skills necessary to make the best steel in the world in the safest way possible. Burns Harbor would also be a good corporate citizen and neighbor, supporting local communities and organizations in their fund-raising efforts and working full-time to improve its environmental performance.

The economic and social impacts of Bethlehem Steel's presence in Burns Harbor were extraordinary, even before the first plate mill started up in 1964. Today, there are four support and service jobs for each job in the local steel industry. During the 1990s, the company invested more than $1.5 billion to modernize and upgrade equipment and training. High technology is in full flex at Burns Harbor, where computerized controls and state-of-the-art processes are key to the production of steel of exceptional precision and quality.

The layout of the facility itself is a model of logistic efficiency. Iron ore, coal, and limestone, the three ingredients necessary for the manufacture of steel, arrive and are stored at the western end of the three and a half mile long plant. They are transported via conveyor to the coke ovens and blast furnaces.

Molten iron leaves the blast furnaces in transfer cars on its way to the BOF where it is processed into steel. The still-liquid steel is carried in ladles to the continuous slab caster to be converted into a solid form. The next stop is the finishing end of the plant, where the slabs are rolled into sheet or plate product. The sheet steel is coiled and shipped to customers directly from the hot strip mill or sent on to the cold mill for further processing to meet customers' requirements. Slabs destined for plate product are sent to the plate mill where they are rolled to widths and cut into lengths specified by customers.

Earning Worldwide Recognition

Burns Harbor is recognized worldwide for the quality of its light flat-rolled sheet and plate steel. High-tech processes in the plant's hot mill, cold mill, hot-dip coating line, and plate mills have contributed to the company's ability to prosper in a highly competitive marketplace where quality product made to exacting

Nighttime view of Bethlehem Steel's blast furnaces and coal injection plant as seen from the Port of Indiana (top).

The Deerfield Woods Center for Education and Training is Burns Harbor's 40,000 square foot craft and safety training facility (bottom).

specifications and delivered on time means economic success.

Burns Harbor combines advanced technology and computerization with highly trained people to make clean steel of tightly controlled, uniform chemistry. This, in turn, produces finished products with superior cleanliness, surface quality, and formability. Steel made at Burns Harbor is used in the production of cars, appliances, office furniture, heavy machinery, construction, farm and construction equipment, railroad cars, marine vessels, and pipe and tube.

Burns Harbor's commitment to quality is no secret. Customers have acknowledged the Division's success in achieving its quality goals by bestowing quality and service awards. From the top down, employees work together to keep the facility at the top of its game. Burns Harbor has achieved international ISO 9002 and QS 9000 certifications that testify to its intent to meet or exceed the most exacting and globally recognized quality standards. The plant's core of application engineers work with individual customers to match products and process for maximum economy and performance in the marketplace. The benefits of this

collaboration are enjoyed by consumers everywhere.

A Gentle Giant

Although Bethlehem Steel's Burns Harbor plant enjoys national recognition as a producer of quality steel, it is viewed locally as the best kind of neighbor. For more than three years Burns Harbor employees and Bethlehem Steel have contributed more than $1 million to United Way agencies in northwest Indiana. Bethlehem Steel, through the Burns Harbor Division, is the only integrated steel producer to form a Citizens Advisory Committee, an outgrowth of the company's participation in the Environmental Protection Agency's Common Sense Initiative. Burns Harbor contributes to the support of many community programs, festivals, and events held throughout the region. Representatives from the plant routinely work with local schools to present informative programs, underwrite special projects, and support initiatives like the national "School-to-Work" program that qualifies selected high school students for technical careers as millwrights.

Environmental initiatives supported and practiced by Bethlehem

Steel are among the most demanding in the industry. The company was the first domestic steelmaker to endorse the CERES Principles, a comprehensive environmental code of conduct promoted by a coalition of national environmental groups and socially responsible investors. The foresight that led Bethlehem Steel to northwest Indiana in the sixties is evident today as the company continues its efforts to ensure that the land and environment prosper in the new millennium and beyond.

After 30 years, Bethlehem Steel's vision for Burns Harbor is still clear and focused. A number of ingredients are necessary to maintain the company's position as a responsible employer and good corporate citizen: commitments to safety, quality, customer satisfaction, responsible environmental performance, and civic responsibility. These, like the ingredients mixed and melted to make Bethlehem's steel, are available in ample supply at Burns Harbor.

Trained staff monitor the progress of steel strip through the five-stand tandem mill (top).

Molten iron is charged into a basic oxygen furnace (bottom left).

Finishing train at Burns Harbor's 80-inch hot strip mill (bottom right).

BETHLEHEM STEEL CORPORATION/ BURNS HARBOR DIVISION

P.O. Box 248
Chesterton, Indiana 46304
www.bethsteel.com

BP AMOCO
WHITING BUSINESS UNIT

the region. Constructed in 1889 on 235 acres of land, the plant employed most of the residents of Whiting, Indiana. It was a star in the constellation that was the Standard Oil Company and a facility often visited by John D. Rockefeller. The city benefited from the largesse of the founder, who built its community center— an Italianate villa now listed on the National Register of Historic Places—and donated the land for the Whiting Public Library.

Production Leader

Today, BP Amoco occupies approximately 1,400 acres of land in the heart of northwest Indiana's Calumet industrial region and employs 1,200 workers. A leader in the production of low-sulfur clean fuels, the refinery produces 16 million gallons of product daily, half of it gasoline. In fact, an average day's output produces enough product to fully fuel 430,000 automobiles, more than 10,000 farm tractors, 22,000 semi-trucks, 2,000 commercial jetliners, and to fill 350,000 propane cylinders. The Whiting Refinery

also makes eight percent of all asphalt used in the U.S.

Now ranked as the fourth largest refinery in the country, the facility maintains 220 tanks, the largest holding 600,000 barrels (21.4 million gallons) of crude oil. Product manufactured by the refinery is shipped via barge, rail, and truck, and also along ten pipelines serving the midwest.

Power is produced on site. The refinery's power station supplies 75 percent of the plant's steam demand and 60 percent of its electrical demand, amounts equal to the power that would be required to supply 90,000 homes with electricity and 200,000 with steam heat. The Whiting Refinery also maintains its own fire department with a full-time chief and inspectors, state-of-the-art fire fighting and emergency equipment, and an available brigade of 75 firefighters.

A Number of Firsts

While the Whiting Refinery contributed much to the history and progress of the region, it also was instrumental in the history of the petroleum industry.

A number of firsts can be credited to the refinery. In 1913, engineers devised a "thermal cracking" process which used pressure and high temperature to cause a chemical change that increased the gasoline yield from crude oil. In 1923, research at Whiting led to the discovery that the addition of tetraethyl lead to gasoline eliminated the power-robbing "knock" of car engines. Research at Whiting in 1941 was the foundation of a process that made high-grade aviation fuel from low-grade naphtha. Coming just four days before the bombing of Pearl Harbor, this technology—as well as the company's development of a new all-weather, heavy-duty motor oil—helped the war effort considerably. In 1987, Whiting's Total Isomerization Process unit began operation. This unit was able to upgrade lower octane light naphtha, a by-product of petroleum distillation, by rearranging its molecular structure, thereby producing higher-octane fuel. In 1999, the refinery led the industry in introducing the next generation of low-sulfur premium gasoline.

BP Amoco's Whiting Refinery (top) made its home in northwest Indiana in 1889. Today it employs 1,200 highly trained workers (bottom) such as Kathryn Brtko and Kevin Clark, chemists who help the company process an average of 16 million gallons of product daily.

Today it is committed to supplying mid-grade and regular unleaded lower-sulfur gasoline to the Chicago metropolitan market by the year 2001.

Innovation is Company Landmark

Innovation continues in the new millennium. Currently a focus of BP Amoco's Whiting Refinery is the Whiting Clean Energy Project, an initiative expected to generate 525 mega-watts of electric power and produce high-pressure steam for use by the refinery and area customers.

One hundred and eleven years have passed since the Standard Oil Company decided to stake its claim to land along the marshy rim of Lake Michigan. Fourth and fifth generations of families have worked at the plant.

Today the Standard Oil Annuitant Club of Whiting, Inc. is one of the largest annuitant associations in the country with 400 members. BP Amoco continues to be committed to a safe, environmentally sound atmosphere for employees and neighbors; competitively priced, quality products for its customers; and economic support and leadership for the northwest Indiana region.

THE BRANT COMPANIES

The Brant Companies has earned a reputation for quality in both commercial construction with facilities like J & F Steel (top) and residential projects with developments like Cobblestones (bottom right) in Munster.

Attractive homes in Autumn Creek (bottom left) continue The Brant Companies tradition. The Schererville residential development was the site of the 2000 Lake County Parade of Homes.

commercial, and industrial development and construction services.

A New Generation

William J. Brant Jr., President of The Brant Companies, learned his trade from his grandfather and father. After his discharge from the United States Navy in 1956, Brant took over the family construction business with his uncle, George Brant. The pair began building homes in Highland and since that time the company has created homes, from single-family dwellings to townhomes, with the Brant signature throughout the midwest and in Florida. The firm's extensive research into the needs and wants of potential homeowners, its innovative design ideas, and the application of the latest technologies combine to

make a Brant home an excellent value. Among the many standard features found in Brant homes are spacious eat-in kitchens, generously-sized rooms, wood-burning fireplaces, and ample closet space.

George and William Brant followed up their success in home construction with residential development in 1960. Tanglewood Apartments in Hammond, as well as University Estates and White Oak Manor subdivisions in Munster, stand as testaments to the vision the Brant family brought to its work. Brant also partnered with famed area developers Don Powers, Harold Rueth, and Florian O'Day to create Fairmeadows, an 1,800-home subdivision in Munster.

Since then, The Brant Companies has continued to turn vacant land throughout Indiana, Illinois,

and Florida into communities where families can live and grow.

A hallmark of The Brant Companies' residential development is the variety of housing styles and types it develops—single-family homes in East Chicago, Munster, and Highland; townhomes in Flossmoor, Illinois, St John, Merrillville, and Munster; condominiums in Munster; and duplexes in LaPorte. Each Brant community is designed with the homeowner in mind—from young professionals to growing families to empty nesters and the handicapped.

The company's work in residential development has also expanded to Tampa, Florida, where Brant has developed and built nearly 200 townhomes. These townhomes, located along the Gulf Coast, feature spectacular

design, luxurious detailing, and innovative technology.

Autumn Creek in Schererville is the latest Brant residential development in the region. The site of the 2000 Lake County Parade of Homes, this 305-lot subdivision continues the company's tradition of providing attractive amenities that nurture today's busy families.

Commercial and Industrial Expansion

Since the 1980s, The Brant Companies has also made a name for itself in the fields of commercial and industrial development and construction throughout the United States and Canada.

Brant serves a wide spectrum of clients with a full range of construction services from design to completion: the manufacturer who plans a new plant or desires to expand or modernize current facilities, the health care provider who needs to add new technology, the commercial investor/developer who is planning a shopping center, a warehouse, or an office building. Brant Construction Management, Inc., one of The Brant Companies, was incorporated in 1984 in Florida to provide those services, which company officials call "single source

responsibility." That means better control of design, construction, costs, and scheduling.

The company's initial construction management contract in 1984 called for the coordination of 33 trade union contractors in the com-pletion of the $36 million East Chicago Central High School. Dozens of contracts, ranging from a $158,190 fire station for the Town of Schererville to a $10 million medical clinic. A primary customer from 1984 through 1992 was J.I. Case Company, for which Brant developed and built facilities in 19 states and in Canada. The Veteran's Administration also tapped The Brant Companies to design and build outpatient VA clinics in Evansville, Indiana; Grand Rapids, Michigan; Bettendorf, Iowa;

Rochester, New York; and San Jose, California. In addition, Brant's Florida office has successfully completed three large shopping centers under construction management contracts, and the northwest Indiana office continues to design and build industrial and commercial buildings.

The Brant Companies is today still a family-owned, family-run business with William J. Brant Jr. at the helm. His sons carry on the four-generation tradition of quality construction with Jim Brant heading the Tampa, Florida office of Brant Construction Management, Inc. and Jeff Brant working in sales and marketing at the northwest Indiana location.

Employee loyalty has also been a major factor in the success of The Brant Companies. Many employees have been part of this family company for up to 30 years, and new workers are consistently being groomed for the future. According to William Brant, those employees have made this company a standout.

A hands-on approach to everything the company does has been another key factor in Brant success. From the most fashionable residential building to the most technical industrial construction, The Brant Companies has access to the professional talent, architects, engineers, management staff, and construction craftsmen to complete a project on time and on budget. That was the promise of yesterday. It remains the promise for tomorrow.

Public facilities round out the company portfolio. In 1984, The Brant Companies was awarded the contract for the $36 million East Chicago Central High School (top).

Commercial construction undertaken by The Brant Companies ranges from industrial plants, schools, and medical facilities to shopping centers and restaurants. A Jalapeno's restaurant in Schererville (center) was constructed by the company in 1999.

The Brant Companies has made contributions in the region—and beyond. For the Veteran's Administration, the firm has developed and built outpatient veterans facilities in San Jose, California (bottom); Evansville, Indiana; Grand Rapids, Michigan; Bettendorf, Iowa; and Rochester, New York.

THE BRANT COMPANIES

1947 Woodlawn Avenue
Griffith, Indiana 46319
(219) 838-2300
www.brantco.com

BULK TRANSPORT CORPORATION

Expanses of Sand and a Model A

Unlike the west with its rich stores of raw lumber or the east with deep deposits of ore and coal, the northwest quadrant of the Hoosier state took its cues from Lake Michigan. While farmers found fertile ground in outlying reaches, more rugged settlers first tamed the swampy land along the lake, wresting homes and stores and roads from marshes, just as their Chicago neighbors had. It took vision to see that the lake itself was a valuable resource, one that could accommodate not only parks and boat docks, but also manufacturing. But to domesticate the land and earn a profit from it would also require hustle.

Leonard Brown had both in ample supply. As a young man in the 1930s, Brown looked at the expanses of sand supplies making up most of the region and knew local

In 1986, Bulk Transport Corp. developed Eastport Centre for Commerce and Industry on U.S. Hwy. 49 in Valparaiso. Fully improved industrial and office lots are available to new and relocating businesses that find the Centre's proximity to airports, highways, and midwest trades a major convenience (top).

Headquartered in Michigan City, Bulk Transport Corp. and Brown, Inc. maintain a fleet of more than 500 specialized heavy vehicles (bottom).

companies could use it for making glass, or mixing mortar, or as an ingredient in the recipe for baking brick. In the Town of Pines where he lived, Brown converted an early Model A Ford into a stake bed truck. In trips throughout the county, along the lakeshore property,

digging basements for homeowners, Brown built an aspiring trucking company from grains of sand.

Construction Company Started in 1950

By 1950, Brown, Inc., a construction company that was spun off to focus on the flurry of postwar heavy and highway earth moving projects, grew in tandem with the era's economic expansion. Brown, Inc. now supplies complete site preparation for new commercial and industrial projects, and acts as a cargo handler at the Port of Indiana for bulk commodities. It also maintains a warehouse division at the crossroads of Highways 149 and 20 serving steel companies with just-in-time deliveries.

Headquartered in Michigan City, not far from their birthplace in the Pines, Bulk Transport Corp. and Brown, Inc. maintain a fleet of more than 500 pieces of equipment. Here, extensive in-house shop facilities accommodate component fabrication, paint and body restoration, trailer

manufacture, and all other work necessary to keep the fleet operating.

The region's dominant steel producers form the nucleus of Bulk Transport Corp.'s customer base today. Within the confines of the mills, specialized heavy off-highway trucks move raw materials to production facilities while finished slabs, plates, and coils are hauled outbound to other steel processors, port facilities, and warehouses. Some steel mills choose to have these services handled by Bulk Transport Corp. and Brown, Inc.'s staff of about 100, while others lease equipment—short or long term—for their own employees to operate.

The Choice for Material Handling

Either way, Bulk Transport Corp. and Brown, Inc. remain the choices in the region for industries that require material handling, including commodities in bulk such as stone, slag, and—as ever—mounds of sand.

Leonard Brown now leaves the business in the hands of his children but has stayed involved to

advise and oversee special projects. According to Barry Brown, the success of both businesses owes much to the vitality of the northwest Indiana marketplace and the steel mills and manufacturing plants that operate in it.

"Our growth has gone hand in hand with the growth of the region," Brown explains. "We were fortunately situated to assist other businesses and to prosper from association with companies here."

Leonard Brown began in business as Brown Trucking Co. in the 1930s (top).

Inside regional steel mills, Bulk Transport trucks load up raw materials for delivery to steel processors, warehouses, or the Port of Indiana (bottom).

BULK TRANSPORT CORPORATION
720 West U.S. Highway 20
Michigan City, Indiana 46360
(219) 872-8618

C & C Iron, Inc.

"IT REMAINS THE AMERICAN WAY FOR A SMALL BUSINESS TO GROW INTO A MAJOR COMPETITOR IN OUR COMMUNITY," SAYS L.J. BUD CRIST AS HE REFLECTS BACK TO THE EARLY YEARS OF THE COMPLEX BUSINESS THAT HE AND HIS SON, MICHAEL, NOW MANAGE. C & C IRON BEGAN IN 1963 AS AN ORNAMENTAL RAILING FABRICATION BUSINESS. TODAY, C & C IRON, INC. IS A LEADING

fabricator and erector of structural steel in the region. Its projects run the gamut from commercial buildings to industrial plants and from hospitals to schools.

Crist, who had worked in sales as a grocery manager and as a meat cutter, developed C & C Iron as a sideline business until 1965. As an ornamental design and steel fabricating shop, the company fashioned railings and gates for institutional and residential customers, as well as produced basement beams and lintels for developers of subdivisions during the years of rapid subdivision growth in the Merrillville area.

As the region grew, so did the demand for Crist's expertise. Not only could C & C fabricate railings, but it also fabricated the structural beams and components needed to construct the framework of buildings. By 1971, C & C Iron was incorporated, and it expanded its operations to structural steel fabricating and erection. Now, C & C Iron, Inc. was working exclusively with major builders and

developers in the area. A 7,500 square foot under-roof fabricating plant on a six-acre site with yard and loading facilities was erected. The privately held, family-owned business continued to grow with the community.

Ready for Future

Today, C & C Iron provides steel fabrication and erection services for hospitals, many local schools, colleges and universities, industrial plants, utility compa-

nies, banks, and major retailers in the region. C & C Iron can be credited for its work on facilities highly recognizable to the public: the Star Plaza Theater, Southlake Mall entrances, Methodist Hospitals, retail stores including four Meijer's and 11 Walgreen's stores, buildings on the campuses of Indiana University Northwest and Purdue University Calumet, and hotel facilities such as the Holidome in the former Holiday Inn.

The well-managed union shop uses a Whitney beam line with a controlled overhead handling system and support equipment to expedite the fabrication process. The production process entails cutting steel to specified dimensions, welding, sandblasting, and painting or finishing the final product. The production loop runs in a circle: conveying steel in at one end, fabricating at stations in the plant, finishing at the end of the loop, and then sending the finished product to the trucking area. Two 10-ton, overhead Gantry cranes hoist steel, load, and unload materials for the production line. The company

Major regional clients, such as Southlake Mall in Merrillville, appreciate C & C Iron's expertise in structural steel fabrication and erection (top).

In-house engineers provide design services (bottom left) while union ironworker field crews make sure final placement meets specifications (bottom right).

operates its own trucks for short-haul deliveries and works with trucking firms in the region for longer trips. It may require as many as ten trips a day to ship C & C Iron, Inc. materials to their final destinations.

Spanning the Midwest

Though some destinations may be as close as Merrillville where the company is located, other shipments may take the firm's steel as far away as Indianapolis, neighboring Illinois, or construction sites throughout the midwest region. On one recent job, C & C Iron received 600 tons of steel from a fabricator in Connecticut, then fabricated the steel to specifications and shipped it to a client in Dubuque, Iowa.

Field erection crews are composed of union ironworkers

equipped with field trucks assisted by a 25-ton or larger crane, a 60-foot manlift, a six-ton forklift, and other machinery necessary to erect the steel on the site.

Special computer software tracks each project undertaken by C & C Iron. In-house engineering staff works with clients to fine-tune specifications and fabricating procedures. Since 1992, C & C Iron has been category 1 certified for conventional steel structures by the American Institute of Steel Construction.

Excellent Working Relationships

Crist and his family, who all contribute to the business, operate the company as a close-knit, teamwork enterprise where the focus is on making sure each customer is completely satisfied with the final product. Affiliated with Iron workers Local 395, Shopmen's Local 473, and Operating Engineers Local 150, C & C Iron enjoys excellent working relationships with all the parties in its enterprise: customers, employees, and suppliers.

"Top quality fabricated steel, delivered when and where it is needed, is our daily work," Crist says. "It takes the combined efforts of every person here to serve our clients well, and we value the

longstanding relationships we have with many customers."

Current projects include steel fabrication and erection services on a variety of buildings in the region: the Merrillville Post Tribune facility, the new Crown Point High School, Lowell School Natatorium, Boone Grove schools, Plum Creek Center, Ultra Foods, and the City of East Chicago's cutting edge Public Safety Center, among others.

As the Crist family travels throughout the region, Bud, his wife Sharon, and their son Michael, who is now president of C & C Iron, can see the fruits of the family's efforts. The company's work is not, like an ornamental railing, visible to the naked eye, but it forms the very backbone of buildings used by the public every day. That sense of community is important to the Crists who are lifelong residents of Merrillville. Sharon Crist has served as a teacher in the Merrillville Schools for 36 years, and Bud Crist was elected to the Merrillville Board of School Trustees for 16 years where he contributed his expertise on new school building and remodeling projects. Youngsters in the neighborhood continue to be seen sporting jerseys printed with the C & C Iron, Inc. logo, another testament to the company's commitment to the community.

C & C Iron projects run the gamut from steel bridges to buildings. The production process involves all phases of fabrication from initial metal cutting, welding, sandblasting, painting, and finishing to erection of the steel components at the construction site.

C & C IRON, INC.
6409 Hendricks Street
Merrillville, Indiana 46410
(219) 769-2511
www.cnciron.com

CALUMET ABRASIVES COMPANY, INC.

3039 169th Place
Hammond, Indiana 46323
(219) 844-2695

Trained staff follow exacting specifications in the manufacture of cutting wheels at Calumet Abrasives Co., Inc. Each batch of abrasives is submitted to a battery of tests before shipment to customers (top).

Sparks fly when the company's steel-cutting abrasives get a trial run on test strips of metal. Cutting wheels are routinely burst-tested at speeds up to 60,000 rpm (bottom).

and relocated to Hammond in 1998, is a high end producer of abrasives serving a clientele of major manufacturers in the midwest.

Synthetics Take Hold

George and Edna Anderson founded the company in 1945. George Anderson, a chemical engineer, spent most of his professional life as a problem solver in a variety of industries. The last company for which he worked before establishing his own firm was in the abrasives field, a manufacturer of rubber-bonded abrasive wheels. Anderson devised a method for substituting synthetic rubber as a bond in place of natural rubber which the war in the Pacific had made a scarce commodity.

Realizing his knack for problem-solving, Anderson decided to go into business for himself. Edna and George moved from Philadelphia to East Chicago to start the company. Working together, the couple developed Calumet Abrasives into a cutting

edge company specializing in creative solutions for specific industrial applications. Current president John Anderson took the reins when George passed away in 1963.

"From the very beginning, my father liked finding solutions to specific problems," John Anderson recalls. "The company was never a commodities producer, but a specialty company able to produce abrasives to meet certain needs on the part of clients."

Exacting Standards

Today, Calumet Abrasives serves about 40 major manufacturers and industrial distributors. Exact recipe chemistry, precise production, and thorough testing are routine at the company. Its current contract with 3M, for instance, requires the firm to produce abrasives to an exacting standard, even burst-testing the wheels at up to 60,000 revolutions per minute.

The abrasives are used in industrial applications in which metal must be cut or slit with great accuracy and for sustained periods of time. The wheels produced by Calumet Abrasives are heavily

tested before shipment to verify the product will perform according to specification. The formulas—the exact "recipe" of solid and liquid resins, fiberglass, filler, and granular materials—fluctuate depending upon the intended use of the abrasive. Mixed and molded like pancakes with a hole in the middle, the wheels are produced both by hand and in automated machinery, cured in large industrial ovens, coded by batch number and production date, tested and recorded, and finally shipped to the customer.

The rigorously manufactured and meticulously tested wheels produced by Calumet Abrasives are not the wheels used by the majority of companies who need abrasives, but the select minority for whom superior performance is critical. Calumet Abrasives, for example, is the firm that got the call from an Illinois utility company looking for abrasives needed at a nuclear power plant.

"We're oriented in such a way as to engineer abrasives for specific purposes," Anderson says. "That has always been our special niche in the marketplace."

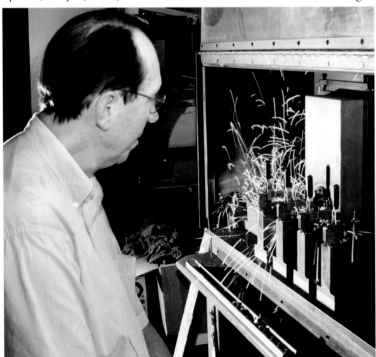

C ALUMET COLLEGE OF ST. JOSEPH, PERCHED ON THE SHORES OF LAKE MICHIGAN, STANDS OUT AS THE PREMIER PRIVATE, ACCREDITED COLLEGE IN LAKE COUNTY. THE CATHOLIC COLLEGE SERVES STUDENTS WHO WANT TO EARN A SOLID EDUCATION AND LAND A GOOD-PAYING JOB AFTER THEY GRADUATE. BACCALAUREATE AND ASSOCIATE DEGREES, ALONG WITH CERTIFICATES

CALUMET COLLEGE OF ST. JOSEPH

and accelerated four-year degree programs, are conferred by the college in areas such as paralegal studies, law enforcement management and accounting. Employers know that CCSJ grads can do the job—and do it well!

Small Classes, Personal Attention

C alumet College of St. Joseph strives to make a college education possible for all, despite today's fast-paced lifestyles. Classes are held during the day and evening at the college's main campus, 2400 New York Avenue in Whiting, and at its Merrillville campus, 51 West 80th Place in Georgetown Plaza near the Merrillville Post Office. The Whiting campus boasts a child drop-off center.

Though a private institution, Calumet College of St. Joseph promises that all who apply for financial aid are given full consideration. Approximately 90 percent of students receive some form of financial aid, and there is no out-of-state tuition differential. Small classes, usually limited to about 15 students, allow professors the constant opportunity to provide each student with personal attention. Students also can stay in constant contact with professors through e-mail, voice mail, and on-campus office visits.

Adults who have already earned approximately 60 college credits can earn a four-year degree in 18 months through the college's Degree Completion Division. Classes are held only one night a week at convenient locations throughout Northwest Indiana and Chicago. Accelerated degree programs include Law Enforce-

ment Management, Organization Management and Healthcare Management. Students also can earn college credit for life experience through the college's Life Experience Assessment Program (LEAP).

Catholic-Sponsored College

S tudents are encouraged to take full advantage of the college's computer lab, library, writing lab, bookstore, art gallery, chapel, student center, child drop-off center and deli. Students also can enjoy Alumni Park, a beautiful setting of lush trees and flowers and benches and picnic tables, which lies to the north of the main campus. Its centerpiece is a three-story cross.

The college, founded in 1951, is sponsored by the Cincinnati Province of the Missionaries of the Precious Blood. It's a college that breeds success! Calumet College of St. Joseph students are the leaders and innovators of tomorrow. They make a huge difference in Northwest Indiana—and beyond.

2400 New York Avenue
Whiting, Indiana 46394

51 West 80th Place
Merrillville, Indiana 46410

Toll free: 877-700-9100
www.ccsj.edu

Small classes, usually limited to 15 students, allow Calumet College of St. Joseph students personalized attention (top).

Flexibility that accommodates the fast pace of life today is a CCSJ hallmark. In addition to its Whiting campus (bottom), the college offers day and evening classes at a campus in Merrillville.

Anyone who visits old homes or historic public buildings built before the 1940's will notice the cramped square footage of the rooms and offices. It isn't that architects and builders of yore wouldn't have jumped at the chance to experiment with bigger rooms and broader expanses. However, the technology of the time did not

Calumet Flexicore promotes a family-oriented atmosphere at its Hammond plant (top). Employees routinely stay with the company until retirement, and many staffers represent second and third generations of families who have worked at Calumet Flexicore.

Calumet Flexicore's pre-cast, hollowcore concrete roof and floor slabs allow longer spans in residential (bottom) and commercial buildings, as well as promote non-flammability, aesthetics, and cost efficiency.

support the longer floor and roof spans required for the great rooms, atriums, and wide open spaces so prevalent today.

Some measure of thanks rightly goes to Calumet Flexicore Corporation and its subsidiary company, Federal Cement Products. Nestled in the northwest Indiana industrial heartland at 24 Marble Street, Calumet Flexicore helped revolutionize the way buildings are

constructed while making them more attractive, economical, and safer.

Proud History

Calumet Flexicore Corporation was founded in 1946 by Carl R. Carlsson and Eugene Swenson. Carlsson, an immigrant from Sweden, had building in his blood and partnered with Swenson to create a company that would capitalize on the post World War II construction boom.

The corporation became a major player in the evolving technology of manufacturing precast concrete products. It also initiated the Flexicore Manufacturers Association in 1952, the organization that developed the first handbook on the design and application of hollowcore slab. Carlsson's son, Carl L. Carlsson, joined the company in 1956 after serving three years as a Civil Engineer Corps officer in the Navy. With a master's degree in structural

engineering, he soon began research in prestressing Flexicore slab. In 1957, the company—one of 14 Flexicore dealers nationwide—was the first to pre-stress hollowcore Flexicore concrete slabs, transforming the design of modern buildings. Calumet Flexicore's method of manufacturing prestressed Flexicore—a method that improved strength and reliability—was soon adopted by other Flexicore companies throughout North America.

Revolutionizing the Building Industry

Flexicore revolutionized the building industry. The proprietary name for pre-cast, hollowcore concrete roof and floor slabs, Flexicore reduced the slab weight, thereby allowing longer spans in commercial, industrial, and residential buildings. Its fire resistant quality was also a great benefit, leading to multi-family dwelling design incorporating non-combustible floor and wall construction. It had other unique and beneficial qualities as well. The hollow cores of Flexicore permitted easy installation of concealed plumbing, heating, and electrical lines. It also could be painted or finished in a multitude of aesthetically pleasing styles. Noise control between floors was another valuable asset. Unlike wood frame, it could stand the test of time with less maintenance and deterioration— an asset that passed substantial cost savings onto happy building owners and managers. Now a mainstay of large structure and multi-family housing construction, Flexicore continues to provide a solution for architects, developers, and design-build firms looking for longer, more economical spans for new building projects.

Carl R. Carlsson bought out the interests of his partner Swenson in 1955. In 1960, Carl L. Carlsson took over as president of Calumet Flexicore Corporation. Within five years, Carl L. had designed the process and equipment necessary to triple productivity. Originally located at Cline and Chicago avenues in Gary, the company constructed a new plant in Hammond that became a model for Flexicore manufacturing. Its methodology was used by Flexicore manufacturing facilities nationwide.

In 1961, Calumet Flexicore purchased Federal Cement Products, a Hammond company started in the early 1900's that manufactured lightweight concrete roofing. Its product was used for the roofing systems of such well-known landmarks as the Hammond Civic Center and Chicago buildings including the Adler Planetarium, Shedd Aquarium, and Union Station. In 1991, the company expanded further with the purchase of Midwest Flexicore in nearby Franklin Park, Illinois, and eventually transferred its operations to the high-efficiency Hammond headquarters.

Family Culture

Calumet Flexicore is a family business with a decidedly family flavor. Employees who sign on with the company are apt to stay until retirement, becoming part of a committed team that works well together. Forty and 50 year careers with the company are not uncommon for many employees. At Calumet Flexicore, morale is high and turnover low. Creating a great company for both customers and employees has been a goal of the Carlsson family. The Carlssons consider the continued loyalty of second and third generations of employees from local families one of the rewards of its business.

Today, Calumet Flexicore Corporation faces the future as energetic and visionary as ever. From its 23-acre manufacturing site, the company's 90 employees continue to design, produce, deliver, and install flooring and roofing components for customers throughout Indiana, Illinois, Michigan, and other parts of the midwest. Its product is used for many buildings not landmarks to the general public—but also a great many that are, like Oprah Winfrey's Harpo Studios and the Lincoln Park Zoo Reptile House, both in Chicago. The company's product is a critical component in the construction of commercial and office buildings, churches, industrial and public complexes, and

condominium developments throughout the region.

Promising Future

The company that revolutionized the building industry isn't finished by a long shot. Carl L. Carlsson's son Carl J. joined the company in 1980 and is active in Flexicore and other business activities. In 1986, Carl's daughter Elizabeth, after receiving a master's degree from the University of Notre Dame, joined the Flexicore family. Carl L. Carlsson retired in 1996, officially handing the reins of the respected company over to the third generation of Carlssons, Elizabeth.

The best may be yet to come. The company is excited about a brand new technology in development that would again triple manufacturing productivity and reduce cost. New prestressed products are also in the development phase that would provide designers with more choices in the selection of building materials. In Calumet Flexicore Corporation, the Carlssons have built a strong family business that continues to build the region.

Product manufactured by Calumet Flexicore has been used in the construction of such landmark buildings as the John G. Shedd Aquarium in Chicago (top).

Carl L. Carlsson (bottom) joined the company in 1980 and retired in 1996. His daughter, Elizabeth Carlsson, is now president of the firm.

CALUMET FLEXICORE CORPORATION
24 Marble Street
Hammond, Indiana 46320
(219) 932-3340

THE CHICAGO SOUTHSHORE & SOUTH BEND RAILROAD IS A STRATEGICALLY LOCATED LYNCH-PIN IN THE EXTENSIVE TRANSPORTATION NETWORK OF NORTHWEST INDIANA. THE ANTECEDENT OF A FIRM THAT PROVIDED ELECTRIC TROLLEY SERVICE BETWEEN EAST CHICAGO AND WHITING AT THE TURN OF THE CENTURY, TODAY THE COMPANY IS A SHORT LINE CARRIER CONNECTING NORTHERN

From short hop passenger service at the turn of the century, SouthShore has grown into the region's premier short line rail service (top).

SouthShore Freight is customer-focused. Clients get a rapid response from staffers (bottom) and can schedule service for 5 or 6 days per week.

Indiana's industrial complex with 20 transcontinental, regional, and local railroads. The Chicago South Shore & South Bend Railroad—dubbed "SouthShore Freight"—provides critically important rail transportation services to a who's who list of companies and industries.

One Hundred Years On the Rails

While the railroad got its start providing short hop service between northwest Indiana cities, it wasn't long until regular freight service was inaugurated to serve the growing industries in the region. Service between South Bend and Chicago was greatly expanded after formation of the original Chicago South Shore & South Bend Railroad in 1925. Construction of the line to steam railroad standards helped assure its survival to this day as an important link in the national transportation network.

In 1967, the railroad was acquired by a predecessor of CSX (the Chesapeake and Ohio). The South Shore was operated as an independent subsidiary until 1984, when it was sold to Venango River Corporation. Through the efforts of the railroad development firm Anacostia & Pacific Company, Inc., the railroad was reorganized and by 1990 featured separated services for freight and passenger lines. Today, SouthShore's management responsibilities extend to the line's freight service while the Northern Indiana Commuter Transportation District (NICTD) provides the railroad's Chicago to South Bend passenger rail service.

Superior Freight Transportation

SouthShore Freight is geared to provide a superior response to the needs of regional customers for reliable freight transportation services via rail. Expert train

crews assure that cars are not delayed in classification yards for switching, but go directly from the customers' facilities to interchange points with Class I carriers. A model of efficiency, SouthShore Freight conducts interchange operations within as few hours as possible and conversely routes received cars directly to customers. Round-the-clock train dispatchers maintain close communication with customers and connecting railroads to ensure that all cars are handled expeditiously.

Trackage extends from South Bend westward to Kensington Yard in Chicago and south from Michigan City to Stillwell and Kingsbury Industrial Park. Other principal cities served by South-Shore include Gary, Hammond, East Chicago, Burns Harbor, Portage, and LaPorte. SouthShore also serves the Illinois International Port District's Lake Calumet Harbor.

With 10 high-horsepower GP38-2 locomotives and a railroad freight car fleet in excess of 550 gondola, covered coil steel, and flat cars, SouthShore is able to tailor services to its on-line clients. Freight car and locomotive shops, located in Michigan City, are modern repair and maintenance centers where SouthShore equipment is kept in tip-top condition. Not only do the shops keep the fleet in excellent repair, but they also have the ability to perform special services for customers, such as making modifications to cars to meet special customer needs. SouthShore assists customers by providing a pool of railroad cars for regular shippers, thereby reducing the number of cars those clients must acquire from a third party.

The railroad's main lines are well-maintained and equipped with an automatic block signal system. Track segments with the heaviest traffic density are laid with 115-pound continuous-welded rail. Because the company's track structure meets—and often exceeds—Federal Railroad Administration Class 4 standards, SouthShore Freight trains may travel at speeds up to 60 miles per hour.

Helping Customers to Compete

SouthShore Freight executives and crews know that efficiency means cost savings for customers. Prompt movement of materials by rail car—both to and from a customer location—helps regional businesses to compete in an increasingly fast-paced, global marketplace.

Metallurgical coal and steam coal account for the greatest percentage of the railroad's freight revenue. In addition to coal, other commodities include steel, iron and scrap, roofing materials, paper, industrial chemicals, industrial minerals, and export food grains.

Steel-making facilities in SouthShore's service area account for one-fifth of America's total steel

production. Two of SouthShore's largest steel customers are Bethlehem Steel at Burns Harbor, the nation's second largest producer, and National Steel at Portage, which ships flat-rolled steel outbound and also receives inbound chemical shipments for its pickling lines via the SouthShore.

SouthShore provides 5 or 6 day per week service to customers such as Isaac/Reserve Iron & Metal, Metron Steel, Arro-Windy City Packaging, The Sweets Mix Company, Reserve Marine Terminal, Hoogewerff Reserve Terminal, ADE, Inc., and numerous grain export facilities. Other major customers include MidCorr, Unifrax, Georgia-Pacific, Behr Iron & Metal, Rollcoater, Inc., and Alexander Chemical Corp.

Freight service provided by SouthShore means direct access for these and other companies to major transportation lines from coast to coast throughout the U.S. and Canada. SouthShore's strong and well-established traffic base includes two Northern Indiana Public Service Company(NIPSCO) generating stations: one in Michigan City and the other in Baillytown in Porter County.

Approximately 65 men and women operate the SouthShore. Non-management employees are represented by the various national rail unions with agreements tailored to meet the service needs of

customers. All freight trains are operated by three-man crews, trained and qualified to operate throughout the SouthShore Railroad and Chicago Terminal.

At SouthShore, the focus is always on the end user. "Serving our customers well is the reason for our existence," says president H. Terry Hearst, who has been at the helm of the company since 1990. "Expert rail service, provided as efficiently as possible, is what customers have come to expect from SouthShore."

In the new millennium, SouthShore intends to stay on track with its record of superior freight service for customers in the industrial heartland. One hundred years of history have given the company experience few can match. The possibilities of the future provide the zeal to remain the region's premier short line.

SouthShore's track serves two Northern Indiana Public Service Company plants: one in Michigan City (top) and one at Baillytown in Porter County.

SouthShore Freight provides timely service to regional customers, aided by high-power GP38-2 locomotives (bottom) and a fleet of more than 550 freight cars.

CHICAGO SOUTHSHORE & SOUTH BEND RAILROAD

505 North Carroll Avenue
Michigan City, Indiana 46360
(219) 874-9000
(800) 873-1486
www.southshorefreight.com

THE COMPANY'S CLAIM TO FAME IS MAKING STEEL FLAT. BUT ITS MARKET PROSPECTS ARE ANYTHING BUT. CHICAGO STEEL, FOUNDED BY BRUCE MANNAKEE IN 1989, HAS EARNED A NATIONAL REPUTATION FOR TENSION LEVELING, A PROCESS BY WHICH STEEL IS UNIFORMLY FLATTENED TO ENHANCE THE QUALITY OF PRODUCTS IN WHICH IT IS A COMPONENT. AS A YOUNG MAN

Mannakee initially pursued a law degree but was drawn back to the steel industry he had come to know as a student at Indiana University. Working full-time during the day while attending college in the evening, Mannakee learned about metal manufacturing at U.S. Steel and was both awed and challenged by the massive equipment and manpower required to produce steel. He was also inquisitive, a trait that later led him and two partners to form Chicago Steel and explore new opportunities in the industry.

Three Plants Serve Industry

Today, Mannakee oversees three plants that serve as toll processors offering tension leveling for mills, service centers, and end users. The flagship Gary facility, with 317,000 square feet of industrial processing space and 94 employees, serves the Midwest. The 165,000 square foot Fairless Hills, Pennsylvania plant employs 37 and serves customers on the East Coast. The third facility, in Gadsden, Alabama, caters to clients in the South.

Chicago Steel, established in 1989, has earned a reputation in the steel processing industry for its high standards and cutting edge technology (top).

Users of Chicago Steel's tension leveled steel coils include appliance and roofing manufacturers, office furniture producers, and automotive companies (bottom).

Chicago Steel owns no inventory, but its Gary facility houses approximately 20,000 tons or more of in-process material and about 35,000 tons of mill-owned material for "just-in-time" delivery. Applications for its tension leveled steel coil include appliances, building and roofing components, motor laminations, office furniture, automotive components, and other products for which flatness is critical.

Using state-of-the-art Herr-Voss tension leveling equipment, Chicago Steel lines process hot-rolled pickled and oiled, and cold-rolled steel; galvanized, Galvalume, silicon steel, terne plate, and pre-painted steel; aluminum; and selected stainless steel in gauges ranging from 0.012 and 0.125 inches, widths from 20 to 72 inches, and coil weights up to 72,000 pounds.

Steel that has been tension-leveled, or flattened, by Chicago Steel provides a more reliable material for end-user production. An unknown science and hidden process to the majority of consumers, tension leveling leads to the removal of product variability. Steel coil that has been flattened

can be slit, punched, sheared, drawn, notched, or subjected to other cold-form methods with no "memory" in the strip and no springback. In other words, the steel performs with greater reliability, predictability, and quality.

Raising the Industry Standard

Mannakee's company is known not only for tension-leveling itself, but also for raising the industry standard. While American manufacturers since the 1950's adhered to guidelines for flatness contained in the American Society for Testing & Materials (ASTM) Standard Number 568, Chicago Steel believed it could do better.

"That standard described shape in terms of the height of a wave with no reference to the frequency of occurrence," Mannakee explains. "We created a new standard—the Five I Unit Flatness Standard—that translates into flatness parameters of one-eighth inch wave height at 28 inch intervals—or less."

While the I Unit method of describing shape has been more widely used in Europe and the Far

East, Mannakee said, acknowledgement of its superiority is rather new in the U.S. Chicago Steel is currently lobbying for formal ASTM recognition of the tougher standard industry-wide.

End-user customers have been supportive of Chicago Steel's quest for higher flatness quality.

"We've had many accounts where the customer recognized the value of this material and requested that the supplier have the steel leveled at Chicago Steel," Mannakee notes. "That helps us partner with steel producers and end-users to produce products that are superior."

Mannakee anticipates growth in the demand for tension leveling and believes Chicago Steel will remain at the forefront of the steel quality movement. Chicago Steel's process is routinely requested by many quality-focused companies.

"Original equipment manufacturers have found they experience economies in production using steel which is flat by our standard," Mannakee stresses. "That, combined with the removal of variability, is the reason for our corporate existence."

Chemcoaters Provides Finishing

Already Mannakee is eyeing the future. In March, 2000, he announced the formation of a new company, Chemcoaters, LLC, to offer alkaline cleaning, scotchbriting, center-splitting, side-trimming, strand extensioning, and waterborne chemical coating all via

a single, freestanding line. The new coil processing line will be housed at an 80,000 square foot facility adjacent to the Chicago Steel plant at 700 Chase Street in Gary.

The new, state-of-the-art coil processing line has the capacity to process 72,000 pound coils of hot-rolled pickled and oiled, cold-rolled, galvanized, stainless steel, and aluminum in widths up to 72 inches.

"The unique aspect of this particular line is the fact that value-added processes are in-line with the vertical chemical coating and drying section," Mannakee explained. "This is, I believe, the only line of its kind that will be available to customers in the next year."

The chemical coating section is designed to apply each of the new waterborne, environmentally-friendly coil treatments currently in use at speeds up to 600 feet per minute. The coatings include dry film lubricants, anti-fingerprint acrylics, dried-in-place zinc phosphates, and no-rinse organic coatings, among others. Two-side vertical inspection stations both before and after the coating process will ensure quality for products with critical surface requirements. In applications where chemical coating is not specified, the line is capable of a maximum operating speed of 1,000 feet per minute.

The new facility enables the company to offer value-added processes at significant cost savings over more conventional methods. The ability of customers to obtain

multiple processing service from a single company on a single production line offers numerous advantages in addition to cost efficiency, chief among them being reduced coil transport and potentially shorter lead times.

Mannakee and his companies do not produce steel nor do they construct the end product. As one of the industry's standard-setting, quality-committed partners, Mannakee remains in the middle of the action. And that, he says, is right where he likes to be.

"High quality combined with efficiency in processing is our aim," Mannakee says. "Both Chicago Steel and Chemcoaters will continue to explore technologies that help us to best serve our customers."

Chemcoaters will offer a host of processing and coating services all via a single freestanding production line (top).

Employees at Chicago Steel, whether working with payroll or payloads, aim for quality and efficiency every day (bottom).

CHICAGO STEEL

700 Chase Street
Gary, Indiana 46404
(219) 949-1111
(800) 367-8110
www.chisteel.com
www.chemcoaters.com

W HEN JOHN AND MARTA CICCO STARTED THEIR FIRST STORE, BUSINESS WAS A REAL STITCH. ACTUALLY, IT WAS THOUSANDS OF STITCHES. JOHN HAD BEEN TRAINED AS A TAILOR IN ITALY AND THE ABILITY TO MELD FABRIC, THREAD, BUTTONS, AND TRIM INTO A BRAND NEW SUIT WAS HIS STOCK IN TRADE. IT WAS A SKILL HE LEARNED BEGINNING AT AGE EIGHT. BY THE RIPE OLD AGE

of 12, John Cicco was sewing custom made clothes.

John and Marta came to the United States where they set up their first shop in Gary in 1951. Ready-to-wear clothing was making big inroads in the American apparel industry, but at the Cicco's store, customers could order tailor made suits and accessories or bring in clothing for alterations. Little by little, the Ciccos added off-the-rack inventory to compliment the store's offerings.

Needle and Thread

John and Marta Cicco built a booming business with needle and thread. Today, Cicco's Menswear is a mainstay of men's fashion in the northwest Indiana marketplace. The Ciccos operate two stores—retail store on Mississippi Street in Merrillville and a service location for alterations on Calumet Avenue in Valparaiso.

Customers throughout the region have seen the Cicco's Menswear billboards proclaiming the store's message: "All men are created equal.

Then they get dressed." That message helps sell hundreds of suits each year.

Today, Tina Cicco Popp and Fred Cicco share the administrative duties, with Tina also handling buying and Fred heading the store's Corporate Apparel Division. John and Marta still keep a hand in the family-owned business now managed by their children, including Theresa Cicco who lends a hand on weekends and during the busy holiday season.

"We all feel blessed to have this family business," say Tina and Fred, who added that the business

has been a good way to keep the family close. The Ciccos see each other every day. They also see customers—thousands of northwest Indiana residents who turn to them for top quality menswear, custom work, and expert advice.

"Part of our job is to present the latest styles and help clients put together looks that fit both the times and their personal lifestyles," Tina Cicco says of the store's client-focused strategy. "We want our customers to look good and also be comfortable in everything they purchase from us."

The Cicco family credits its fine staff for dedication and talent, two qualities that have contributed to the menswear store's success (top).

Marta (left) and Tina Cicco help Miguel Arredondo with a custom-made suit (below). Cicco's Menswear sells hundreds of suits to northwest Indiana residents each year.

Largest in Region

Cicco's Menswear has the largest selection of fine menswear in the region. The independent store stocks a wide range of apparel and accessories including suits, formal wear, casual clothing, hats, shoes, ties, coats, and more. Committed to helping every customer, Cicco's carries regular, short, and big and tall size clothing with a size range from 36 to 70 and men's sportswear in sizes medium through 6X.

A separate floor at the Merrillville store is devoted to alterations and custom sewing. The Cicco family still offers individually tailored clothing. A corporate apparel division provides logo wear and customized apparel for restaurants, steel mills, entertainment companies, construction firms, and automobile dealerships.

About 12 tailors and seamstresses are employed at Cicco's to produce custom-made suits and coats for clientele. They also handle contract sewing and alterations for several major retailers. Company pick-up and delivery trucks travel the state, serving companies as far away as Lafayette and Indianapolis.

Winning Staff

The Cicco family now presides over a business that offers the gamut of menswear services: quality menswear sales, custom tailoring, alterations for both men and women, expert dry cleaning, corporate apparel sales, and tuxedo sales and rentals. Cicco's also offers group sales events when Cicco's staffers visit area businesses to show fabric samples and take measurements for custom and ready-made clothing. It takes a talented and dedicated team of employees to accomplish it all.

"We're fortunate to have wonderful, friendly, hardworking, and loyal staffers," Tina stresses.

The Ciccos take time from the hustle and bustle of the family business to share in the life of the community. In addition to other efforts, Fred and Tina are active in Indiana Sports Charities, an organization started by former White Sox player Ron Kittle that raises money for cancer cure research at area hospitals.

In 1999, Cicco's Menswear sold more than 3,000 ties. It was a hot year for ties, when Regis Philbin "revolutionized" the look with solid color satin ties matched up against solid color shirts. While other stores were scurrying to catch up, Cicco's was on the money with its inventory and displays. John Cicco was still upstairs at the Merrillville store, stitching the seam of a suit. It was a year in which one could pattern after television's "Mr. Millionaire"—or talk to the Ciccos about getting a custom suit that truly would be one in a million.

Marta and John Cicco grew up in a small town in Italy (top right) where they opened their first store. By 1951, they had immigrated to the region and set up shop in Gary.

Quality service and personal attention breed long-time customers. John Cicco (bottom) takes the measure of McWally Judge. Mr. Judge was one of Cicco's first customers and is still a regular today.

CICCO'S MENSWEAR, INC.
8250 Mississippi Street
Merrillville, Indiana 46410
(219) 769-1744

MUCH HAS CHANGED SINCE LESLIE I. COMBS ESTABLISHED HIS CONTRACTING BUSINESS IN GARY. IN THE PRE-WAR ERA, A SOLIDLY BUILT HOME IN A FINE NEIGHBORHOOD COST COMBS' CUSTOMERS FROM $6,000 TO $15,000, INCLUDING THE LOT. THAT WAS 1940. THE PRICES OF EVERYTHING HAVE RISEN SINCE THEN, FROM LOAVES OF BREAD TO CARS, HOMES, AND COLLEGE EDUCATIONS.

L.I. COMBS & SONS, INC.

5500 East 81st Avenue
Merrillville, Indiana 46410
(219) 947-2296
www.licombs.com
www.gleneaglevillas.com
www.compasspointe.com

L.I. Combs & Sons, Inc. has built a regional reputation for its residential and commercial properties. Compass Pointe (bottom) in Valparaiso, a luxury apartment home community, is one of the firm's latest developments. The firm is lead by Jim Combs (top), grandson of the founder pictured in front of Gleneagle Villas, another recent residential development located at Aberdeen .

But one thing has not changed at L.I. Combs & Sons, Inc. The company still produces finely built homes and buildings in a professional, timely, and cost effective manner.

Proven Track Record

L.I. Combs has a proven track record in construction and development for residential and commercial properties. A third generation company, the firm is now headed by Jim Combs, grandson of the founder. L.I. Combs operates from offices in Merrillville, but its reach is region-wide. The winner of numerous awards for its communities, L.I. Combs has developed and/or built homes, commercial buildings, or entire neighborhoods in every municipality in northwest Indiana, as well as properties in other midwestern states.

Thousands of people live in attractive homes built by L.I. Combs, in neighborhoods such as Quail Ridge—which earned awards in 1989 from the City of Valparaiso, Greater Valparaiso Area Chamber of Commerce, and Porter County Builders Association. Residents of the region also enjoy other buildings constructed by the firm: the

Chesterton Medical Center, Uno's Pizzeria, Davenport College, and a host of others. The firm's most notable recent commercial land development is the Environ Executive Center in Merrillville, now home to Bank One and Northern Indiana Public Service Corporation.

The secret of the firm's success, Jim Combs says, is that the company has never accepted a commission on which it didn't believe it could deliver excellent construction, cost efficient services, and the highest degree of customer satisfaction.

"Our reputation is important to us," Combs says. "Our aim has been to serve individual clients well, while also improving and beautifying the built environ of the region. That's still our goal on every project."

Home Sweet Home

Two new residential projects will continue the company tradition. Gleneagle Villas offers distinctive homes at Aberdeen, an upscale golf course community in Valparaiso. The villas, Combs said, are perfect for people who value quality homes as well as the spectacular views of the greens, walking

trails, breathtaking landscaping, and community amenities like the Aberdeen Inn and Aberdeen Brewing Co. The homes offer single level living with luxurious master suites, high ceilings in entryways and living rooms, and a host of lifestyle options such as bonus rooms and four-season sunrooms.

Compass Pointe, a luxury apartment home development in Valparaiso, offers rental residences designed for busy people who may not want to mow the lawn, but appreciate on-site amenities such as the swimming pool, workout facility, volleyball courts, fireplaces, and vaulted ceilings. Forging a new style of apartment home living, L.I. Combs has added extras—like cable television service, high speed T-1 internet access, and laundry equipment in each apartment—that afford residents both comfort and convenience.

Quality and service have been company hallmarks since L.I. Combs & Sons, Inc. built its first homes in 1917. For more than eight decades, the company has proven that—no matter how much things change—high quality workmanship never goes out of style.

IF THERE'S A COMPANY THAT KNOWS HOW TO KEEP ITS EYES ON THE DONUT—AND THE HOLE—IT IS DAWN FOOD PRODUCTS, INC. A PRIVATELY HELD INTERNATIONAL BAKERY GOODS COMPANY ESTABLISHED IN 1920, DAWN FOODS STARTED WITH THE DONUT WHEN IT OPENED A PASTRY SHOP IN JACKSON, MICHIGAN. BUT IT WASN'T LONG BEFORE THE FIRM SAW A HUGE HOLE IN THE

DAWN FOOD PRODUCTS, INC.

marketplace for a company that could combine the highest quality products with a passion for customer service.

Worldwide Company

Today, Dawn Foods is a worldwide bakery products and finished foods supplier with processing facilities, distributors, and subsidiaries in North America, Europe, South America, and Australia. Manufacturing plants and distribution centers ring the globe from Denver, Colorado to Weesp in the Netherlands, from Ederbach, Germany to Sydney, Australia, from Hong Kong, China to Buenos Aires, Argentina, and Evesham in the United Kingdom. Dawn Foods has facilities in Dubai, UAE (United Arab Emirates) in the mideast and right here at home in the midwest in Munster, Indiana.

Dawn Food Products staffers Steve Burse, Joe Greco, and David Parks (l to r) know that since the 1920s, the company has always had "flour power" (top).

More than 2,500 items are warehoused at the company's Munster facility where a colorful sculpture welcomes employees and visitors each day (bottom).

The Munster distribution center, which opened in 1987 and employs approximately 70, provides warehouse-to-customer service for retail and wholesale bakeries, restaurants, hotels, donut shops, and other food-aligned businesses. Its service territory stretches from the Chicago metropolitan area as far north as the Wisconsin border and includes the northern quadrant of Indiana. It also serves customers in southwest Michigan. About 80 percent of this northwest Indiana facility's business is in the Chicago marketplace.

According to Steve Burse, general manager of Dawn Foods' Munster facility, the company prides itself not only on the quality of its bakery products and efficiency of its distribution network, but also for a customer orientation that makes excellent service the goal every day.

"Success for the end-user is paramount," Burse explains. "Dawn Foods doesn't just sell to a customer, we help that business by sharing knowledge and know-how that come from years of experience. As long as the customers do well, we know we will, too."

Extensive Inventory

With more than 2,500 line items, Dawn Foods is one of the nation's largest manufacturers and distributors of bakery products and supplies. Inventory is divided into three categories: wet products, dry products, and frozen products. Wet items include pie fillings, baker's jellies, powdered fillings, icings and glazes, fondant, batters and marinades, stabilizers, pie bases, and related products. Dry products include, donut mixes, cake mixes and bases, brownie mixes, pound cakes, donut sugars, stick mixes, sweet dough, cookie mixes, bread and roll concentrates, waffle cone mixes, pizza and pretzel mixes, and many more. Ready-made, frozen product lines include gourmet muffins, cookies, fruit sticks, puff pastry, cinnamon rolls and danish and Dawn frozen Snackees,™ among others.

An inclusive Web site (www.dawnfoods.com) allows customers worldwide to find Dawn Foods locations and research the company's entire product line. Direct links via e-mail make it easy for customers and prospective clients to make inquiries and obtain quick answers.

Finest Products

Nationally known restaurants, hotels, and food chains use Dawn Foods products. So, too—most likely—does the donut shop right down the street. The company serves big accounts and smaller ones with the same "please and thank you service." Its worldwide reputation for fine products timely delivered is sweetened not only with icings and glazes, Burse said, but service that shows every customer is important.

From the Munster distribution center, employees organize all of the products the baker needs to turn out tasty cakes, muffins, pies, donuts, and other delights. Fresh ingredient products like flour, eggs, sugar, and other basics are also available to customers. The center receives its product from Dawn manufacturing facilities and stocks it for delivery to customers in its service area. Inventory is a critical aspect of the distribution center's business as it seeks to fill orders immediately for any product or group of items carried by the company, in whatever quantities are needed by the customer.

The Munster facility is one of a network of distribution centers that ensure no bakery, grocery, restaurant, or hotel is far from a Dawn Foods plant. Manufacturing facilities, distributors, and subsidiaries work closely together to serve customers throughout the world. Dawn Foods may have cakes and cookies down to a science, but its distribution network makes sure customers—and finally consumers—taste the benefit of that expertise.

From Donut to Distribution

That's fitting for a company that started with a donut shop and then added delivery. Back in Jackson, Michigan, customers loved the family recipes for Dawn Donuts so much even competitors begged for the mix. Demand became so large that the owners decided to close the retail store and open the

nation's first bakery mix company. It wasn't long before the company realized the marketplace needed a one-stop-shop where bakers could obtain everything they needed from a single supplier. The distribution network began in Michigan and branched out quickly, as Dawn Food Products, Inc. invested in strategically located centers from which its top-notch products could be shipped to customers.

The company is still a family-owned business. The Jones family—with Ron Jones at the helm—manages the now massive enterprise whose headquarters remain in Jackson, Michigan. The corporate culture is one that encourages personal initiative and rewards effort. Burse said the company philosophy can be boiled down to a simple maxim: "At Dawn Foods, we value every single customer and every single employee."

The Dawn Foods product line has expanded to include a lot more than those original donut mixes. A complete catalog of

mixes, bases, icings, fillings, frozen products, ready-to-sell products, equipment, commodities, packaging, and more provide literally everything any baker needs to bake up a profitable business.

A small business that started with a donut has become the source of satisfaction for the sweet-toothed worldwide. Which just goes to show that sometimes it's a good idea to look past the donut, and focus on the hole.

Georgiann Agnew (left) is one of 70 staffers who provide Dawn's trademark efficient and friendly service every day (top).

Dawn Food Products' distribution system features a 50-unit fleet of refrigerated tractors/trailers (bottom).

Dawn Food Products, Inc.
Chicago Distribution Center
215 45th Street
Munster, Indiana 46321
(219) 922-3660
www.dawnfoods.com

A REGION MAY BE JUDGED NOT ONLY ON THE AMENITIES IT OFFERS TO ITS FLOURISHING CITIZENS, BUT ALSO THE SERVICES IT PROVIDES TO RESIDENTS WHO NEED A HELPING HAND. FOR 25 YEARS, EDGEWATER SYSTEMS FOR BALANCED LIVING HAS BROUGHT BALANCE TO THE LIVES OF PEOPLE IN GARY AND SURROUNDING COMMUNITIES WITH A COMPREHENSIVE PROGRAM OF ADDICTION, MENTAL

health, and healthcare services.

Edgewater came into existence in 1974 after a panel of distinguished Gary citizens studied the needs of the community. The specially convened committee, under the chairmanship of Barbara Leek Wesson, resolved that locally based mental health, intervention, child and adolescent, and other services could promote public health and well-being and serve as an advocate for pro-active programs and outreach.

Beacon of Hope

Today, Edgewater Systems for Balanced Living thrives under the direction of Danita Johnson Hughes, who currently serves as president and chief executive officer. A graduate of Indiana University and the University of Chicago, Johnson Hughes works with a team of 250 staff members at Edgewater. All of them believe it is the agency's mission to shine as a beacon of hope and health in the community.

"To be a neighbor is to be there when the need is greatest, to be a light in the darkest hours," Johnson Hughes says. "Edgewater considers

Danita Johnson Hughes (top) serves as president and CEO of Edgewater Systems for Balanced Living.

Individual counseling services (bottom) help those who come to Edgewater Systems deal with life-changing or stressful events from addiction and depression to divorce or job loss.

itself a neighbor to at-risk children and troubled families, to citizens struggling with drug or alcohol addiction, to men and women working through depression or dealing with the loss of a loved one."

Comprehensive Services

Edgewater, located at 1100 West Sixth Avenue in the heart of downtown Gary, is a haven for people of all ages with all manner of life disruptions. The agency maintains programs in adult services, addiction services, child and adolescent services, crisis intervention, employee assistance, and psychological testing and treatment design. According to Ashvin Sheth, Associate Vice President for Clinical Services, a trained psychiatric counselor who has worked at Edgewater for 15 years, the agency may assist as many as 3,000 clients at a given time with services that range from weekly out-patient counseling sessions to full-time, in-patient residential care and treatment.

Sun House, another Edgewater Systems initiative, is a residential facility serving adolescent males ages 16 to 18 who have been separated from their families for an extended period of time.

"We take pride in the comprehensive nature of our services," Sheth notes. "Trained staff and multiple facilities allow us to make a difference in the lives of those who come to us."

At The Turning Point, an addiction services center, clients can take advantage of a battery of programs including addiction counseling and treatment, individual and family psychotherapy, and self-help and support group programs. The Thelma Marshall Children's Home provides residential treatment and therapy for emotionally disturbed adolescents from ages 6 to 17 who require 24-hour care and services. Even businesses find their way to Edgewater, where the agency's Employee Assistance Program assists their employees in resolving issues involving everything from job stress and "burn out" to depression or pre-retirement counseling.

Accessible and Affordable

Edgewater is partially funded by the State of Indiana Division of Mental Health and also works with Medicare and Medicaid. Fees computed on a sliding scale to accommodate the wage discrepancies of clients make

Edgewater's services accessible and affordable. Through its contractual relationship with The Methodist Hospitals, Edgewater is able to provide services that require medical intervention or in-patient psychiatric evaluation and care.

Edgewater is certified by the Indiana Division of Mental Health and is fully accredited by CARF, the rehabilitation accreditation commission.

Helping Neighbors in Need

Edgewater Systems for Balanced Living is not a business in which success is judged by a growing list of customers. But, Johnson Hughes stresses, it is a sign of hope that mental health and behavioral difficulties once ignored by society are now addressed with positive programs.

"The world is not a utopia," she says. "There will always be friends and neighbors who need someone to talk to, a safe haven in a storm, a place to rest and regroup. Edgewater will strive to meet those needs, now and in the future."

Edgewater Systems for Balanced Living (top), established in 1974, offers a staff of 250 counselors and support personnel and specialized facilities for children and families.

Outpatient treatment, including group counseling sessions (bottom), help people work through psychological, emotional, and behavioral problems. Inpatient care is available, coordinated by Edgewater Systems in partnership with The Methodist Hospitals.

EDGEWATER SYSTEMS FOR BALANCED LIVING

1100 West 6th Avenue
Gary, Indiana 46402
(219) 885-4264
(877) 921-EDGE toll free
www.edgewatersystems.org

EMPRESS CASINO

HAMMOND

IS NOW

HORSESHOE CASINO HAMMOND

Horseshoe Casino Hammond is an impressive sight on the Lake Michigan shore. The massive ship housing this northwest Indiana entertainment powerhouse required 5.9 million pounds of steel and 5,245 gallons of exterior paint (top).

Action-packed fun is the name of every game at Horseshoe Casino Hammond. The casino offers more than 1,600 slots, 50 table games (bottom), award-winning restaurants, and elegant conference and meeting rooms.

games, award-winning restaurants, and elegant banquet and meeting rooms, Horseshoe Casino Hammond continues to be a sure bet for top notch gaming and entertainment.

A gleaming white landmark on Lake Michigan, the 288 feet long by 74 feet wide catamaran plays host to residents of the region and visitors from throughout the world. Before joining the fun inside, visitors marvel at the massive ship designed by naval architects. With a gross tonnage of 1,583, construction of the gaming vessel required more than 5.9 million pounds of steel and 5,245 gallons of exterior paint. The four-story cruiser—with its Emerald, Diamond, Ruby, and Gold level gaming floors—took almost a year to construct. The ship carries 3,240 passengers and is impressive to Horseshoe staffers, too, who keep her in tip-top shape, right down to polishing the light fixtures—of which there are 745.

Voted the Best

W hether it's slots, video poker, craps, blackjack, or roulette,

Horseshoe Casino (seconds off the Indiana I-80/90 skyway at Indianapolis Boulevard) strives to be the premier gaming destination in the midwest. The effort has borne fruit—and not just the slot machine kind. Voted "Best Place to Gamble" by area newspapers and winner of Casino Player

Magazine's "Best Blackjack" award, Horseshoe Casino Hammond is considered one of the very best casinos in the industry. Its "Winners Circle" club offers casino members opportunities to enjoy special promotions and earn points redeemable for cash, meals, and merchandise.

Horseshoe Casino Hammond is the place to go for get-togethers as well as gaming. Professional and social organizations find Horseshoe the perfect place for parties, banquets, and conferences. Exquisitely designed and decorated banquet rooms and private meeting rooms make Horseshoe a convenient, comfortable, and entirely classy venue for any special event.

Touted restaurants provide gaming patrons with expertly prepared cuisine from casual to gourmet. Jack Binion's Steakhouse, the Lake Michigan Deli Company, and the sumptuous Village Square Buffet offer award-winning fare together with top-notch service.

Community Impact

Owned and operated by Jack Binion's Horseshoe Gaming Holding Corp., Horseshoe Casino Hammond is committed to high quality casino entertainment. But it is also focused on the community in which it does business. Regional leaders have applauded the economic impact of Horseshoe Casino Hammond, which has created more than 2,300 jobs, contributed millions in taxes, and supported more than 300 local and regional charitable organizations with donations of money, gifts, time, and talent. Horseshoe executives are currently involved

in more than 50 community groups—from the Lake Area United Way to Tradewinds to Haven House—organizations that strengthen neighborhoods and provide valuable services. It is clear Horseshoe employees at all levels are willing to give even if it hurts— well, just for a second—considering that four blood drives at the casino produced more than 400 pints of blood for area hospitals.

Horseshoe Casino Hammond's commitment to community isn't a bet, it's a sure thing. The casino works to strengthen other businesses in Hammond and the region by utilizing local companies when purchasing goods and services. In hiring and purchasing, the casino is committed to working with minorities and MBE/WBE firms.

It has committed $5 million to residential development in Hammond, and displayed its commitment to education in 1999 with a $100,000 pledge to the capital campaign of Calumet College of St. Joseph in Whiting, Indiana. Its support of the ongoing work of local charitable organizations is supported by a $1.425 million investment, in the Hammond Community Corporation, the interest from which is disbursed to area not-for-profit groups on an annual basis.

When it comes to casino entertainment, Horseshoe Casino Hammond continues to be the destination of choice for residents and visitors. As a business in the region, it also has succeeded in becoming a good neighbor.

Horseshoe Casino's 33-home, $5 million Higgins Park development is bringing new housing to the Hessville neighborhood of Hammond (top left). It is just one of the many projects Horseshoe Casino has pursued to help local communities.

For elegant fare expertly served, the casino is the place to be. Award-winning eateries (bottom left) include Jack Binion's Steakhouse, the Village Square Buffet, and the Lake Michigan Deli Company.

Owner Jack Binion (bottom right) welcomes guests at the top-draw Jack Binion's Steakhouse.

Horseshoe Casino Hammond

777 Casino Center Drive
Hammond, Indiana 46320
(219) 473-7000
(1-866-711-SHOE)
www.horseshoe.com

FAMILY CARE CENTERS
OF INDIANA, LLC

put families and their needs first, and offer the services required for them to enjoy longer, healthier lives.

Two Decades of Growth

In the 1980s, Stemer saw that medical specialty services were in demand in the region. While urban medical facilities mushroomed to great size and medical specialization reigned, often families could not find local physicians to tend to their concerns. Stemer, an infectious disease physician, decided to incorporate Medical Specialists in 1983. Dr Stemer's first associate was Dr. Elliot Stokar, a pulmonologist.

"Our specialties complemented each other," says Stokar. "However, our driving concern was delivery of high quality care to the people of northwest Indiana."

By 1995, the doctors incorporated Family Care Centers, and welcomed several doctors as partners to serve a growing market for not only specialty services, but also primary care focused on families and their needs.

To serve the medical needs of northwest Indiana patients, Dr. Alexander Stemer (top left) and Dr. Elliot Stokar (top right) joined together to deliver high quality medical care.

Dr. Samuel Leather examines a patient at Family Care Center's St. John office (bottom).

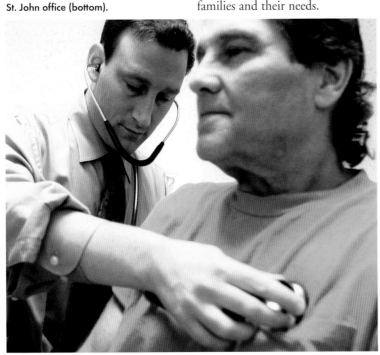

Regional residents responded with enthusiasm. Continuing to monitor the needs of its patients, and striving to provide the finest care, the firm in 1998 opened Women's Health Specialists, a unique care center staffed by female doctors and support staff that caters to the specific health care concerns of women. From adolescence through later adulthood, patients come to Women's Health Specialists for obstetrical and gynecological services, general care, menopause care, and other services tailored to their needs. Women's Health Specialists is located at the Women's Health Center in Dyer, where female patients also find Womankind Imaging, providing services in mammography, radiology, and related diagnostics; family and pediatric care; and dermatological services, all in a supportive environment where doctors, specialists, and support personnel understand the critical healthcare requirements of women.

In 1999, the corporation merged with ProMedCo, a medical management company with expertise in coordination of healthcare services in non-urban communities. In 2000, the merged companies introduced the Ambulatory Infusion Center, the first of its kind in northwest Indiana.

Serving the Community

Today, Family Care Centers enjoys a reputation for medical expertise delivered in customer-friendly fashion. With offices in several northwest Indiana communities, Family Care Centers continues to meet the public's need for top-notch healthcare close to home. This network of community-based primary care offices and specialty medical centers offers the services of certified, board-licensed physicians supported by diagnostic and therapeutic facilities.

The physicians and staff of Family Care Centers believe delivery of superior healthcare services requires personalized doctor-patient relationships and an emphasis on preventative medicine. In other words, Family Care doctors get to know patients and their families, taking time to understand how they can best safeguard the health of each family. Working with local hospitals, out-patient facilities, extended care facilities, and managed care providers, Family Care Centers strives to find the most effective and cost-efficient means

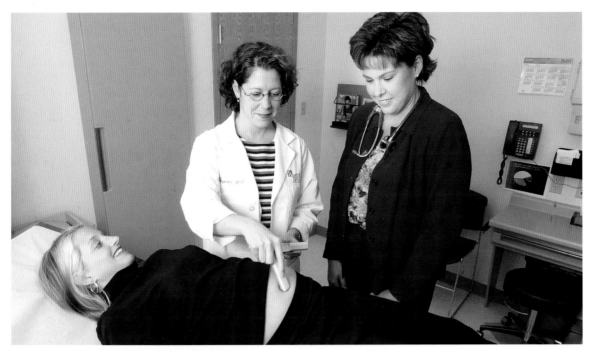

Dr. Dana Carpenter (left) and Dr. Merit Lemke perform an ultrasound examination at the Women's Health Center in Dyer (top).

At the Center (left), female patients can access a host of services provided by women doctors, nurses, technicians, and support staff. Services are designed to help women at every stage of life in a comfortable, convenient setting.

The tree, a signature image in Family Care literature, symbolizes the many branches of medical care provided by the company. Family Care Centers uses this image in regional media to reach out to the community (bottom).

to achieve healthcare goals. Family Care's state-of-the-art ambulatory Infusion and Surgery Center keeps patients well in their own homes whenever possible.

According to Stemer, the organization he envisioned has filled a gap in medical care for residents of the region.

"The patient population of northwest Indiana benefits from an integrated care network capable of providing the highest quality primary care, specialty services, and in-hospital services," Stemer explains. "Expert medical care, combined with the convenience of our many community-based centers and offices, brings healthcare services to those who need it."

Expertise Counts

Family Care Centers doctors are of the highest caliber, are board certified or eligible, and often have specialized training in specific areas of medical care and intervention. The centers' primary care physicians, physician specialists, hospitalists, and advanced practice nurses work together to provide the full spectrum of healthcare, education, and support services that help each individual patient.

In addition to six primary care offices and the Women's Health Center, Family Care Centers operates Medical Specialists, PC providing medical care for Infectious Disease, Rheumatology, Ear, Nose & Throat, and Pulmonary medicine; Indiana Endocrinology Specialists, providing medical care for hormonal imbalances and treatment of disorders of the endocrine system; a Same Day Surgery Center providing outpatient surgical services; the Ambulatory Infusion Center, for out-patient intravenous therapies;

the Munster Radiology Center; and the Munster Sleep Diagnostic Center, where patients obtain diagnostic and treatment services for sleep disorders of all kinds.

Looking to the Future

Dr. Stemer has seen his vision—top quality healthcare in northwest Indiana—take firm root. Today, the corporation is growing and changing to meet the needs of families in the region. But the goal remains the same. At Family Care Centers, every physician, specialist, and service is poised for one purpose: to care for the individual patient with the best medical technology available in the warmest, most helpful manner possible.

FAMILY CARE CENTERS
OF INDIANA, LLC
Main Office
919 Main Street
Dyer, Indiana 46311
(219) 934-2450
www.fcci-llc.com

FIVE STAR
HYDRAULICS, INC.

Four star service isn't good enough for a Portage firm whose claim to fame is helping major industrial clients avoid production down-time. When Timothy Bowgren established Five Star Hydraulics, Inc. in 1977, he had five star service in mind. His company would not only perform exceptional work, but also warranty it for a full year, a guarantee virtually unheard of in the industry. It would also explore new technologies, ever vigilant for materials and methodologies capable of enhancing quality and streamlining production.

Five Star Hydraulics' Portage plant (top) provides expert cylinder repair service to industrial clients (bottom).

Five Star Hydraulics' president Timothy Bowgren (left) and general manager Butch Cunningham discuss an AGC cylinder repair.

Expert Cylinder Repair

Five Star Hydraulics repairs air and hydraulic cylinders from its 20,000 square foot under roof facility in Portage, Indiana. Close to the area's steel mills and nestled in the shadow of the new Portage marina, the company is a major player in the industrial life of the region. Clients for the company's services include such firms as U.S. Steel Corp., Bethlehem Steel, National Steel Corp., Beta Steel, International Harvester, Applied Composites, and Nucor.

Air and hydraulic cylinders are used in every phase of steel production. The basic components of the equipment that processes steel—from initial production through finishing—cylinders also are subject to wear and breakdowns. Five Star Hydraulics has earned a reputation as a speedy source of top-quality repair for cylinders ranging in size from 1-inch bore by 2-inch stroke (the industry term for length) to hefty 50-inch diameter by 292-inch stroke. The repair of AGC cylinders is a company specialty.

Provision of expert, emergency repair service has earned Five Star a reputation of excellence. With steel production down-time costing manufacturers from $5,500 to $10,000 per minute, emergency cylinder repair is essential to profitability.

"We have our own tolerances and quality standards," Bowgren explains. "Five Star is the only company I know of with a one-year warranty on repairs from the date of installation. We can do that because—from our general manager "Butch" Cunningham to all of our employees—quality is number one." "Right the first time" is the company motto.

Innovative Materials

Five Star Hydraulics is an industry leader in exploring new materials for the design and repair of cylinders used in manufacturing. Instead of bronze overlayed pistons, the company now employs Durabar, a cast material that increases cylinder life by as much as 300 percent. Where atmospheric conditions in a production setting may attack chrome-plated cylinder rods, Five Star is using a product called Nitrobar, which lasts as much as four times longer than chrome. The company uses James Walker packing, considered the best material available to seal fluids and ensure smooth and steady operation of cylinders.

Although Five Star Hydraulics makes new cylinders and special cylinders, the company recently entered into an agreement with Hanna Cylinders to represent them in the steel industry, according to Bowgren. "There are many cylinders cheaper to construct new than repair due to their size," he says, "and Hanna produces hundreds of one size at a time, reducing fabricating costs. The timing was right, and Hanna was our choice. With its Chicago manufacturing location, Hanna gives us an edge on the competition, too."

Revolutionary Cylinders

Today, Five Star is exploring new territory representing NSD Corporation's Absocoder, an absolute positioning encoder that allows a unprecedented degree of accuracy and quality in the

Expert repair services are offered by Five Star (top) for cylinders from 1-inch bore by 2-inch stroke to cylinders as large as 50-inch diameter by 292-inch stroke.

Large bore, trunion-mounted cyclinders are a company specialty (bottom left).

Company staffers are excited about the Absocoder (bottom right), a unique linear motion sensing device for which Five Star is the exclusive North American distributor.

manufacture of steel and other products. Its revolutionary "Cylnuc" cylinder features unique linear motion sensors that track every position and are not affected by noise or vibration. Internal coil sensors connected to a computer terminal track position to within one one-thousandth of a millimeter, a stunning degree of precision in the industry. For Five Star customers, the Absocoder allows accurate and consistent product positioning which heightens quality, substantially reduces production down-time, and saves money formerly lost to wasted time and scrapped material.

"Our customers are embracing this new technology," says Cunningham. "The industry is moving away from estimating when failures will occur to an on-going monitoring system that eliminates waste and boosts production." Bowgren agrees. "This is the most reliable sensor on the market, capable of saving time and money for our customers," he stresses. "We're very excited about its prospects in this region and throughout North America."

Five Star will aggressively market the new technology. As the exclusive North American distributor for NSD, Five Star intends to be a partner with its clients in changing the technology of production in the 21st century. Five Star has become the North American repair center for Nambu Company, Ltd. Nambu manufactures rotary expand cylinders for hot strip mandrels.

Five Star Drive and Commitment

Bowgren and his crew understand that they're in the customer service business. Efficient and top-notch emergency cylinder repair service will remain a key component of the 23-year old business. But with NSD and Hanna among its arsenal of weapons, Five Star Hydraulics, Inc. aims to win the war against untimely production failures. It's the five-star kind of commitment that has driven the company since the day it opened its doors.

FIVE STAR HYDRAULICS, INC.

1210 North Crisman Road
Portage, Indiana 46368
(219) 762-1619

WHEN HE STARTED HIS ADVERTISING AND DESIGN BUSINESS IN 1997, GREEN LIGHT CREATIVE PRESIDENT TIM SIMIC HAD A SINGLE DRIVING VISION: "I WANTED TO ATTRACT THE AREA'S BEST CREATIVE TALENT—PEOPLE WITH HIGH-END AGENCY EXPERIENCE—SO THAT WE COULD PRODUCE EXCITING, HARD-WORKING, AND ENERGETIC DESIGN SOLUTIONS FOR OUR CLIENTS."

GREEN LIGHT
CREATIVE

445 169th Street
Hammond, Indiana 46324
(219) 937-2237
green@netnitco.net (email)
www.greenlightcreative.com

Today, Green Light's staff consists of seasoned veterans from the northwest Indiana and Chicagoland market with over 70 years combined experience in concept development, copywriting, design and production services on large, local and national accounts, including State Farm, Sears, Chicago Tribune, Motorola, American Express Financial, Hyatt Hotels, Caterpillar, and others. The agency's specialties include print ads, brochures, direct mail, annual reports, corporate identity, outdoor boards, and Web site design.

"People are bombarded with thousands of advertising messages every day," Simic says. "If you put something out there that's just average you have little chance of cutting through the clutter. Our clients understand that, and they come to us for high quality, creative work—whether they're looking for something conservative or way out there—they want to be noticed; they want to be remembered; they want to make a difference."

A creative company requires a creative environment in which to do its best work, and the minute you walk through the doors at Green Light it's obvious that's been achieved. An eclectic array of green objects covers every available surface in the office: antiques, exotic glass ware, lamps, piggy banks, and even a fish tank with green lights and rocks. Staff, clients, vendors, and visitors have all contributed to the growing collection.

"We wanted to create a different look for our workplace," Simic says. "We want it to be fun as well as stimulating." Work spaces for each of the designers feature low, glass block walls, which provide privacy as well as plenty of opportunity for interaction. Simic explains: "I wanted to create an open atmosphere where it would be easy to talk to each other about our projects and to share ideas. By drawing on the collective experience and talent of all the people we have here, everything we make is the best it can be. A great work environment helps us give our clients great work."

Simic feels that his company's experience and commitment pay off for clients. "Whether it's a corporate marketing campaign or a single postcard, our mission is to take a client's image or message and make it come alive in a unique and creative way. We work hard to hit their target, make their deadline, and stay within their budget. It's all part of a non-stop effort to deliver the kind of service and solutions we know our clients deserve."

I N A WORLD SHAPED BY PROGRESS THAT APPEARS NEVER-ENDING AND TECHNOLOGY THAT
ATTEMPTS TO REMEDY ALL ILLS, DEATH REMAINS THE MOST DIFFICULT FRONTIER. IT IS WITHIN
HUMAN NATURE TO ADVOCATE FOR LIFE, TO REACH FOR ANY HOPE THAT THE ENDING OF A LIFE CAN
BE STAVED OFF FOR ANOTHER YEAR, ANOTHER MONTH, ANOTHER HOUR. HOSPICE OF THE CALUMET

HOSPICE OF THE CALUMET AREA, INC.

Area, Inc. is an organization of people familiar with the rugged terrain of this frontier. Dedicated to a concept of care that brings dignity and comfort to life's last days, the nurses, social workers, pastoral staff, and volunteers of Hospice ensure patients facing life-limiting illnesses and their families have the help and support they need.

A Concept of Care

Hospice of the Calumet Area is not just a place, but also a concept of care. As many as 75 percent of Americans currently meet death in hospitals where the rhythms and routines of an institutional setting mitigate against peaceful and pain-free time with loved ones. The highly trained staff of Hospice of the Calumet Area helps patients in their own homes where a higher level of comfort is achieved. Working with the patient's physician and family, Hospice professionals emphasize effective control of pain and discomfort through a comprehensive plan of personalized care. Regular visits by professional nurses and home health aides ensure patients and their families receive the best possible care and comfort.

While the primary focus is on the physical comfort of the patient, social workers and spiritual counselors address end of life issues and the anticipatory grief of patient and family. Trained volunteers support caregivers by providing relief, companionship, and other supports to the patient and family. This support continues through the bereavement program.

Through its team-oriented approach and wide network of professionals, Hospice seeks to

provide services that help each individual patient. Since its inception, the organization has assisted more than 5,000 patients.

Two Decades of Concern

Hospice of the Calumet Area, a not-for-profit organization, was established by concerned community leaders in 1981. Designed as an alternative program of comfort and care for patients with life-limiting illnesses, it is fully Medicare-certified and a member of the National Hospice and Palliative Care Organization, the Indiana Hospice and Palliative Care Organization, and the Illinois State Hospice Organization. Referrals of patients are made by physicians, family members, health care professionals, and clergy. Hospice of the Calumet Area's programs are open to residents of Lake and Porter counties, and bordering communities in Illinois.

In 1997, the William J. Riley Memorial Residence opened its doors to care for those who desire services but are unable to remain at home safely. The six-suite home provides assistance and care for persons with life-limiting illnesses who want to live out their

remaining time in a home-like environment. Services are provided regardless of ability to pay and the cost of care is significantly less than a hospital stay.

Hospice of the Calumet Area is governed by a volunteer board of directors. Contributions from corporations, churches, and individuals in the Calumet region allow HCA to provide care to all in need regardless of insurance or ability to pay.

Hospice of the Calumet Area helps those individuals with a life-limiting illness and their loved ones to live with dignity in a place where the sights and sounds of life surround them, a place like no other—home.

Hospice of the Calumet Area provides compassionate care in patients' homes and at the William J. Riley Memorial Residence (top), a six-suite home built in 1997. Since its inception, HCA has assisted more than 5,000 patients.

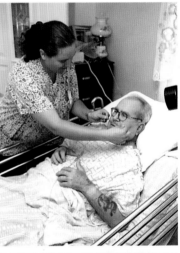

At any given moment in any given day, someone in the world is likely using a product made possible by Hammond Group, Inc. The company has many customers, for its products improve or power a host of items essential to modern life. From fine china and crystal on the table to piezoelectric sensors on the ocean floor and from eyeglasses to batteries, Hammond Group's focus on purity, consistency, and quality contributes to the success of hundreds of industries and to the lives of citizens everywhere.

Quality Culture

Hammond Group, Inc., founded in northwest Indiana in 1930, is today the corporate company overseeing four divisions. While Hammond Group functions as the parent company with centralized purchasing, accounting, and other services that streamline operations, divisions including Hammond Lead Products, Halstab, Hammond Expanders, and Halox manufacture lead chemicals, stabilizers, and additives for a multitude of clients that produce everything from bathtubs to forklifts.

In northwest Indiana, Hammond Group collectively employs 250 at four facilities in the region. A privately held company, it is led by president and CEO Peter Wilke. Its reputation for superior products and workmanship has grown in a corporate culture that actively promotes a sense of responsibility

on the part of all employees. The company's commitment to quality is evidenced by ISO 9001 and 9002 certifications that attest to its adherence to internationally recognized quality standards. Not just meeting but exceeding customer expectations is the goal driving Hammond Group.

In addition to its manufacturing prowess, the companies serve customers through a reliable worldwide distribution network that ensures timely delivery of materials whenever and wherever they are needed.

Hammond Lead Products

One of the earliest of the company's divisions, Hammond Lead Products is a producer and marketer of specialty lead chemicals for the glass, ceramic, electronics, and battery industries. Three facilities, in Hammond, Pottstown, Pennsylvania, and in Malaysia, manufacture lead oxides, lead silicates, and lead borates in a variety of particle sizes, treatments, and packages to meet increasingly specialized demands for performance and safety.

Hammond Lead Products is the company to credit for setting purity standards. It developed the means to produce ultra-high purity—up to 99.99 percent—to satisfy the needs of the optical industry and emerging fiber optic markets. Hammond's in-house technical and engineering groups developed 400Y, a dedusted granular litharge, to meet the environmental and batching needs of the television glass industry. Its low-solubility lead frits, Ceraflux® and Bisilicate B-15, responded to the occupational safety requirements of the ceramic industry. The company's participation with the World Health Organization and the International Standards Organization has helped establish international standards for the safe use of lead for ceramic foodware.

Today, Hammond Lead concentrates more specialized attention on lead chemicals and their end users than any other supplier. For industries throughout the U.S. and the growing global export market, that commitment is essential in the development of new and better products for citizens worldwide.

Quality consciousness and constant monitoring (top) ensure Hammond Group products meet high standards. The company has earned both ISO 9001 and 9002 certifications.

Halox (center) produces lead-free, stain-inhibiting pigments for a variety of industries, while Halstab (bottom) manufactures lead stabilizers used in a host of products from credit cards to automotive parts.

Halstab

Lead and nonlead stabilizers for PVC (polyvinyl chloride) products are as critical as the products themselves. Without stabilizers, cable insulation would fail, vinyl building and automotive components would deteriorate, and products from upholstery to credit cards wouldn't last nearly as long or function so well.

The Halstab division was created in 1971 to ensure that PVC formulators can get the variety and quality of stabilizers needed.

Halstab produces some 25 different types and grades of PVC stabilizers to perform well in a multitude of applications: under high process temperature, to minimize moisture pick-up, to reduce agglomeration, and to disperse more uniformly in the finished plastic product.

Automated processes and sophisticated equipment are hallmarks of the Halstab plant, re-engineered in 1983 to set industry standards for quality, productivity, and safety. Halstab's processes and environmental controls not only surpass existing EPA and OSHA standards, but also should comply with stricter standards anticipated for the future.

Halox

Priding itself on its ability to respond to the needs of the marketplace, Hammond Group established Halox in 1972. Restrictions on red lead pigments created a need for new, lead-free corrosion and tannin stain inhibiting pigments for coatings industries. Red lead pigments had been effectively protecting bridges and other structures against corrosion for decades in the U.S. and abroad. But new Halox pigments proved just as effective and safer.

Halox lead-free pigments add corrosion protection to paints for structural steel, industrial equipment, railcars, farm equipment, appliances, and a wide variety of paints and coatings used by contractors and consumers.

To maintain a clean and bright finish over wood substrates that bleed tannins into the paint film, Halox pigments effectively inhibit discoloration and unsightly stains.

Today Halox is a leading producer of tannin stain inhibiting pigments. As coatings technology develops over time, Halox continues to explore new chemistries and methodologies in partnership with the industries it serves.

Hammond Expanders

As a producer and marketer of additives for the battery industry, Hammond Expanders serves customers in the industrial, automotive, and communications markets. To meet the rising demand for higher battery reliability, this division developed several

specialized expander products: for the deep cycle service and varying temperature ranges of industrial batteries, to enhance cold cranking power and battery life in automotive applications, and even a special non-organic formulation for calcium batteries employed in communications, solar power, and emergency lighting systems. The expander division also produces expanders according to specification for proprietary use by a number of national battery companies. Hammond Expanders operates two facilities, one in Hammond and another in Newcastle in the United Kingdom.

Hammond Expanders' pledge of consistency is backed up by its use of high-purity materials, precise blending techniques, and thorough quality control. That leads to higher reliability in batteries—the end goal of the enterprise.

The breadth and depth of Hammond Group's work improves the lives of consumers. Whether starting up the car, talking on the phone, getting out the dishes for dinner, putting on spectacles to read the evening newspaper, or enjoying a bubble bath, people come into contact with materials likely manufactured by the firm's divisions every day.

Hammond Group's divisions ensure many commonly used consumer products—from dishes and crystal (top) to car batteries—perform better.

Hammond Expanders (center) operates plants in Hammond, Indiana and also in Newcastle in the United Kingdom.

Automated processes and sophisticated equipment (bottom) are hallmarks of Hammond Group, Inc., established in northwest Indiana in the 1930's.

HAMMOND GROUP, INC.

1414 Field Street, Building B
Hammond, Indiana 46320
(219) 931-9360
www.hmndgroup.com

HARDINGS INC.

E MIL HARDING WAS A HARDWORKING FARMER WHEN A BOUT OF RHEUMATIC FEVER WEAKENED HIS HEART AND MADE MANUAL LABOR DIFFICULT. BUT HE WAS ALSO A BRIGHT YOUNG MAN WHO SAW AN OPPORTUNITY TO HELP OTHER FARMERS BY STOCKING AND SELLING THE PLOWS, DISKS, HARNESSES, AND OTHER EQUIPMENT THEY NEEDED TO WORK THEIR FIELDS. IN 1923, HARDING SET

up shop in his hometown of Lowell and began to build his future.

The business that Emil Harding built is still going strong. Today, Hardings Inc. operates from a large facility not more than two blocks from the company's original location. Hardings created a lot of futures for family members and townspeople, too. Now owned and operated by Emil's grandchildren Clarence Harding, Jr. and Cathy Harding Marshall, the business employs about 30 people and over eight decades has earned a reputation as one of the town's best corporate citizens.

New Era, New Equipment

Hardings grew and prospered serving farmers from throughout northwest Indiana and communities in nearby Illinois. Emil Harding stocked the latest Caterpillar and John Deere lines throughout the 1930s and 40s. It was an era of unprecedented technological advances in farming when new machines were created to do work once handled by hand and horse. Hardings was officially incorporated in the 1940s and Emil's son Clarence, after serving as soldier in the WWII European campaign, joined the family

Emil Harding (immediately behind Clarence Harding Sr. (the man in light-colored suit) visited the Caterpillar farm equipment factory in Peoria, Illinois in the mid-1930s (top).

Hardings earned an early reputation for top-notch equipment and expert repair services, as well as timely delivery (right) of machinery to the job site.

Cathy Harding Marshall and Clarence Harding, Jr. (below) now run the family-owned and operated heavy construction equipment business.

business. The father and son team focused on agricultural machinery and equipment, but its specialty was service. Customers who came through the doors at Hardings appreciated the expert care Emil and Clarence doled out, whether the purchase was large or small.

The marketplace has changed since those early days. Around Lowell and throughout the nation, there are more neighborhoods and fewer family farms. Today, Hardings still specializes in top-notch equipment, but the emphasis is on machinery that helps contractors, developers, and homeowners accomplish residential and commercial projects. The building boom of the past two decades in northwest Indiana brought a whole new roster of customers to the Hardings business on Commercial Avenue. An elder statesman of the regional business community, Hardings was able to grow and change with the times.

Sales Backed by Service

Hardings serves area contractors and builders with a complete line of construction equipment available for sale or rent. The inventory includes everything from vibratory compactors

and construction lights to large dozers and excavators. The Wacker and Yanmar lines of equipment carried by Hardings offers state-of-the-art job site machinery, and used heavy construction equipment is available in a wide variety of makes and models.

Hardings' claim to fame isn't just that it gets construction crews going—but that it keeps them going. The company is widely known for its expertise in repair and its extensive inventory of parts. In fact, while sales and rentals of new and rebuilt equipment constitute 30 percent of Hardings' daily work, service is the grease that keeps Hardings—and its clients—moving forward.

At Hardings, contractors are able to have engines rebuilt, hydraulic cylinders resealed and rebuilt, steering clutches and brakes repaired, transmissions serviced, and much more. Services run the gamut from work on engines, undercarriages, and cooling systems to transmissions and drive systems, hydraulic systems, and bucket and blade repair for all makes of construction equipment.

"Service is really our bread and butter," says Clarence Harding. "We have a corps of highly trained mechanics and we always strive for top quality workmanship. Taking care of customers is the priority at Hardings."

Cathy Harding Marshall agrees. "We don't farm out any of the repair work, which is why many customers come to us. Even if an area isn't high profit for us—like our engine machine shop—we provide the service because our customers want it done right, and right away."

From a Building to a Block

Hardings' original location was a small building in downtown Lowell. Today, the Hardings business encompasses an office

and showroom structure built in the 1930s, several additions for warehouse space, a paint shop, machine shop, welding shop, track shop, and other facilities. In all, the Hardings built seven additions since moving to its current location. The business has literally grown from a single building to a city block.

Customers hail from throughout Lake County, Indiana, southern Cook County in Illinois, the Kankakee area, and beyond. Word of mouth advertising has helped the company grow into a regional resource for contractors and builders within a 100-mile radius of the Hardings location.

As for the future, both Clarence and Cathy believe the family business will prosper as long as it stays focused on the customers.

"We listen to our customers, we're in the business of serving their needs," Clarence says. "Hardings is bound to keep growing and changing with the times as it has for the last nearly 80 years."

Always a Good Neighbor

Around Lowell, the Harding family is known and respected not only for its business acumen, but also for its commitment to the community. From the beginning, Hardings Inc. has been a good neighbor, supporting community improvement projects, youth groups, town events, and charities of all sorts. The tradition began with founder Emil Harding and continues to this day.

The list of recipients is long indeed: youth sports teams, Pop Warner football, 4-H clubs and scout troops; charities from the Lake Area United Way to the March of Dimes; and a host of northwest Indiana initiatives such as improvements at Hoosier Boys' Town and renovation of the Lake County Courthouse in Crown Point.

A recent project that got a boost from Hardings is the Lowell Public Library, for which the company provided financial support large enough for it to receive a matching state grant. The monies are being used to establish an endowment fund that will allow ongoing enhancements and capital improvements to the much-visited library. Emil Harding, Clarence Harding, and Clarence Harding, Jr. and Cathy Harding Marshall have all been committed to the same philosophy: giving to the community is the right thing to do.

Customers come from a 100-mile radius for the expert repair service and wide inventory of parts provided by Hardings (top).

Hardings grew from a single building in 1923 to a city block today that allows room for the company's dozers, excavators, and other equipment (bottom).

HARDINGS INC.

**109 West Commercial Avenue
Lowell, Indiana 46356
(219) 696-8911**

THE YEAR 2000 MARKS THE FORTIETH ANNIVERSARY FOR HESSVILLE CABLE & SLING. THIS COMPANY, A FAMILY BUSINESS STARTED BY BOYD RANDALL AND NOW OWNED AND OPERATED BY HIS SONS GEORGE AND KEN, HAS BEEN A PIVOTAL PLAYER IN THE GROWTH OF NORTHWEST INDIANA. THE COMPANY MANUFACTURES CABLE AND CHAIN SLING PRODUCTS FOR HEAVY INDUSTRY AND

construction. Few major projects have been achieved without the high-strength wire rope, chains and fittings, nylon, and wire rope slings the company produces at its plant in Gary.

Trained workers produce the wire rope, chain, and nylon slings needed by contractors and heavy industry in the company's production, welding, and sewing shops (top).

Boyd Randall established his business in a small building in Hessville (below). Randall is pictured circa 1955 (bottom left). Today, Hessville Cable & Sling is located in a 60,000 square foot facility on Cline Avenue in Gary (bottom right).

Help for Heavy Construction

Wherever a building is being constructed, a boat is being hoisted into the air, deep tunnels are being dug, or cranes are removing earth at a mining site, Hessville Cable & Sling products are likely to be on the job. The company is now the number one supplier of Python wire rope—rope capable of lifting tons of material into the air easily and safely. Some of the firm's largest customers are the northwest Indiana steel mills though the company ships to industries across the U.S. Hessville Cable & Sling routinely tackles custom orders, hand-splicing wire rope to specification and finishing it with the hooks, rings, eyes, or other hardware required for a specific job. Technological innovation has produced several proprietary products including HessLink® chain slings and HessFlex® nylon slings.

Hessville Cable & Sling maintains several operational areas

within its plant. In addition to production areas dedicated to the manufacture of sling and wire rope, the facility also houses a sewing shop for custom nylon fabrication, and welding and tool repair divisions.

Quality is key. The company tests its own cable, chain, and sling before shipment. Slings produced by Hessville Cable & Sling is certified at twice its workload limit.

Today, 50 employees work at the plant, some of whom have been with the company for two decades. The firm is still a

family-owned business where cooperation and teamwork make for felicitous conditions. The emphasis on customer service and quality remains unquestioned. Here talents are developed in the art of hand-splicing wire rope and specialty items like braided sling.

Boom Period for Building a Business

It would make founder Boyd Randall proud. Randall had a knack for splicing. His special skill was honed in the forties and fifties when he worked on the Wattsbar Dam in Tennessee, the Kentucky Dam, and on numerous Tennessee Valley Authority projects. After Randall settled in northwest Indiana in 1954, word of his expertise traveled quickly. The region's steel and construction industries were in a boom period and quality cable was a key ingredient in every major building project. While Randall worked as an ironworker on a crew that constructed, among other structures, the Prudential Building in Chicago, he devoted his off-hours to cable splicing.

The family business was born when he brought sons Ken and George on board. Four other sons contributed to the growth of the new company. Contracts were nearly doubling year over year and the Randalls decided to give the company the time and space it needed to grow. The Randalls rented a small building in Hessville. Two years later, they used a $500 loan from the Inland Credit Bureau to purchase cable they could use to mass produce slings.

Still a Family Company

The year 1966 was a test not of the strength of the company product but of the family itself. Boyd Randall was killed on the job at a steel mill at the age of 54. The community was saddened at the story of the hard-charging ironworker taken too soon from his family, friends, and bustling business. Ken and George turned grief into a renewed commitment to the vision of a top-quality, family-oriented company strong enough to survive the setback.

"We had a choice to make that was difficult but also clear-cut," Ken explains. "Running the company without our father wasn't something we had ever imagined. But we knew he'd want us to keep going, to finish what he started."

Now located at 1601 Cline Avenue in a 60,000 square foot manufacturing facility, the firm is still the area's top choice for cable, rope, and sling products. It is now one of the largest, oldest, and most respected of cable companies in the region.

"As long as there's loading and lifting to be done, Hessville Cable & Sling will be on the job," George says. "We owe our success to our customers and our aim is always to make products they can trust."

HESSVILLE CABLE & SLING

1601 Cline Avenue
Gary, Indiana 46406
(219) 944-7200
(773) 768-8181

A SEARCH OF THE ENTIRE REGION WOULDN'T TURN UP A BANK MORE LIKE THE ONE IN FRANK CAPRA'S 1946 CLASSIC "IT'S A WONDERFUL LIFE" THAN HFS BANK IN HOBART. LIKE THE BAILEY BROTHERS BUILDING AND LOAN ASSOCIATION OF MOVIE FAME, HFS BANK HAS ALWAYS BEEN COMMITTED TO THE COMMUNITY. ESTABLISHED IN 1934—A DOZEN YEARS

before Jimmy Stewart won an Oscar for his portrayal of banker George Bailey—HFS Bank is still the "hometown team." Though not the biggest bank in the region, it strives to be the best in delivery of financial services for families and businesses in the communities it serves.

Six Decades of Service

Sixty-six years ago, a group of local businessmen organized the bank, originally chartered as a savings and loan association. It moved from its location at the corner of Main and Third to a new building on Third Street constructed in 1960.

Financial services have changed immensely since HFS opened its doors. Today, the bank's customers use new technologies like ATM cards. But at HFS they also enjoy more time-honored traditions— like savings account passbooks, which the bank still issues. A trip to the Hobart facility proves another adage about caring, concerned locally-owned banks: customers and bank staffers know each other. Like the bank the Bailey brothers ran, HFS is home to loan officers and tellers who know if a customer's son is on the high

school basketball team or has a daughter planning to be married. Customers who apply for a home equity loan to remodel their house likely obtained their mortgage at HFS and may live down the street from their loan officer. Most customers turn to HFS for the full variety of services available to them: checking, savings, IRA accounts, auto loans, and Christmas Club savings, too.

"We have a genuine concern for our customers and we want them to be happy with our bank," says James H. Greiner, president of HFS since 1981. "What we do, we do well. What we can't do, we don't pretend to do."

For HFS customers, it's the friendly, hometown, no-nonsense kind of banking that makes them feel cared for and comfortable.

Hometown Banking

HFS may be a smaller, hometown bank, but it has definitely grown with the community. In 1934, the predecessor savings and loan began business with $3,314 in seed money—an impressive amount in those post-depression years. Today, HFS records approximately $205 million in assets and serves customers across the region from its headquarters in Hobart as well as four branches. HFS offices are located

HFS Bank's home was at the corner of Main and Third (top) until a new bank was constructed in 1960.

At the helm of the financial institution throughout the 1960s was William M. Hebert (above). He encouraged the bank's tradition of support for community events and programs that continues today. In 1959, HFS celebrated its 25th anniversary with a parade (bottom) in downtown Hobart.

Leading HFS Bank into the new millennium is James H. Greiner (top right), president since 1981. While advancing technology, Greiner maintains the bank's focus on personalized customer service (top left).

HFS Bank is an institution in the community—and not just for banking. Many city residents have worked at the bank throughout its 66-year history. This photograph taken in the 1960s (bottom) captured HFS Bank staffers Joyce Griesel (immediately left of Santa), who still works at HFS and Linda Buzinec (second to last row, second from right), who began her second term as mayor of Hobart in 2000.

in Crown Point and Griffith, and also in Portage where the bank maintains two branches. Plans are currently in the works for expansion of the Crown Point branch and construction of a drive-up facility. Employees now number about 80 full- and part-time staff.

Family lending and small business banking constitute the bulk of the financial institution's daily work. From mortgage and consumer loans to investments and savings, HFS Bank helps customers to finance the most important moments in their lives: a college education, a new home, a small business, retirement.

"Ninety nine percent of our customers are able to have all their needs taken care of at HFS," notes Shirley Campbell, a vice president

of the bank. "Our strengths in family lending allow us to serve as an important financial center in the northwest Indiana community."

Trusted Neighbor and Friend

HFS Bank is an institution in the community, in the broadest sense of the word. It's the place where many of the city's residents worked their first jobs. Where young people opened their first passbook savings accounts. And also where bank employees strive every day to give something back to the community.

There are few community-oriented projects that haven't gotten a boost from HFS, which donates both money and volunteer

hours to more than 70 area programs and charitable initiatives. From the Boys & Girls Clubs in the region to Meals on Wheels, HFS is a partner in efforts to lend a helping hand to others and to build strong neighborhoods. Many of the bank's board members, officers, and employees serve in the organizations dedicated to doing good in the community.

A Wonderful Life

James Greiner anticipated more fallout from the mega-mergers and acquisitions that defined banking in the 1990s. As it turns out, HFS has found that being the smaller, friendlier, more customer service-focused alternative has helped differentiate the bank in the marketplace.

"We spend time with people, we emphasize service, we actually answer the phone," Greiner says, smiling. "I think we're positioned just right in the marketplace, doing the things that are valued by customers."

No room for any "Pottersville" as far as HFS is concerned. Greiner has been known to watch "It's A Wonderful Life" from time to time. He also watches as longtime customers of the bank bring in their passbooks on Friday to deposit earnings from their paychecks into their savings accounts. The buzz in banking may be high-tech, but HFS hasn't lost its hometown ambience. And that's worth wings any day.

HFS BANK

555 East Third Street
Hobart, Indiana 46342
(219) 942-1175
HFSbank.com

Hoosier Boys' Town, Inc.

is now Campagna Academy

The stained glass artwork in the new Campagna Center (top) shows Father Campagna passing on his love and compassion to a boy who then has "the world at his fingertips."

The land and facilities of Hoosier Boys' Town were purchased in 1946. It opened in 1947 under the direction of founder Father Campagna (center) and was filled to capacity within one week.

Counseling and group discussions are critical components of life at Hoosier Boys' Town. Psychologists, counselors, and teachers help youngsters take responsibility for positive changes in their lives (bottom).

A Dream Fulfilled

Father Campagna, a Catholic priest with a parish in East Chicago, was convinced that a place offering positive adult role models and a second chance to succeed at home, in school, and in church could make the ultimate difference in the lives of countless boys. The young men Father Campagna had in mind were society's "lost children"—boys abandoned by home or community, boys having trouble in school, boys who had lost sight of life's essential goodness and who had turned to violence or crime.

Father Campagna and his team located a well-built house, a small cottage, a barn, and a two-room cabin, all situated on a 47-acre site in Schererville. Purchased in 1946, the land and buildings were the foundation of Hoosier Boys' Town. The facility officially opened within one year. Within one week it was filled to capacity.

Father Campagna is now gone, but his vision lives on. Hoosier Boys' Town, located in northwest Indiana's Schererville community, has been serving young men for more than five decades. Established as a residential facility providing full-time services to

about 20 boys, the organization has grown immensely. Today, Hoosier Boys' Town offers residential programs, day treatment services, and transitional living programs to help troubled boys become exceptional men. Community-based programs dealing with a variety of situations that affect families are offered to children and parents.

Serving the Region

Hoosier Boys' Town is a not-for-profit residential and day treatment facility licensed by the Indiana Division of Family & Children Services and accredited by the Council on Accreditation of Services for Families and Children, Inc. It provides a continuum of services to youth ages 6 to 21 and their families. Initially, the facility

served about 20 young people at a time. Today, it has grown to accommodate as many as 160 in a variety of programs. Youth in the region deemed candidates for Hoosier Boys' Town programs are referred to the facility by the Department of Family & Children Services, Juvenile Probation, special education departments, and other youth-serving agencies.

While Father Campagna referred to his beloved Hoosier Boys' Town as a refuge for "boys with emotional difficulties," the children who are helped at Hoosier Boys' Town today represent a wider cross-section of difficulties and behaviors. Some of the youth may be the victims of abuse, neglect, or abandonment. On the other hand, many come from loving families where depression, learning disabilities, or clinically diagnosed conditions have made outside assistance advisable. Help at Hoosier Boys' Town is also available for young men who display aggressive behavior, are habitual truants, or whose lives are currently diminished by drug abuse, family conflict, or delinquency problems.

Anita Dygert-Gearheart serves as the CEO, working with a staff of 100 residential counselors,

teachers, master level clinicians, case managers, and support personnel dedicated to the futures of those who turn to Hoosier Boys' Town. The organization is governed by a volunteer board of directors and is funded by grants, Lake County, and the State of Indiana.

The Boys' Town Vision

Hoosier Boys' Town continues to strengthen and reunite families, giving young men the opportunity to make positive life changes that lead to respect, social responsibility, and personal success.

Statistics show that intensive, focused programs like those offered at Hoosier Boys' Town can have a huge impact on young men at a critical stage in their lives. Hoosier Boys' Town is proud of its record of achievement. For instance, of the 24 youth served by the organization's GED (General Education Diploma) program in 1998, 66 percent of those who took the exam passed the test. In that same year, there was a 95 percent attendance rate for youth in both on-campus and off-site educational programs. In the fall semester, 70 percent of students averaged a "C" or better record in their courses of study. These positive outcomes—from a group of 153 boys formerly delinquent from school or in school but falling below minimal achievement standards—represent a substantial contribution to the futures of the boys, their families, and the community at large.

Focus on Outcomes

Hoosier Boys' Town is committed to positive results. In order to help its participants reach goals, the agency has developed both residential and day treatment programs. Boys admitted to the residential program receive intense supervision in a 24-hour setting. Academic programs and related services—from diagnostic psychological testing and treatment to

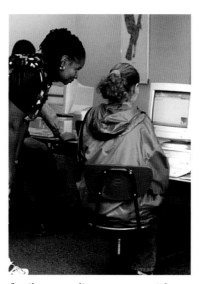

family counseling—are essential for placing participants on a productive path.

Day treatment offers help to young people—both boys and girls—with behavior or emotional problems interfering with life at home or progress in school. These youth live at home, but attend Hoosier Boys' Town year-round for their educational and therapeutic needs. All youth participate in a holistic menu of services provided to restore balance: educational, therapeutic, vocational, and psycho-educational programs—and even assistance with transitions from home to independent living. An emphasis is placed on following a comprehensive individualized plan for each and every young person.

Facilities at Hoosier Boys' Town are designed to support the achievement of academic and interpersonal goals. From the classrooms and computer labs to the athletic fields, gym, and swimming pool to the residential quarters, the organization has worked with the northwest Indiana community to continually upgrade the infrastructure supporting these youth.

The regional community also contributes by participating in special programs of Hoosier Boys' Town. One such program—Personal Adult Linkage (known as "PAL")—brings adult volunteer mentors together with the youngsters who need them. Many of these relationships continue throughout the child's life.

Hands-on Commitment

A world in which no child is at risk would be ideal. In the meantime, Hoosier Boys' Town fulfills its mission of responding to reality by restoring hopes and building dreams. The stated philosophy of the organization contains seemingly simple ideas: that respect is the underlying value in life, that every interaction has the potential to be therapeutic, and that every moment is a learning opportunity. To live by that philosophy, however, requires hands-on commitment. Hoosier Boys' Town helps youth in classrooms, in the gym, in the cafeteria, in counseling sessions, and in mentor relationships. It also helps by sending the message that there are many adults willing to lend a hand in the healing of a young person. For the youngsters who come through the doors of Hoosier Boys' Town, that may be the most life-changing lesson of all.

Girls as well as boys (top left) participate in Hoosier Boys' Town's day treatment programs that help troubled youth and their families get back on track.

The residential program provides housing, counseling, and classes for about 72 young men (top right). Hoosier Boys' Town facilities now include computer labs, a gymnasium, athletic fields and a swimming pool.

For many residents of Hoosier Boys' Town, the facility offers a safe haven (bottom) where quiet reflection and positive new relationships help them create new possibilities and a new sense of self.

CAMPAGNA ACADEMY
7403 Cline Avenue
Schererville, Indiana 46375
(219) 322-8614
www.campagnaacademy.org

S URROUNDED BY A CANOPY OF TREES ON 100 WOODED ACRES IN CROWN POINT, INDIANA, HYLES-ANDERSON COLLEGE FOCUSES ON STRONG ACADEMIC INSTRUCTION COUPLED WITH PRACTICAL CHRISTIAN TEACHING. STUDENTS RECEIVE A BALANCED EDUCATION THAT GOES BEYOND THEORY. IN ADDITION TO THE EXCELLENT ACADEMICS, HANDS-ON MINISTRIES AND EVANGELISM

play a major role in the lives of faculty and students.

Through the ministries of the First Baptist Church in Hammond, Indiana, students have the privilege each week to put into practice the principles they learn in college. First Baptist Church's well-organized bus ministry enables an average Sunday school attendance of more than 20,000 each week. More than 40 different ministries offer a wide range of training experiences and opportunities.

Vision Takes Shape

Hyles-Anderson College has grown and prospered since its founding on August 21, 1972. It stands as a testimony to the glory of God and the vision God implanted in Dr. Jack Hyles back in 1970. Dr. Hyles had long desired to build a college that could train and equip men and women for full-time Christian service. In 1970, as Dr. Hyles was walking and praying along a freeway in Los Angeles, his fervor to start the college became stronger.

Dr. Russell Anderson, a Christian businessman from Ypsilanti, Michigan, took a trip with Dr. Hyles, and the vision began to take shape. In January 1972, the First Baptist Church of Hammond purchased 21 acres of land in Schererville, Indiana, to establish the school. Work began on the 10th of that same month and was completed on August 21, 1972. The electricity was turned on at 4:00 a.m., and registration began at 8:00 a.m. the very same day.

More than 300 students enrolled in 1972. Enrollment nearly doubled within a year to 590 students in 1973. The rapid growth caused the college to search out larger facilities. A seven-building property in Crown Point, a former Catholic seminary on 71 wooded acres valued at $5 million, was the property of choice. The members of First Baptist Church dedicated themselves to raising the money and made great sacrifices to reach the goal. Many sold wedding rings, mortgaged homes, and even took out personal loans to fuel the vision. The property was purchased on December 31, 1975, at a reduced price of $2.8 million. The value

of the campus today is estimated at over $22 million. Current enrollment averages approximately 2,000 students per year.

Pastors and Missionaries

There are more than 720 graduates of Hyles-Anderson College pastoring today in churches across America. There are also more than 340 Hyles-Anderson College graduates working as missionaries in 40 different countries, spreading the Gospel. It is part of the commitment of Dr. Hyles to assist in establishing great soul-winning churches from coast to coast and around the world. The

The 100-acre campus features a beautiful lake where students can reflect, meditate, and enjoy each other's company.

training and equipping of pastors at Hyles-Anderson College are key factors in that mission. Each year the college receives more requests for pastors than the college graduates.

While academics and Christian service are taken very seriously, campus life is still fun and fulfilling. A strong intramural sports program gives students the opportunity to compete in football, basketball, and soccer. In addition to events on the college's picturesque campus, many off-campus activities are planned each year. Trips to Chicago, regional shopping malls, and professional sporting events are a few of the annual outings in which students can participate.

Dating is an important part in the life of a college student. Hyles-Anderson College offers a healthy environment in which couples can date and, in many cases, provides a foundation where lifelong relationships in marriage can be built. The Activities Department provides numerous opportunities for young couples to have an enjoyable time together. Such occasions include the Christmas Lights activity in Chicago, the Valentine Banquet, boat rides on Lake Michigan, trips to the Lighthouse Museum, and tours of historic sections of Chicago.

Faith in the Future

What does the future hold for Hyles-Anderson College? According to Dr. Hyles, it offers a continuing commitment to the call of God to prepare godly men and women for Christian service. Whether students become pastors, teachers, evangelists, housewives, or professionals in any other field, the mission of Hyles-Anderson College is to establish in the hearts of its students a passion and fire for God and for the lost. As Dr. Hyles states, "God has always blessed those individuals and institutions who have firmly stood for the fundamentals of the faith." Hence, Hyles-Anderson College has determined to maintain Biblical standards of conduct and practice. No school is better than its product. The Apostle Paul put it best when he said in II Corinthians 3:2, "Ye are our epistle written in our hearts, known and read of all men."

HYLES-ANDERSON COLLEGE

8400 Burr Street
Crown Point, Indiana 46307
(219) 365-4031

A UNIVERSITY HOLDS CLASSES AND CONFERS DEGREES, BUT ITS STOCK IN TRADE IS DREAMS. FOR GENERATIONS, EDUCATION HAS BEEN THE DREAM OF MILLIONS OF AMERICANS SEEKING MORE UNDERSTANDING, A BETTER LIFE, A PROMISING CAREER. INDIANA UNIVERSITY NORTHWEST HAS EVOLVED INTO A HIGHLY RESPECTED INSTITUTION HELPING STUDENTS IN THIS REGION ACHIEVE

their dreams. Dynamic programs, top-notch faculty, and a commitment to community have become the hallmarks of the university.

Proud History

Though IU Northwest was formally dedicated in 1959, its story can be traced back to 1917. That's when Indiana University, seeking to serve the growing population of northwest Indiana, decided to offer extension classes in Gary, Hammond, and East Chicago. In 1922, the university established a permanent office in Gary. Ten years later, the Hammond-Whiting-East Chicago Extension Center was founded, renamed in 1939 as the New Calumet Center of Indiana University. In 1948, Gary College was formed, later called the Gary Center of Indiana University.

As demand for higher education increased, the need for expansion was evident. Recognizing the need for—as well as the benefit of—a quality institution for residents of the region—the City of Gary in 1955 donated 27 acres of land in Gleason Park for the construction

of a central campus. The Gary Center and Calumet Center were merged as a regional campus. The first commencement was held in 1967 and, a year later, the campus was renamed Indiana University Northwest (IU Northwest).

Wide Range of Programs

Today, IU Northwest offers students from northwest Indiana and northeastern Illinois a wide range of quality programs from four-year bachelors degrees in more than 30 fields to associate degrees and certificate programs in 40 more. The master's degree program provides an opportunity for post-graduate studies in accounting, business, elementary and secondary education, public affairs, and social work.

IU Northwest is a place where students—of all ages, races, cultures, and interests—can pursue many different dreams. From a major in French to a teaching certificate, from a degree in criminal justice to training for a career as a respiratory therapist, from a Bachelor's in nursing to a certificate in public safety, residents of the region find at IU Northwest the most comprehensive and cutting-edge of the region's educational offerings.

From the creation of its first building in 1959—Tamarack Hall—the campus has continued to meet the academic needs of the student population through the construction of additional buildings. Facilities on the beautifully landscaped campus, which has grown to 38 acres, include Hawthorn Hall, Marram Hall, Raintree Hall, and the Moraine Student Center. The Library Conference Center houses a three-story

library, the Calumet Regional Archives, the Lake County Law Library, the chancellor's office, and a conference center that hosts many community meetings and activities. Also significant to the campus environment are the Dental Education Center, the Child Care Center, the Indiana Police Academy, the Northwest Center for Medical Education, Lindenwood Hall, Sycamore Hall, and Swingshift College for students needing flexibility while working a variety of shifts.

Top Teaching, High Tech

IU Northwest faculty members are known for their excellence and have garnered multiple teaching and research awards throughout the Divisions of Allied Health, Arts and Sciences, Business and Economics, Continuing Studies, Dental Education, Education, Labor Studies, Medical Sciences, Nursing, Public and Environmental Affairs, Political Science, and Social Work. More than 85 percent of the faculty have earned doctorates or the highest degrees in their disciplines, and many are known nationally and internationally in their fields.

Supporting the efforts of students and faculty are facilities at IU Northwest designed to provide

IU Northwest students, who receive personalized instruction and guidance from faculty, are encouraged to participate in extracurricular and community service organizations (top).

In addition to the beautiful 38-acre campus in Gary (bottom), IU Northwest offers classes at instructional sites in Portage and Schererville, as well as at several high schools in the region.

state-of-the-art tools and technology. More than 200 computer work stations are available to students in 11 tech labs on campus; enrolled students are assigned their own e-mail accounts and invited to create personal Web pages. IU Northwest's partnership with software companies allows students to purchase personal copies of software for as little as $5 per CD and to obtain training in free software workshops. Interactive classrooms on the campus enable students to participate in courses and seminars offered at other Indiana University campuses throughout the state.

The IU Northwest library houses nearly half a million books and other publications. Via electronic connection with university libraries statewide, easy access is available to more than five million books, reports, periodicals, and other materials.

Rich Resources

Campus life at IU Northwest is made richer by the resources available to students. The university's new Academic Activities Building (Savannah Center) houses a bookstore, art gallery, lecture/performance hall, gymnasium with a running track, dance/aerobics area, Wellness/Fitness Center, Women's Center, Student Activities offices, and seminar rooms. With a panoply of options for student actualization—from campus government and community service to theater performance or the Biology Club—the university encourages all students to expand their horizons outside of the classroom, too.

IU Northwest offers both intercollegiate and intramural sports for men and women. The university has National Association of Intercollegiate Athletics (NAIA) teams in men's basketball, golf, and baseball. Women's NAIA basketball, golf, and volleyball were initiated in 2000. Intramural options run the gamut from basketball to other fun sports like bowling and

badminton. Personal fitness can be pursued at the gym housed in the Savannah Center.

Future-focused and Flexible

Pursuing dreams can be a difficult business if all the pieces can't be brought together. For students, IU Northwest is a partner in "making it happen." For starters, tuition at IU Northwest is reasonable and within the reach of students, many of whom qualify for financial assistance through federal, state, and university programs as well as the federal work study program. After cost comes the question of convenience. A new and expanded on-site Child Care Center allows parents to take classes while children are safe in a new facility managed by trained care professionals.

Flexibility is also an issue that IU Northwest has tackled. In order to accommodate working students, the university established two off-campus instructional sites—in the Portage Commons Mall and at Deer Creek in Schererville—offering several degrees and a variety of classes. Classes are also offered at Portage High School, Lowell High School, and Lake Central High School.

At IU Northwest, the focus is on the future. That future, according to university chancellor Dr. Bruce W. Bergland, means more flexibility, more interactivity, more personalized attention, and more community outreach. Students at the university find themselves in a setting purposely designed to provide all the tools for success.

After coming to the campus as chancellor in 1999, Dr. Bergland immediately began working with students, faculty, staff, alumni, and community members from seven counties the university serves: Lake, LaPorte, Jasper, Knox, Porter, Newton, and Starke. After a year of hard work, planning, and community meetings in all seven counties, a strategic team gathered ideas and input for the university's

goals in the new millennium and a Shared Vision was created. The vision has identified eight areas of focus beneficial to both the campus and the communities it serves.

"As a university, we are committed to our Shared Vision and excellence in education while reaching out to as many people as possible," Bergland says. "We consider ourselves a partner with every student in the quest for an education and make it a priority to answer student needs, whatever they may be." He adds, "We also consider ourselves a partner with communities we serve in order to enhance quality of life for all in northwest Indiana."

An old song suggests that dreams are "wishes the heart makes when a person is fast asleep." At Indiana University Northwest, dreams are plans people make when they're fully awake, ready to embark on the journey of a lifetime.

Graduation is a dream come true for IU Northwest students for whom education is the path to better lives and fulfilling careers.

INDIANA UNIVERSITY NORTHWEST
3400 Broadway
Gary, Indiana 46408
(219) 980-6991
Toll free: 1-888-YOUR-IUN
www.iun.edu

Nestled along the shoreline of Lake Michigan, amidst the nation's largest steel producers, is the engine that drives much of the northwest Indiana economy. Indiana's International Port/Burns Harbor at Portage is the region's gateway to the world. The port, situated in Porter County, opened to international trade in 1970.

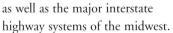

Ocean-going vessels from more than 40 foreign ports carry cargo to Indiana's International Port at Burns Harbor/Portage (top).

An array of sophisticated material handling equipment is used at the port to unload ships and barges of their cargoes (bottom).

The port offers Indiana's farmers and manufacturers unparalleled access to the marketplace via low-cost water transportation. This access is via the Saint Lawrence Seaway to the trade routes of the Atlantic Ocean and Mediterranean Sea, and through the inland water-way system via the Mississippi River to Gulf ports where goods are transported from barges onto ocean-going vessels serving Pacific rim nations. Additionally, through the inland waterway system, the port services the hinterland of our nation. On lake vessels, it services Canada, the United States' largest trading partner.

Partnering for Prosperity

The success of Indiana's International Port is also dependent on land-based transportation. Recognized as a transportation hub, the port has access to industrial America via major rail corridors, as well as the major interstate highway systems of the midwest.

In recent years, the port has developed a 500-acre maritime related industrial park. Port tenants such as Beta Steel, Cargill, Chicago Cold Rolling, Feralloy, Frick Services, and Steel Ware-house are but a few of the tenants that process and handle millions of tons of commodities every year. Port tenants ship and receive grain, fertilizer, machinery, steel prod-ucts, and dozens of other cargoes. The port's Foreign Trade Zone allows shippers and receivers addi-tional savings by deferring or amending customs' duties.

The port provides independent stevedores and terminal operators who utilize a complex array of cargo-handling equipment at the International Port to move mil-lions of tons of cargo each year. Continuing investment in tech-nology and training, as well as teamwork in relationships with the International Longshoremen's Association Local 1969 and the International Union of Operating

Engineers Local 150, have earned the port its well-deserved reputation as the most productive, efficient, and cost-effective port on the Great Lakes.

Federal Marine Terminals (FMT) handles steel and general cargo. A division of Fednav, Ltd., the world's fifth largest steamship company, FMT is the largest carrier on the Great Lakes. Through the services of its parent company, FMT has forecasted continued growth in cargo at Indiana's International Port. In anticipation of this growth, the port is making major infrastructure improvments: new docks, new warehouses, and additional outside storage capabilities. With the ever-growing maritime traffic, the new International Seafarers Center has become a valuable amenity providing recreational, religious, and transportation services to visiting seamen.

Three decades ago, Indiana's International Port was little more than a dream in the minds of northwest Indiana visionaries. However, the State of Indiana and the U.S. Army Corps of Engineers transformed a small area on Lake Michigan into the most modern port facility on the Great Lakes. Over the years, the port has serviced thousands of barges, Great Lakes carriers, and ocean-going vessels flying flags of more than 40 different nations. Few then could have envisioned the bustling

maritime industrial complex that the port has become.

Benefits across the Region

The port's impact, like the waters to which it makes connection possible, is wide and deep. A recent study by researchers at Indiana University estimated that the port's direct economic impact exceeds $40 million per year. The predominant share of that total is felt locally, from companies that benefit from the raw and processed materials shipped into and out of the port to the local school systems that are recipients of property taxes paid by port tenants. Unlike many ports, the International Port is self-supporting. No state subsidies are appropriated to underwrite the facility's annual operations.

The port is administered by the Indiana Port Commission, a seven-member board appointed for a four-year term by the Governor of Indiana. The commission is committed to enhancement of Indiana industry and agriculture, not only through the International Port, but also via Indiana's two riverports: the Southwind Maritime Centre in Mt. Vernon and the Clark Maritime Centre in Jeffersonville.

The International Port will handle more than three million tons of cargo in the first year of the new millennium. Today it is clear the port has positioned itself to help the region and the State of Indiana play a key role in the competitive global marketplace of the 21st century.

Indiana's International Port has earned its reputation as one of the most efficient and customer-friendly ports in the world. In anticipation of growing global shipping, the port is investing in infrastructure from new docks and warehousing space to outside storage facilities.

INDIANA'S
INTERNATIONAL PORT
BURNS HARBOR
AT PORTAGE

6625 South Boundary Drive
Portage, Indiana 46368
(219) 787-8636
www.portsofindiana.com

ALTERNATIVE DISTRIBUTION SYSTEMS, INC.

AT INDIANA'S INTERNATIONAL PORT

Internet access, bar code tag reading, customized inventory management systems, customized computer reporting, EDI, AISI, Compord, TDCC, Ansi X.12, and facsimile transmissions are a few of the technological efficiencies that enhance Roll & Hold's full service operations (top).

The Area "Lite," designed to increase payloads while reducing customer costs, can haul larger material loads before reaching maximum hauling weights. The trailer is built from non-corrosive aluminum and requires less mainte-nance (bottom).

Alternative Distribution Systems, Inc. (ADS) is bound to get the call. An industry leader in the logistics field, the 30-year old firm is the parent company of Area Transportation Company, Roll & Hold Warehousing & Distribution Corp., and Western Intermodal Services, Ltd. Each of the subsidiary companies has offices or operations in northwest Indiana. The companies provide fully integrated services, including transportation, warehousing, dis-tribution, and logistics services to the metals producing and con-suming marketplace.

A privately held business with approximately 600 employees and independent contractors, ADS began simply as a trucking compa-ny, hauling materials for suppliers and OEM's throughout the region in the late 1970s. Growth in the steel and metals industries led to needs for off-site warehousing and delivery services to maximize storage space, handle inventory,

and expedite delivery of metal to manufacturing lines exactly when required, known in the industry as "just in time" (JIT) delivery.

ADS primarily serves the metals industry with its transportation, warehousing, and logistics services which are expertly matched with the firm's knowledge of the trends in and needs of ferrous and

non-ferrous metal producers and processors. The company handles mostly steel, aluminum, and other metals.

Capitalizing on the growing need for JIT services to the manu-facturing sector, the subsidiaries have steadily extended their reach across North America by focusing on customer service and taking advantage of new technologies that increase efficiency and reduce costs for clients.

Northwest Indiana Operations

ADS is a pivotal player in the booming northwest Indiana manufacturing marketplace. Area Transportation Company, with offices in Munster, is a 48-state customs bonded motor carrier specializing in the transport of metal and other products in pro-prietary trailers designed for metals hauling. Roll & Hold Warehous-ing & Distribution Corp., with operations in Hammond and Portage, is a metals products ware-houser providing the highest quality facilities, service, and

technology with emphasis on JIT delivery and electronic communications. Western Intermodal Services, Ltd., with offices in Munster, specializes in materials movement management and packaging of services combining rail, truck, and barge transportation, primarily between the midwest and West Coast.

That ADS is a company on a roll can in large part be attributed to its investment in the future. Roll & Hold's 133,000 square foot facility in Hammond constructed in 1997 was designed to handle sensitive material such as cold-rolled and coated materials. It augments the firm's 300,000 square foot facility that warehouses commodity hot-rolled steel. The new facility features tight environmental controls, 35-ton cranes, and a rail service line that allows the plant to service northwest Indiana and the greater Chicago area.

Roll & Hold's facility at Indiana's International Port at Burns Harbor/Portage includes a 206,000 square foot facility with

Roll & Hold signature features: environmentally controlled storage space, double airlock access, direct rail, through-building truck lanes, material-sensitive cranes, and its proprietary computer system. Roll & Hold has partnered with Fednav Limited of Montreal, to serve as a general cargo terminal operator and stevedore at the port, and in 2000 began providing steel processing services at this facility through its partnership with Flat Rock Metal of Flat Rock, Michigan.

Service Is Key

Ever alert to the needs and opportunities in the industry, the company stresses ongoing improvements, especially with its technology solutions. For instance, the firm's proprietary software, LoMaS™, provides customers a supply chain management solution through its integrated applications that manages inventory, order processing including rating and dispatch, commodity tracking, billing,

and freight payments as well as equipment management. Electronically shared freight bills and electronic billing help to increase efficiency.

In 2000 ADS brought many of its technology solutions to the Web. Area Transportation launched its e-tranzit™, an online transportation marketplace dedicated to flatbed shippers and carriers. This system provides shippers a streamlined transportation procurement process, and provides carriers with instant access to new shippers. Roll & Hold Web-enabled its Inventory Management System© providing producers and consuming end users real-time access to their inventory at Roll & Hold facilities. Leveraging the company's technology know-how on behalf of customers has been a key component of the success of ADS and its subsidiary companies.

The little engine that could—a small business that started with several trucks—has become a big engine helping move manufacturing in the midwest and throughout the country.

Roll & Hold facilities offer heat and humidity controlled environments for product storage. Additional services include a full range of customized export and domestic packaging, inspection services, repairs, upending/downending, palletizing, and weighting.

ALTERNATIVE DISTRIBUTION SYSTEMS, INC.
935 West 175th Street
Homewood, Illinois 60430
(708) 799-4990
www.adsinet.com

If Andre Joseph were writing an advertisement for the International Longshoremen's Association Local 1969, he might alter a line from a well-known car commercial: "This is not your father's union." Stationed at the Port of Indiana, loading and unloading millions of tons of cargo carried by ships from nearly every

INTERNATIONAL LONGSHOREMEN'S ASSOCIATION

At Indiana's International Port

6613 Compass Drive
Portage, Indiana 46368
(219) 787-9189
www.ilaindiana.org

Members of the International Longshoremen's Association Local 1969 consider themselves business venture partners with their customers at the port. More than 350 residents of the region work at the Lake Michigan port as terminal head checkers, walking bosses, signalmen hatch bosses, CDL drivers, forklift operators, and holdmen.

country in the world, the association sees itself not as an adversary of business—as unions have often been historically portrayed—but as a partner in promoting the promise of the port.

Today, there are as many as 350 residents of the northwest Indiana region at work as longshoremen at the port on an average day. Whether they're employed as terminal head checkers, walking bosses, signalmen, hatch bosses, CDL drivers, forklift operators, or holdmen, the longshoremen use their training and skills to help the port succeed.

Joseph, who is an expediter—the guy who rounds up qualified longshoremen to serve the stevedores of the cargo ships and terminal—is proud of his union today. While it exists to represent the workers at the port, ensuring good-paying jobs and top-notch benefits, it also regards itself as a joint venture business partner with employers and their customers.

"We all enjoy success if the port enjoys success," Joseph says. "Our approach is positive and pro-active."

As a partner, the association has pursued a number of successful strategies. For starters, the union makes it a point to understand the businesses it serves. Longshoremen on the docks are educated on the complexities of steel-making and the ins and outs of other industries to better service clients. The association's apprenticeship training programs—in areas that range from safety to equipment maintenance to cultural diversity—have marked the Port of Indiana's longshoremen as some of the best trained in the field. Its commitment to customer service draws kudos from stevedores and businesses that work with the

union. For instance, Joseph and his workers used their autonomy to design a cargo unloading system requiring only one dock superintendent. The cost savings were passed on to customers.

"It matters to us that our clients make money," Joseph explains. "We consider ourselves a partner in the enterprise, able to help solve problems and come up with the right solutions."

It's no small matter to customers of the longshoremen's services, for whom the transportation and handling costs of goods shipped along the St. Lawrence Seaway make a big impact on the bottom

line. Joseph said his union—which boasts a very high 80 percent or better attendance at scheduled meetings—has worked hard to help the Port of Indiana gain recognition as the most cost-effective, qualified port on the Great Lakes.

The association also focuses on family. From the longshoremen's buddy system that ensures worker safety to holiday parties where workers and their families celebrate together, the union helps build the bonds of community. And the longshoremen invite employers to those parties—whose children play with their children.

"It's not your normal stereotype," admits Raymond Sierra, vice president of the International Longshoremen's Association organization that represents the chain of ports throughout the Great Lakes region and Canada. "We focus every day on building the kind of relationships that will make the port the most productive in the industry."

It's a unique new model that puts the union family and its customers on the same side of the success fence.

Acount of stars certifies Isakson Motor Sales as a leading dealership—and nearly as its own constellation. Isakson has 75 golden stars, five for each time it has been selected a top-ranking Chrysler dealership, a notable achievement for a business that opened in 1928 to sell DeSotos and Case tractors. One of the midwest's oldest dealerships,

**3530 North Hobart Road
Hobart, Indiana 46342
(219) 962-3681**

the award-winning firm has a long history in the region. Established by Clarence and Walter Isakson, the company opened as Isakson Brothers in 1928. One of the original DeSoto dealerships, Isakson Brothers also sold Plymouth models to customers as well as Case tractors to farmers in northwest Indiana. Clarence Isakson's son Bill took the reins in 1968 and today, at the age of 75, can still be found working in the dealership's showroom and service areas several days a week.

Today, Rob Isakson—Bill's son and the grandson of the founder—is at the helm of Isakson Motors. The business remains one of the oldest, continuously family-owned and operated automobile dealerships in the midwest. Rob's sons Eric and Steven are now working at the dealership, learning the ropes and helping the family business to deliver satisfaction to customers.

New Times, New Showroom

In many ways, Isakson Motor Sales is a role model for the modern car dealership. From a gleaming, spacious 17,000 square

Since 1928, Isakson Motor Sales has offered the northwest Indiana driving public excellent service. A Five Star Chrysler dealership, Isakson Motors constructed a cutting edge showroom in 1999 (top), one of the largest and most accommodating sales and service facilities in the region.

foot facility built in 1999, management and staff work hard to make the business one of the best in the industry.

Customers enjoy the airy, spacious quarters at Isakson Motors. But they're truly smitten by the service. For 16 of the last 18 years, Isakson Motors has been selected a Five Star dealership by the Chrysler Corporation, an honor bestowed upon only the top dealerships in the country. To earn Five Star status, dealerships must earn high marks in customer service, automotive repair, technology and training, and other key areas.

Record of Achievement

"We're proud of our record of achievement," says Rob Isakson. "We work diligently to keep service levels high so that customers are always happy."

Isakson believes success has come from the company's philosophy of balancing the high tech world of automobiles today with "good, old-fashioned service." Sales, service, and support staff

spend hours in training on such topics as customer service, financing, etiquette, ethics, the Internet, and more. Classroom and hands-on training sessions help Isakson Motor's 22 employees hone skills in every facet of the business.

"We treat our customers like human beings," Isakson explains. "Many people come to us reeling from bad experiences, or are tired of the circus-like atmosphere at other dealerships. We turn that around by taking time to answer questions and deal with customer concerns. In a fast-paced world, the customer still deserves top service."

It's a boom market for Chrysler models. At Isakson Motors, superior service combines with popular series—like the new PT Cruiser, Chrysler minivans, the Sebring series, and sporty 300M—to form an unbeatable one-two punch.

Isakson trusts there will be more gold stars in the company's future. Once you've achieved a constellation, goes the thinking, the goal becomes a galaxy.

I F EDUCATIONAL OPPORTUNITY IS THE CROWN OF NORTHWEST INDIANA, IVY TECH STATE COLLEGE NORTHWEST MUST BE RANKED AS ONE OF ITS JEWELS. A PUBLIC, STATEWIDE, OPEN-ACCESS, COMMUNITY COLLEGE PREPARING STUDENTS WITH GENERAL AND TECHNICAL EDUCATION, IVY TECH IS PART OF A STATEWIDE COLLEGE SYSTEM COMPRISED OF 13 REGIONS AND 23 CAMPUSES. THE COLLEGE

Northwest Indiana Region Campuses in Gary, East Chicago, Valparaiso, and Michigan City (800) 843-4882 or (219) 981-1111 http://gar.ivy.tec.in.us

Students are prepared for the challenges of the real world upon graduation (top). Microbiology, Welding, and CNG (Alternative Fuels Programs) are a few of the areas of training available to students at Ivy Tech (bottom).

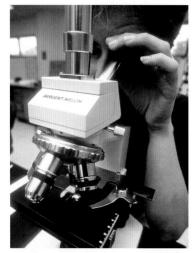

developed an educational partnership with Vincennes University in 1999 to form the state's first Community College system. The Northwest Region Gary Campus was selected as one of four pilot sites statewide to implement the new system. The other campuses in Valparaiso, East Chicago, and Michigan City are expected to become Community College sites in 2001.

Combined, the four campuses offer more than 30 programs and specialties designed to help area citizens meet their educational and career goals. Programs are offered in the technologies, health services, human services, and business. Ivy Tech Northwest offers personalized instruction that promotes student academic success. Classes are small and are taught by faculty with a broad range of experience in their respective fields. Placement, financial aid, and career counseling—as well as other support services—are available to meet students' academic and personal needs. An Alumni Association and many other student-related organizations exist which offer a variety of extracurricular activities.

In keeping with its mission and goals, the college serves persons

with educational programs consistent with projected job requirements and personal interests. Ivy Tech programs complement secondary programs, four-year programs, and adult basic education programs. Credit programs culminate in an Associate in Applied Science degree, an Associate in Science degree, or a Technical Certificate.

Ivy Tech State College maintains articulation agreements with a number of public and private institutions throughout the state that allow students to transfer individual courses or entire programs. Opportunities are available to Ivy Tech students to transfer and complete a baccalaureate program as a resident or commuting student.

Vincennes Programs

The College now offers eight new programs through its Community College of Indiana partnership with Vincennes University. The Vincennes programs are English, History, Liberal Arts, Philosophy, Political Science, Pre-Law, Psychology, and Sociology. These programs became available for the first time during

fall semester 2000 at the Gary campus. Also offered are numerous program-related courses.

Customized classes

Short-term training is available in selected credit courses, in sequences of credit courses, and in custom-designed courses for local businesses and industries. These courses are designed and delivered through the Region's Business and Industry Training Division (BIT). BIT works closely with Indiana businesses to offer customized training, retraining and continuing education in response to specific company needs. Also available are contract training programs and non-credit institutional activities such as seminars, workshops and conferences.

In addition to program and custom-designed courses, Ivy Tech State College offers basic skills instruction for students who require academic support and need to strengthen their study skills. Additionally, enrollment in certain basic skills courses is designed to prepare the student for the GED examination.

L AKE AREA UNITED WAY BRINGS TOGETHER THE RESOURCES OF THE NORTHWEST INDIANA COMMUNITY TO ASSIST PEOPLE IN HELPING THEMSELVES AND ONE ANOTHER. A COMMUNITY-BASED, NOT-FOR-PROFIT ORGANIZATION, IT RAISES AND ALLOCATES FUNDS FOR HEALTH AND SOCIAL SERVICE AGENCIES IN LAKE COUNTY, INDIANA, AND LANSING, ILLINOIS THAT PROVIDE CRITICAL

assistance from subsidized child care to occupational training.

The size and scope of today's United Way—now that the national organization has big name sponsors and advertising spots during National Football League telecasts—lead many to think United Way has always been around. In fact, it took a great deal of work and dedication for United Way to become a force in support of charitable and community initiatives. The growth of Lake Area United Way (LAUW), too, required the dedication of many to attain its current status as the quality leader among nonprofit health and human service organizations.

LAUW traces its history to 1969 when Judge William J. Obermiller of East Chicago founded an organization called United Drive with the intent of uniting seven separate fund-raising groups into one. The vision took tangible shape in 1971 when Lyndon R. Milliken became the first executive director of the Lake Area United Appeal. The new organization combined the activities of the Northwest Indiana United Fund and the United Calumet Community Chest. This became the forerunner of Lake Area United Way, officially

established in 1973. Milliken is still fondly remembered as the founder of LAUW.

Commitment and Dedication

N othing significant happens without the strong commitment of many dedicated people. LAUW was no exception. Julian Colby, a Hammond businessman, donated the current LAUW building in Griffith, providing needed office space to house

the new organization. It was this type of commitment and sacrifice that gave LAUW its start, attributes that continue to be instrumental in the growth and work of the organization.

Major support of LAUW originated with heavy industry and organized labor in Gary, East Chicago, and Hammond. When the steel mills began to reorganize in the early 1980s, it was clear that a wider base of financial support was needed. LAUW—in the

Fourteen staffers (top) manage the operations of Lake Area United Way, keeping community impact high and overhead costs low.

Programs funded by the nonprofit organization assist a broad range of people in the region including the handicapped and elderly (bottom).

precarious position of balancing declining revenues with an increasing demand for services—searched for new streams of revenue to support its important work. Relationships with banks, hospitals, retailers, and service organizations were cultivated to help build a solid foundation of financial support.

Today, LAUW is much more than a fund-raising and funds-distribution organization. Its mission is to establish value-added services for the organizations it supports. Not only a provider of funds for vital services, LAUW is also a source for the leadership training, personnel development, and skill-building that help supported agencies improve efficiency and deliver more effective services.

One function of LAUW is to ensure that needed services are being provided by the member agencies it supports. Coordination and collaboration of services mean that every dollar donated to LAUW is helping to make a difference in the community. LAUW helps lower the expenses of supported agencies by reducing the costs of fund-raising and providing valuable training. These types of value-added services keep quality organizations alive and well in Lake area communities.

LAUW's mandate is to constantly improve its level of service to the community. By continuously monitoring the organizations it funds, the LAUW assures individuals and companies that their donations are put to the best possible use. The State of Indiana recognized LAUW's superior performance when it awarded the organization the 2000 Indiana Quality Improvement Award.

Volunteers Serving the Community

The largest source of revenue its LAUW's current budget of about $6 million comes from its payroll deduction program. Employees voluntarily elect to have small deductions taken each payroll period, which over time constitute significant contributions. An extremely effective and efficient fund-raising method, it is the main reason why only 13 cents per dollar is allocated for overhead and marketing expenses.

A healthy United Way is a sign of a healthy local economy. When prospective entrepreneurs look to open factories and shops in a community, they often look at the viability of the local United Way as a gauge of the business environment. While the LAUW is not responsible for creating jobs, it plays an important role in serving the business community by providing workers and citizens with a variety of needed support services.

With only 14 full-time employees to manage the intricacies of its operation, a large volunteer base is critical to the success of the LAUW. The Board of Trustees and hundreds of community volunteers assist in annual fund-raising, allocation research, marketing, training, and much more. The time, talents, and commitment of LAUW volunteers help to maintain low overhead and truly serve the community. Lake Area United Way means it literally when it says—as is its motto— "Thanks to you, it's working."

Community leaders like Julian Colby (top), who donated a Griffith building to Lake Area United Way, and Lyndon Milliken (above) LAUW's first executive director, were instrumental in the organization's growth.

A large share of the LAUW's $6 million annual budget is earmarked to help families and youngsters in the region.

LAKE AREA UNITED WAY
221 West Ridge Road
Griffith, Indiana 46319
(219) 923-2302
www.lauw.org

FRANCES DUPEY IS CURRENTLY SERVING AS LAKE COUNTY'S FIRST FEMALE COMMISSIONER. IT IS A ROLE SHE RELISHES. DUPEY HAS LIVED IN THE REGION MOST OF HER LIFE, IS SMITTEN BY ITS BEAUTY AND AMENITIES, AND ENJOYS THE DAILY CHALLENGES OF SERVING HER CONSTITUENTS. DUPEY ATTENDED HAMMOND TECHNICAL VOCATIONAL HIGH SCHOOL AND THEN MOVED TO

Frances DuPey relishes life as a public servant, but had to break through barriers to become the first woman elected to the Lake County Council and later the first woman voted in as a Lake County Commissioner (top).

Lake Michigan is one of DuPey's true loves. A resident of Hammond, DuPey spends as much time as possible along its shores (bottom).

Lamoni, Iowa where she graduated from high school in 1959. Though she appreciated the opportunity to see another part of the country, DuPey missed the diversity and hustle-bustle of life in Lake County and returned to Hammond shortly after graduation.

Business college was next for DuPey. After studying a business machines curriculum at Hammond Business College, she landed a job with Kraft Foods in Chicago. One of only three women to work in the Central Division of the corporation, DuPey worked in the shipping and production department. Tiring of the long commute, DuPey left Kraft to take employment with Youngstown Sheet and Tube in East Chicago where she worked as a comptometer operator in the payroll department.

Frances Gilbertson DuPey met and married Frank DuPey, a Hammond police officer. Frank became the Police Chief of Hammond under former Mayor Edward Raskosky. Retired from the force after 27 years, Frank now works at Mercantile Bank. DuPey and her husband have two children, Veronica DuPey and Frank DuPey. They also have one grandson, Allen.

DuPey left Youngstown Sheet and Tubing to work as a secretary for Mayor Raskosky. From that day on, DuPey began a love affair with politics that helped her destiny take shape. She found government exciting, and realized she could make a difference in people's lives as well as act as a positive force in public service.

DuPey decided to run for public office. Although she lost her first race, successive campaigns proved fruitful. DuPey broke the barrier to become the first woman elected to the once male-dominated Lake County Council board. She broke another barrier in 1997 when she was elected as Lake County Commissioner. DuPey currently serves the Third District, encompassing Hammond, Whiting, East Chicago, Munster, Highland, and Griffith. DuPey also serves as Hammond's first

female head of the Hammond Democratic Precinct Organization.

DuPey is reflective about her role as barrier-breaker and public servant. "Perhaps being a woman made me more resilient or perhaps I was just stubborn enough to carve out a place for myself in politics," she says. DuPey has learned that politics are not for the faint of heart, as the work involves long hours, difficult decisions, and the stamina to stay the course. Although more women populate the landscape of politics today than at any other time in history, DuPey embarked on her journey in a different era when few females held elected office.

Today, DuPey advocates for financial stewardship, neighborhood improvements, and fairness in issues like taxation and transportation that affect all of the county's citizens. With the end of federal revenue sharing, DuPey has focused on responsible use of casino funds. Her insistence that revenue be spent on capital improvements and projects that improve quality of life have won her high marks from constituents. DuPey believes that the funds are better used for long term improvements, not the excessive job creation that undercut the federal revenue sharing program.

DuPey's success can be attributed to her willingness to discuss and negotiate, and to listen to different points of view. "You have to keep an open mind and be willing to change your mind based on the facts," DuPey believes. This sensitivity, dedication, and quest for harmony has made DuPey a careful and calming force in Lake County government. DuPey said she is proud of her record as a public official.

Throughout her career, DuPey has depended upon her family to assist her and boost her spirits. Her family includes four sisters and a brother, all of whom reside in the Calumet region. She also still relishes the familiar northwest Indiana landscape and Lake

Michigan. The region's golf courses, DuPey remarked, are some of the best in the midwest and she has recently taken up the sport. The lake, DuPey said, is one of the region's finest assets. Sometimes she is content to sit at the water's edge, appreciating the beauty of tranquility, the sun dancing on the waves. But she's just as apt to take the plunge. Not only is the swimming good exercise, DuPey said, but it adds an interesting twist to her political life. For if someone tells DuPey to "go jump in the lake" (it comes with the turf), she's likely to invite him to join her.

DuPey serves a diverse constituency of residents in Lake County's Third District, which includes Hammond (top), Whiting, East Chicago, Munster, Highland, and Griffith.

Public life has taught DuPey one can never hear too many ideas. She spends as much time as possible traveling throughout her district discussing important issues with residents (bottom).

**FRANCES DUPEY
LAKE COUNTY
COMMISSIONER**

Lake County Government Center
2293 North Main Street
Crown Point, Indiana 46307
(219) 755-3200

GERRY SCHEUB IS A DEMOCRAT, BUT HE TAKES A LEAD FROM ONE OF THE GREATEST REPUBLICANS IN HISTORY, ABRAHAM LINCOLN. IT WAS LINCOLN WHO SAID, "LET THE PEOPLE KNOW THE FACTS AND THE COUNTRY IS SAFE." AS THE COMMISSIONER FOR LAKE COUNTY, INDIANA'S 2ND DISTRICT, SCHEUB HAS MADE HEADLINES AND ENDEARED HIMSELF TO THE PUBLIC INSISTING

on open meetings and forums on all issues, advocating for tax reform, and attending to the concerns of his constituency.

Northwest Indiana Roots

Not bad for a small town boy who grew up in the Tolleston community of Gary and who once planned to be an accountant. Today when Scheub opens a manila folder, what he finds is not a company's balance sheet, but letters of congratulation and support from representatives and senators. Scheub's propensity to pursue the common sense solution, to cleave to the time-honored American values of good government and fair outcomes, has brought the 65-year old public servant kudos from all political parties and citizens from every walk of life.

Scheub was born for the people-packed, rough and tumble life of politics. Gregarious and curious, he found that hearing different points of view and seeking common ground was often hard work, but always exhilarating and critical to the well-being of his community.

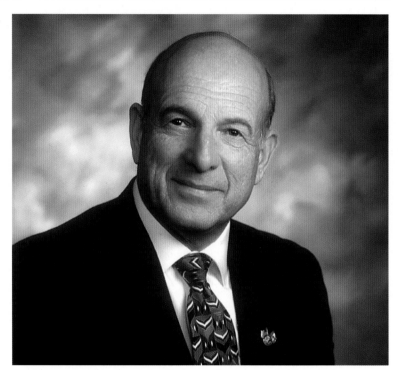

"There's never a dull moment, never a day without an issue of some sort," Scheub says. "We have big issues, like taxation, that affect everyone. We have small issues, like one farmer's drainage problem. I've tried to focus on finding solutions for every single person who walks through my door."

Scheub has spent most of his life in government. As a young man, he served as an apprentice bricklayer, worked at U.S. Steel and the American Bridge Company, and tried his hand as a salesman for a manufacturer of corrugated shipping cartons. By the time he was 33, Scheub was acting as a Democratic precinct committeeman and not long after became a St. John Township Trustee, a post he held for 20 years.

Challenging the Standards

It was during Scheub's tenure as trustee that he first felt the power of good ideas to transform public life. Scheub lobbied aggressively for a system of relief for the

county's needy that would pay wages for honest work, not simply function as a public dole. His philosophy was simple: that hand-outs never helped a human being in the long run as much as could a job. His philosophy was also respectful of all parties involved in poor relief, from the recipient who would get assistance and work to the taxpayer who would get something tangible in return. Now a pivotal part of the national platform on welfare reform, Scheub's proposal was unprecedented in the seventies. His idea anticipated the current climate by two decades and earned him a mention when Ronald Reagan stumped for presidential office in New Hampshire in 1976.

"I'm still very proud of that initiative," Scheub says. "We were a small township in the middle of the country, but we did have the power to affect government and to contribute to the national dialogue." In other words, little guys sometimes win. It was a lesson

Since entering public life at the age of 33, Gerry Scheub (top) has tried to make a positive impact. His proposal for changes in welfare relief grabbed the attention of Ronald Reagan in 1976 and anticipated eventual legislation by two decades.

Indiana Governor Frank O'Bannon (left) presents Scheub with an Innovative Leadership Award, an honor Lake County earned in 1999 (bottom).

The community facility (top) in St. John Township was a project near and dear to Scheub's heart. He put together a vacated police post, county revenue sharing funds, and volunteers to build the community center. In 1999, it was renamed in his honor as the Gerry Scheub Community Center.

Family comes first with Scheub, who gathered in 2000 with his wife, children, grandchildren, and close family friend Father Roy Beeching for a family reunion (bottom).

Scheub learned from his years of coaching football at St. Michael's Grade School in Schererville and at Andrean High School in Merrillville. The point in politics—just like football—is not to fret about the size of the team, but to get to the goal.

A Man Who Believes in People

Today, Scheub pursues the goal of good government. The St. John Township community facility, recently renamed the Gerry Scheub Community Center, is another

stripe on his helmet. The center was built on a five-acre plot vacated by a police post using county revenue sharing funds. A new patio and gazebo were constructed by volunteers—including many of Scheub's former high school football players. Other of Scheub's initiatives, like the first ever Lake County Impact Plan, earned the county an Innovative Leadership Award in 1999 from the Association of Indiana Counties, Inc.

Scheub hopes the future will bring welfare tax reform and a trade school and day care center

in Lake County so that mothers receiving welfare support can more easily pursue new skills and job opportunities. He works for regional cooperation on transportation issues and economic development. And Gerry Scheub still makes sure every call that comes into his office gets a rapid response.

"Every citizen counts," Scheub explains. "According to my view of politics, that means more work and more accountability. What I have been given by the voters isn't a prize, but a duty."

**GERRY SCHEUB
LAKE COUNTY
COMMISSIONER**

Lake County Government Center
2293 North Main Street
Crown Point, Indiana 46307
(219) 755-3200

W HEN DEVELOPMENT WAS IMMINENT FOR THE EASTERN LEG OF U.S. HIGHWAY 30 IN MER-RILLVILLE, ENGINEERS IN 1989 PROPOSED INFRASTRUCTURE INCLUDING AN 18-INCH SEWER LINE TO SERVICE NEW COMMERCIAL ENTERPRISES. THE LAKE COUNTY COMMUNITY ECONOMIC DEVELOPMENT DEPARTMENT HAD BIGGER IDEAS. CREATING A TAX INCREMENT FINANCING DISTRICT

(known as a "TIF") and issuing 20-year bonds to pay for construction, the department specified a 36-inch line big enough to handle the businesses its staffers knew would inevitably flock to the area.

It is the kind of pro-active, forward-looking work done by the Lake County Community Economic Development Department (LCCEDD). Today travelers along that once vacant corridor shop at the stores of major retailers now an important part of the economic vitality of the region. Hundreds of jobs were created for Lake County citizens. And—to sweeten the deal—those 20-year bonds will be retired in ten.

For the LCCEDD, spurring the right economic development in Lake County is more than a mandate, it's a mission. The LCCEDD has initiated numerous programs to attract commercial and industrial businesses to the county. Chief among them is the Lake County Revolving Loan Fund that provides $100,000 to $2 million short-term construction financing loans for the establishment or expansion of an industrial business. Loans from the fund can be used to acquire buildings or machinery, to acquire land on which a facility will be

constructed, to make leasehold improvements, for energy conservation, for pollution control, and for on-site infrastructure.

The LCCEDD also uses its arsenal of assistance programs that range from federally funded Community Development Block Grants (CDBG) and loan programs spearheaded by the Small Business Administration, Indiana Department of Commerce, TIF program, Industrial Revenue Bonds, and cooperation with numerous commercial lenders in the region.

In recent years, for instance, the LCCEDD used Revolving Loan Fund monies to help clients

including a steel processor, institutional laundry business, a sterile medical kit assembly company, and others. Funds from the CDBG program were channeled into water and sewer lines to help small manufacturing firms grow. The U.S. 30 TIF District, once a sparsely populated tract with about nine businesses, today is home to seventy companies and retailers such as Home Depot, Target, and Barnes & Noble.

Committed to the County

I t makes sense for Lake County to toot its own horn. Ideally situated close to three major interstate highways, within minutes from

Once a vacant tract of land, the TIF District along U.S. 30 (top) in Hobart was spurred in part by the department's foresight in up-sizing new infrastructure which has lured national retailers like Home Depot, Target, and Barnes & Noble (bottom right).

Families like the Ramos' of Hobart (bottom left) are now homeowners, thanks to the LCCEDD's programs for first-time buyers.

Gary-Chicago Airport and an hour from Chicago's O'Hare Airport, and with access to rail lines and the International Port of Indiana, the county can capitalize on convenience features. Nearly one hundred truck lines serve the area. Add singular amenities like the county's location along Lake Michigan, a bevy of cultural institutions and public parks, excellent schools and nationally-known universities, and Lake County looms as a very real competitor in the economic development

marketplace. In addition to its proximity to urban resources, much of Lake County's most productive lands have been retained in agricultural production. Lake County has about 80,000 acres of corn and 50,000 acres devoted to soybeans.

Help for communities

While it focuses much effort on economic development in the broadest sense, the LCCEDD also takes pride in its work to enhance communities and the existing housing infrastructure

in the county. As the only such county-wide agency in Indiana, the department works with 17 cities and towns to enhance infrastructure and housing.

The Department oversees a multitude of Lake County initiatives that offer financial assistance to homebuyers; weatherization; counseling on housing matters; public infrastructure improvements; demolition of outdated building stock; and low-interest loans and grants for housing rehabilitation and emergency repairs for low and moderate income applicants. Its homebuyer assistance program has helped more than 170 Lake County families purchase their own homes since 1998. Funds from the U.S. Department of Housing & Urban Development (HUD) are divided among county communities for eligible neighborhood improvements like sidewalk repairs, sewer projects, street renovation, and other refurbishment of public infrastructure.

A tall order, but not an impossible one for the ambitious and dedicated staff of the Lake County Community Economic Development Department.

LAKE COUNTY
COMMUNITY ECONOMIC
DEVELOPMENT
DEPARTMENT
2293 North Main Street
Crown Point, Indiana 46307
(219) 755-3225
www.lakecountyin.com

LAKE COUNTY CONVENTION & VISITORS BUREAU

spend all its resources producing brochures with pretty pictures. When it comes to forward-thinking, proactive advancement of Lake County, the Lake County Convention & Visitors Bureau has become a national model for agencies of its type and a force in economic development in the region.

A variety of information on Lake County attractions is available to visitors at the bureau's new center in Hammond (top).

Kids learn "crime doesn't pay" and other historical lessons at the center's John Dillinger Museum (bottom).

Unique Visitor Center

The groundbreaking nature of its work became literal in 1999 when the organization introduced the new Visitors Information Center in Hammond, located directly off the Borman Expressway (I-80/94) at Kennedy Avenue. One of the country's most unique and touted visitor centers, the building pays homage to the most salient characteristics of Lake County. Designed by a northwest Indiana architectural firm, the award-winning center honors steel and sand and industry and innovation.

Visitors from near and far are smitten by the center's ability to convey facts while keeping things fun. Consider the structure itself, an impressive melding of form and function. The large exhibition space is created in the form of waves, fabricated of northwest Indiana steel and glistening in the sun, a reference to the importance of Lake Michigan in the region. Concrete is used to create

undulating sand dunes. The natural terrain rolls into sections of the building that depict plains and farms, and the free-flowing Kankakee River. Outside, evocative landscaping conveys a sense of place with plantings of prairie grass and tall green corn.

Inside, expertly conceived displays relay the history of Lake County in the John Dillinger Museum. The center features the grand 6,500 square foot W.F. Wellman Exhibition Hall, a state-of-the-art fiber optic theater, bureau offices, a gift shop, visitor information desk, and other service areas. Friendly staff help tourists collect the information they need on the county's attractions, amenities, and festivals, as well as the perfect places to dine, play, and rest.

James McDaniel, chairman of the bureau's board of directors, believes the building will prove a key investment in the growth of Lake County tourism.

"The talents and vision of many people have created a tourism center of enormous impact and long-lasting value," McDaniel says. "The new center packs a wallop when it comes to educating the public and promoting Lake County as a great place to visit and do business."

Aggressive Strategies

Established in 1983, the Lake County Convention & Visitors Bureau is a major player in the growth of Lake County as a destination for tourists from throughout the midwest and country at large. Funded through a hotel/motel tax and per capita casino visitor tax, the bureau has an annual budget of about $2.5 million and a staff

of 40 including part-time visitor center staffers. It is governed by a board of directors composed of business and industry leaders, many of whom are involved in the leisure marketplace as owners and operators of hotels, restaurants, and various other tourism related businesses.

The bureau aggressively courts businesses and events that can expand the tourism marketplace in Lake County. It was instrumental in the passage of legislation that brought gaming to northwest Indiana. The casinos in Lake County today bring in millions of dollars spent by tourists on recreation, dining, hotel and motel accommodations, and other goods and services.

Another major accomplishment was the organization of the Gus Macker 3-on-3 basketball tournament that, over the course of its nine-year run, has raised more than $300,000 for area charities. In 1996 the bureau opened a satellite visitor center, a cooperative venture with the Indiana Department of Transportation and Indiana Department of Tourism on I-65 northbound at the Kankakee River.

Partnering with the local hospitality industry, the Lake County Convention & Visitors Bureau

has brought hundreds of business and association conventions to Lake County. It works with charter tour companies that wish to bring visitors to the county's casinos, the Radisson Hotel at Star Plaza, or recreational facilities. And nabbing major annual events—like the National AAU indoor track and field competition and the Men's State Bowling Tournament—has helped boost tourism numbers beyond anything envisioned a decade ago.

"It's been a tourism growth market in Lake County," says Katie Holderby, vice president of

tourism marketing for the bureau. "The natural amenities here in the county, combined with an aggressive program of outreach, have been essential in the sustained growth in both visitor numbers and dollars spent here."

The work of tourism goes on. If there's something that can be done to bring more visitors to Lake County, bureau staffers are busy doing it. The strength of the bureau's approach isn't just that it knows who is visiting today. The real punch is that its focus is always on who can be lured to Lake County tomorrow.

Stunning in design, the Lake County Interstate Visitors Information Center pays homage to all that is northwest Indiana: from steel and sand to farms and rivers (top).

Because it provides so much historical and geographical information about Lake County, the Visitors Information Center (bottom) is becoming a popular destination not only for tourists, but also school and organization field trips.

LAKE COUNTY CONVENTION & VISITORS BUREAU

7770 Corinne Drive
Hammond, Indiana 46323
(219) 989-7770
(800) ALL-LAKE
www.alllake.org

WHAT HAS OVER 5,700 ACRES, SHELTERS AVAILABLE FOR PICNICS OF ALL SIZES, TWO STRUCTURES LISTED ON THE NATIONAL REGISTER OF HISTORIC PLACES, RIVERS, STREAMS, PONDS, AND LAKES, TENNIS COURTS, BALL FIELDS, BOAT LAUNCHES, BEACHES, WALKING TRAILS THROUGH WOODS, PRAIRIE, AND MARSH, STATE DEDICATED NATURE PRESERVES, A CHAMPIONSHIP GOLF COURSE,

creative playgrounds, Vietnam Veteran's Memorial, the largest wetland restoration in the state, dozens of special events, a fantastic wedding gazebo, and Indiana's premiere waterpark?

That's right: the Lake County Parks, where the benefits are truly endless.

Balancing Nature and Recreation

On June 1, 1968, only three years after the Indiana Legislature authorized the creation of county park departments throughout the state, the Lake County Parks and Recreation Department was formed. With the goals of providing a balance of open space and recreational development, enhancing the living environments in urban and suburban areas, and meeting the leisure needs of present and future generations, the park board set about creating one of the most progressive county park systems in the nation. The

first park board purchase was 160 acres near Cedar Lake, now Lemon Lake County Park. Soon after that, 69 acres were acquired on the Deep River park site. This was the official start of developing the present Lake County Park system.

Throughout the years, hundreds of volunteers giving thousands of hours have worked together with park department personnel and board members to provide a versatile park system balancing recreation, preservation, and restoration. Environmentally, the Lake County Parks has been instrumental in preserving significant natural areas at Gibson Woods and restoring prairie ecosystems at Oak Ridge Prairie. The Grand Kankakee Marsh County Park, dedicated over 20 years ago, was the forerunner of one of the largest conservation projects in the state of Indiana.

The Grand Kankakee Marsh Restoration Project, funded by the North American Wetlands Conservation Act, is a partnership that includes almost 30 organizations, small businesses, and corporate partners from throughout northwest Indiana. These partners have a ten year plan to acquire, restore, and enhance 26,000 acres

Since 1968, the Lake County Parks and Recreation Department has earned a reputation as one of the most forward-thinking and diverse park systems in the nation. The park system offers residents everything from golf courses to a cutting edge water park.

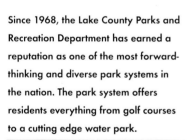

of historic wetland areas through-out the eight counties that make up the Kankakee River Basin.

Partnerships are key, too, in bringing recreational facilities to the public. An early coalition was established in 1977 when the Lake County Parks assumed management of Lake Etta under an inter-local government agree-ment with the Indiana Department of Natural Resources. Today, that relationship continues with the Little Calumet River Basin Development Commission, pro-viding for a variety of recreational opportunities. Whether it's festi-vals, hikes, learning history firsthand, enjoying an active day on a creative playground, or just contemplating the wonder of nature, the Lake County Parks has something for everyone. And when it comes to fun, there's no better place than Deep River Waterpark, where it's simply "splashtastic."

Benefits for Everyone

Sure, parks and recreation are fun, but they are so much more. Recognizing the impor-tance of parks to the quality of life, the Lake County Parks takes pride in managing more than 5,700 acres of marshland, wood-land, native prairie, historic sites, and recreation areas—and one of the largest and most successful public water parks in the country. Parks and recreation are wise investments that provide benefits, both immediately and for decades to come.

Historically, public parks and recreation programs have been a critical part of our heritage. The Lake County Park system is constantly evolving, adapting to changing cultural, societal, and demographic demands and desires in an attempt to meet the leisure needs of the com-munity. Often the value of public parks is taken for granted, but the benefits they provide are truly endless.

Fun for all seasons is one of the goals of the Lake County Parks and Recreation Department. Its offerings range from fishing in spring, to Deep River Waterpark in summer, to nature hikes in fall, to snow skiing in winter.

LAKE COUNTY PARKS AND RECREATION DEPARTMENT

8411 East Lincoln Highway
Crown Point, Indiana 46307
(219) 945-0543
(219) 769-PARK Park Information
www.thetimesonline.com/org/lcparks

Buckley Homestead
3606 Belshaw Road, Lowell

Deep River County Park
9410 Old Lincoln Hwy., Hobart

Deep River Waterpark
9001 East Lincoln Hwy., Merrillville

Gibson Woods Nature Preserve
6201 Parrish Ave., Hammond

Grand Kankakee Marsh
21690 Range Line Rd., Hebron

Lake Etta
4801 West 29th Ave., Gary

Lemon Lake
6322 West 133rd Ave., Crown Point

Oak Ridge Prairie
301 South Colfax St., Griffith

Stoney Run
142nd and Union St., Leroy

Three Rivers
2600 Nevada St., Lake Station

Turkey Creek Golf Course
6400 Harrison St., Merrillville

Whihala Beach
1561 Park Rd., Whiting

TALK ABOUT SIGNS OF THE TIMES. THOUGH THE U.S. POPULATION HAS INCREASED 25 PERCENT SINCE 1970, THE NUMBER OF VEHICLES ON THE HIGHWAYS HAS INCREASED BY 147 PERCENT. WHEN IT COMES TO REACHING MOTORISTS WITH MESSAGES, LAMAR ADVERTISING IS THE NATURAL CHOICE. LAMAR ADVERTISING OPERATES MORE THAN 113,000 ROADWAY BILLBOARDS NATIONWIDE.

LAMAR ADVERTISING COMPANY

1770 West 41st Avenue
Gary, Indiana 46408
(219) 980-1147
www.lamar.com

One of the oldest outdoor advertising companies in the country, Lamar is today also one of the largest with more than 113,000 billboards nationwide.

The firm also has built a niche in privatized logo signage, the blue signs that provide information on food, lodging, and camping on state-awarded public rights-of-way near highway exits. Over the past decade, Lamar Advertising has branched into transit advertising, providing design and placement services for major U.S. companies on buses, bus shelters, benches, and kiosks. The company now provides transit advertising in 17 states. Lamar Graphics, a state-of-the-art printing facility, utilizes the latest in large format digital printing techniques to faithfully reproduce each customer's advertising message.

Strong Indiana Presence

Lamar Advertising has a strong presence in northwest Indiana. Headquartered in Baton Rouge, Louisiana, it currently owns and operates billboards along all major expressways from the Illinois state line east to Michigan City, Indiana

and from the lakeshore south to the Lowell-DeMotte area. Large scale outdoor advertising, including what is known as "30-sheet" coverage posters as well as the innovative electronically operated rotating or permanent bulletins, are offered by Lamar Advertising throughout the region. Since it also operates in Illinois, the company is uniquely poised to coordinate advertising in northwest Indiana with outdoor bulletins in the greater metropolitan area.

One of the oldest and most respected outdoor advertising companies in the United States, Lamar Advertising is a publicly traded company on the Nasdaq Exchange (LAMR). A period of acquisitions starting in the mid-90s leap-frogged the company from third largest to first in the nation. Its purchase of Chancellor Outdoor Media in 1999 made Lamar the largest outdoor company in the nation in terms of number of display signs.

Committed to Technology

Today, Lamar Advertising has operations in nearly every state. Its success has been built through ambitious targeting of new venues for outdoor advertising and a commitment to the latest and best technologies. Of all the publicly traded outdoor companies, Lamar remains focused on its core competency: providing information to the driving public.

Not bad for a company that began with the flip of a coin. It was Charles W. Lamar, Sr., the great grandfather of the company's current CEO Kevin P. Reilly, Jr., who in 1908 dissolved a partnership with J.M. Coe. One partner would take the Pensacola Amusement Company, the other a poster advertising business called Pensacola Advertising. The flip proved Lamar would take the advertising company, the name of which he changed to Lamar Advertising in 1926. The firm has grown every year since.

THERE ARE 57 MILLION DOGS AND CATS IN AMERICA. SOME DAYS, DR. PAMELA J. VERGIN-GREEN FEELS AS THOUGH SHE HAS SEEN EVERY ONE OF THEM. THAT'S BECAUSE HER ENTERPRISE, LINCOLN 'WAY ANIMAL COMPLEX, HAS SINCE ITS OPENING IN 1985 GROWN TO BE ONE OF THE LARGEST AND BEST EQUIPPED VETERINARY CLINICS IN NORTHERN INDIANA.

LINCOLN 'WAY ANIMAL COMPLEX

The Cat's Meow

Lincoln 'Way Animal Complex, with its state-of-the-art variety of services under one roof, is a leader in modern veterinary care—and a very busy place. Dr. Vergin-Green practiced for 11 years before she decided to build a new facility, one that would encompass all of the amenities needed for superior pet care as well as conveniences for customers.

"I didn't start with a budget, I began by thinking from the client's point of view," Vergin-Green recalls. "I simply asked myself one question: if I could have the facility of my dreams, what would it have and how would it function?"

Today, customers believe Lincoln 'Way Animal Complex is "the cat's meow" in animal care. The complex, in excess of 10,000 square feet, contains ample room for veterinary care, boarding, training, pet food and supply sales, grooming, and storage. Top technology was employed in its design. For instance, the isolation area for sick pets is truly isolated at Lincoln 'Way, with no air exchanges between it and the animal examination rooms, boarding areas, or other areas. Boarding areas have access to outdoor runs that are under roof and, therefore, free of snow in winter and dry on rainy days. No detail was too small for Vergin-Green to incorporate into the plan for a model veterinary complex.

Cutting Edge Care

The ever-changing technology of veterinary medicine was also important to Dr. Vergin-Green. The plans for Lincoln 'Way provided four examination rooms (most facilities in 1985 still had one or two) and laboratory offices

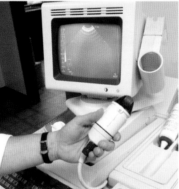

where blood sample testing and analysis could be conducted on site, a service rare in the industry. Today, x-ray scanning and computer software that allows data compression enables ultrasound files to be sent to any radiologist in the nation, greatly speeding the receipt of results.

Today, Lincoln 'Way's customers number more than 10,000. The pet roster includes dogs, cats, snakes, hamsters, gerbils, ferrets, birds, lizards, iguanas, and other small animal species. Vergin-Green has a devoted customer base that appreciates not only the excellent facilities, but also the kind and caring veterinary services she and staff members give to pets.

"We take the time to talk to people about their pets and give them the information they need," says Vergin-Green. "Our services

come with education on how to feed, train, and care for pets."

Vergin-Green is focused on cutting edge veterinary care. That's why in 2000 she received certification in the growing field of animal chiropractic medicine. She also explores the offerings of alternative medicine and treatment—an arena that is offering more and more herbal and environmental treatments for common problems from pet allergies to skin ailments. An animal lover herself, Vergin-Green also emphasizes preventative medicine and measures that reduce the risk of pet disease or disability.

What started as the doctor's dream—"if I build it they will come"—became a definite reality, and a success story in veterinary care in the region.

6400 West Lincoln Highway
Crown Point, Indiana 46307
(219) 865-1201
www.lincolnway.net

The staff of Lincoln 'Way Animal Complex (top) employ state-of-the-art diagnostic equipment including on-site ultrasound (center) in the care and treatment of pets.

Dr. Pamela Vergin-Green (bottom), a pet owner herself, is known as a kind and caring veterinarian who doles out good advice with every visit.

SINCE 1932, MERCANTILE BANK HAS GROWN FROM A ONE-OFFICE BANK TO A NATIONALLY RECOGNIZED FINANCIAL INSTITUTION. THE ONLY FAMILY OWNED AND OPERATED NATIONAL BANK IN LAKE COUNTY, THE BANK HAS EARNED A REPUTATION AS A SERVICE-ORIENTED COMPANY CATERING TO ALL SEGMENTS OF THE MARKETPLACE. IT IS ALSO REGARDED AS THE BEST KIND OF CORPORATE NEIGHBOR.

The Hometown Choice

Mercantile Bank has grown and changed since it opened its doors in Hammond more than six decades ago as a family-owned financial institution. With assets now topping $600 million, Mercantile Bank reigns as the bank that can "put together the big deals" for corporate customers in the region. But it is also still the hometown choice for family banking for thousands of local citizens. Its broad reach, together with its commitment to local communities, has earned it a place as a pivotal player in the marketplace.

Today, Mercantile Bank headquarters remain in Hammond. Its affiliations with First National Bank of Illinois in Lansing, Illinois and Home State Bank in Crystal Lake, Illinois have allowed it to also serve customers in the south suburban Chicago region. Collectively, these three sister banks have combined assets of more than $1.3 billion. In 2000, Joseph T. Morrow, now chairman emeritus of Mercantile Bank, handed the reins to his son Christopher M. Morrow who serves as chairman of the board, continuing a

longstanding tradition of hands-on management by the family owners of the bank. Thomas A. Galovic, III serves as president and CEO.

More than 230 employees assist customers at 15 full-service offices throughout northwest Indiana. A sixteenth office is soon slated to open in Valparaiso. It will house the bank's Center for Small Business, a center dedicated to the burgeoning numbers of small businesses and entrepreneurs for whom specially tailored banking services can mean the difference between success and

struggle. The Center for Small Business was established in 1997.

Relationship Bank

According to Christopher Morrow, Mercantile Bank has prospered because its customers have prospered. While banking in the late twentieth century tended toward the impersonal—with mergers and mega-deals dominating the headlines of the financial pages—Mercantile Bank focused on its relationships with customers.

"We have the sophistication and size to handle larger loans," Morrow says, "but also the commitment to local companies and communities that's so important. We really listen, and we really look for ways to be a partner."

Investments in the people and technology required to build relationships have kept Mercantile Bank at the top of its game. Morrow believes the institution's investment in knowledgeable banking staff and specialized service differentiates Mercantile Bank. So does the U.S. Small Business Administration, which honored the bank as the state

Christopher M. Morrow (left), Mercantile Bank's chairman of the board with his father Joseph T. Morrow who now serves as chairman emeritus of the family-owned and operated bank (top).

Mercantile Bank has been visible in helping such regional projects as expansion of Gary-Chicago Airport get off the ground (bottom).

and region's Number One lender in New Markets and Urban Lending in 1999. Thorough and quality-focused, Mercantile Bank is also consistently named as one of the nation's safest banks by independent ratings bureaus across the country.

Growing companies in the region appreciate the talents and resources Mercantile Bank offers. The bank is responsive and committed to local growth, but also has the assets and sophistication required for major loan packages. Mercantile Bank, together with its affiliate banks and sometimes in coordination with other financial institutions, routinely processes corporate loan requests in the millions.

A Good Neighbor

It is not only Mercantile Bank's know-how that distinguishes it in the region, but also its heart. Consider the fact that, while other financial institutions fled urban areas during the difficult days of the recessionary 1980s, Mercantile Bank stayed put. Today, it is the only community bank serving the City of Gary.

In keeping with its strong philosophy of service, Mercantile Bank's directors and officers collectively serve on the boards of more than 200 hospitals, educational institutions, service clubs, community foundations, and charitable organizations throughout northwest Indiana. It is a commitment

not to be taken lightly, as bank personnel balance long hours on the job with evenings spent in community meetings and planning sessions. The investment of time is well worth it, says Morrow, who believes in "the obligation to give something back."

"I have been fortunate growing up in northwest Indiana and am proud to serve the community through loyal community service and strong financial leadership," Morrow notes. "It's important to be active in the community, helping to spur growth, make improvements, and safeguard the wonderful amenities of the region."

A vocal partner in economic development in northwest Indiana, Morrow has been a steadfast proponent of such critical regional

initiatives as the expansion of Gary-Chicago Airport and the growth of the Lake County parks system. Mercantile Bank staffers are regulars at local chamber of commerce meetings. And there's hardly a charitable drive or community fundraiser that doesn't count on consistent support from Mercantile Bank.

"I would say it's one of our strong suits," says Morrow. "When we say we're community-oriented, we mean it. Those are important relationships, too."

Looking to the Future

Mercantile Bank will continue to be a critical component in the future growth and prosperity of the region. The "hometown commitment"—together with rich resources in family banking, corporate services, and financial management—has made Mercantile Bank the bank of choice for more and more customers in the region.

Morrow believes the mission of the bank and the mission of the region are one and the same: to grow, to perform, and to serve. Together, Mercantile Bank, businesses, and communities can achieve a future that respects northwest Indiana's rich past and invests in its bright future.

"We're invested in this community," says Morrow. "And it's exactly where we want to be."

While other banks fled urban areas in the recessionary 1980s, Mercantile Bank moved in. Today it is the only community bank serving the City of Gary (top and center).

Helping small businesses survive and thrive is the aim of Mercantile Bank's Center for Small Business, established in 1997 (bottom).

Your **BUSINESS** *is Our* **BUSINESS**

SOLUTIONS FOR YOUR BANKING NEEDS

MERCANTILE BANK
5243 Hohman Avenue
Hammond, Indiana 46320
(219) 933-8220
(800) 599-3636
www.mercantileweb.com

THE METHODIST HOSPITALS

MISS MARGARET PRITCHARD WOULD BE PROUD TO SEE THE METHODIST HOSPITALS TODAY. IT WAS PRITCHARD, A REGISTERED NURSE, WHO CAME TO GARY IN 1910 WITH A VISION TO ESTABLISH A HOSPITAL IN THE EMERGING "STEEL CITY." THAT VISION, COMBINED WITH SPUNK AND $2,000 IN DONATIONS FROM LOCAL PHYSICIANS, CREATED GARY GENERAL HOSPITAL.

Within a decade the demand for the hospital's services had grown so much, it was clear a new and larger facility would be needed. By 1923, in association with The Methodist Board of Hospitals of Indiana, plans were laid for what has become the premier medical institution in the region.

In 2000, The Methodist Hospitals celebrated its 77th year of service. Through each year spanning more than three-quarters of a century, the organization has grown and changed, and continued to meet the community's need for excellence in health care.

The Methodist Hospitals strives to be the preeminent provider of comprehensive health care. More than 400 physicians representing 34 specialties are on staff, together with 3,000 employees and more than 400 volunteers. A not-for-profit, community-centered medical institution, it operates two full-service hospital campuses— Northlake in Gary and Southlake in Merrillville—and is affiliated with allied health and nursing education programs throughout the region.

Its Family Practice Residency program assures the availability of primary care physicians who provide coordinated care for their patients.

Today, a hospital is far more than a building with beds and nursing care for inpatients. The Methodist Hospitals has been a leader in the creation of "continuum of care" services and facilities. Because of rapid technological advances, many patients can now be treated on an outpatient basis. Because of the growth of medical research and expertise, patients can receive care for health problems– from sleep disorders to addictive behavior–untreated less than a generation ago. And because of The Methodist Hospitals' commitment to the well-being of the entire community, residents can now obtain wellness information and services that make a real difference in daily lives.

Care for Life-threatening Illness or Injury

A fully accredited hospital system affiliated with major health plan providers, The Methodist Hospitals provides a broad range of services to a wide marketplace. Critical care, providing highly sophisticated levels of services, responds to life-threatening illness or injury. Emergency facilities at both the Northlake and Southlake campuses are renown for trauma care. Urgent care services for minor illnesses and injuries are also available. Since 1976, The Methodist Hospitals has served as the Regional Coordination Center for emergency medical services and paramedic education, providing critical training to first-responders throughout a seven county area.

The Methodist Hospitals has always provided specialized care for heart patients. One of the medical facility's initial "Centers of Excellence," The Heart Institute performed its first open heart surgery in 1984. At the same time, Methodist made substantial medical investment in heart care for northwest Indiana residents. Its services now include a panoply of state-of-the-art heart-related diagnostics, surgeries, treatments, and rehabilitation for patients with cardiovascular diseases and conditions of all types.

Medical specialists in neurosurgery provide trauma services for delicate head, brain, and spinal injuries; surgeries are followed by specialized nursing care through The Neuroscience Institute. The

Doctors, nurses, and benefactors created Gary General Hospital (top) in the early 1900s to serve the growing City of Gary. By 1923, the facility underwent the first of many expansions.

Excellence in caring for women and children is a hospital hallmark (bottom). The Methodist Hospitals' maternal-fetal care program draws upon the expertise of medical specialists in neonatology and perinatology. Neonatal, Intermediate, and Wellborn Nurseries are available.

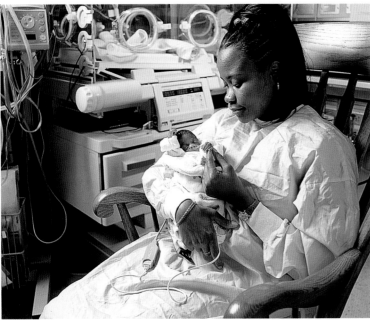

Institute also provides outpatient care for patients suffering from chronic pain, headaches, and neurological conditions such as Multiple Sclerosis and Parkinson's Disease. In an effort to educate youngsters about safe play, the Institute also targets children from 8 to 16 with its "Think First" head and spinal cord injury prevention program, offered free to local schools.

The Choice of the Region

The Methodist Hospitals has been a top regional choice in health care for women and children. A broad and unique range of mater-nal-fetal services administered by medical specialists in neonatology, perinatology, intermediate and wellborn nurseries, and other fields provides excellent care. Through the services of The Women's Health Resource Center, women find care throughout a lifetime–in maternity care, cancer prevention, wellness and fitness, surgical inter-vention, and gerontology and caregiver issues.

Seminars designed especially for females provide the latest informa-tion on a broad range of women's health care issues and developments. For special needs, The Children's Developmental Center offers neuro-developmental assessment, diagnosis, treatment, and referral for children with developmental, physical, or learning difficulties.

Extensive Rehab Services

The first Physical Therapy Department in Lake County opened at Methodist in 1947 in response to patients suffering the effects of the polio epidemic of the late 1940s and 50s. By 1971, Methodist's Rehabilitation Center was established as the first hospital-based service in Indiana.

Inpatient care units at both campuses provide rehabilitation diagnosis and treatment for adults, children, and adolescents recover-ing from a wide range of medical situations, from stroke, spinal, or head injury to paralysis due to accidents. Progressive Care units at both campuses offer transitional skilled care, providing inpatient services for those who need them. The Rehab Centers help regional patients achieve their maximum levels of function and fitness through a coordinated effort and consolidated facility providing a holistic approach, all on an outpa-tient basis. The Wound Treatment Center has given Lake County its only hyperbaric oxygen chamber for medical therapies. The Women's Incontinence Center is the newest program. Since 1986, the Metho-dist's Gerontology program has provided continuous, comprehen-sive, and caring treatment and resources to older adults and their caregivers. From screening pro-grams to support groups, medical specialists help seniors to make smooth transitions into later life, even assisting families with infor-mation on appropriate long-term care needs and available facilities.

The Methodist Hospitals has long provided psychiatric and

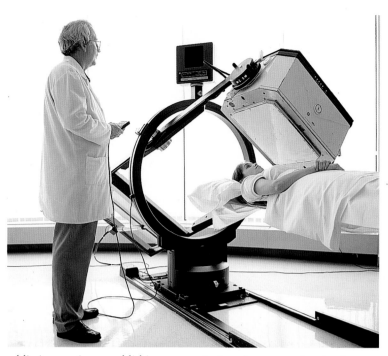

addiction services, establishing some of its most sophisticated programs in the last two decades. The Child and Adolescent program, created in 1984, offers inpatient care and therapeutic classes, as well as continuing outpatient counseling.

Concern Beyond the Numbers

Medical institutions are often described "by the numbers." An increasingly complex and glob-al marketplace, changed daily by technology, makes sense of health care by citing the numbers of patients, the number of beds, the number of dollars, the number of health plans, the number of pro-grams. That is why, according to John H. Betjemann, president of The Methodist Hospitals, his insti-tution strives to always remember the mission behind those numbers.

"Each patient is number one," Betjemann has said. "Our mission has been to provide comprehen-sive health care in this community. We want every individual who turns to us to be healed, to be helped, to be whole."

In other words, Margaret Pritch-ard's vision lives on. She had one clear idea: "This community needs a hospital and it has to be good." Today, The Methodist Hospitals continues to honor that vision every time a patient walks in the door.

Cutting edge care combined with compassion is the goal at The Methodist Hospitals where the latest medical technologies and imaging equipment help patients (top).

The Methodist Hospitals operates two facilities in northwest Indiana: Northlake in Gary (bottom) and Southlake in Merrillville (center).

THE METHODIST HOSPITALS

Corporate Office
600 Grant Street
Gary, Indiana 46402
(219) 886-4000
www.methodisthospitals.org

R.L. MILLIES & ASSOCIATES, INC. CONSULTING ENGINEERS

R. Lee Millies and Ronald L. Millies, both alumni of Valparaiso University's School of Engineering, are partners in R.L. Millies & Associates, Inc.

The respected and experienced northwest Indiana consulting engineering company designs quality and innovative HVAC and lighting systems for numerous educational facilities and churches. Recent projects include Harrison School in East Chicago (BDP&P Architects) and St. Paul's Lutheran Church in Munster (J.F. Architects).

A S A STUDENT AT HAMMOND TECHNICAL HIGH SCHOOL, RONALD MILLIES DEVELOPED A PASSION FOR CREATIVE ART AND TECHNICAL DRAFTING. HE WON SEVERAL AWARDS FROM THE FORD FOUNDATION FOR HIS TECHNICAL DRAWINGS AND THEN BEGAN TO CONSIDER A CAREER IN ENGINEERING. DURING HIS ENGINEERING STUDIES AT VALPARAISO UNIVERSITY, HE ENJOYED THE framework of logic that developed into an equal passion for problem-solving. As a principal of the firm he founded, Millies daily draws from both spheres of passion to—as he puts it—"serve clients with innovative and creative engineering solutions."

Known for Quality Engineering Services

Today, R.L. Millies & Associates, Inc., is a consulting engineering firm that designs environmental systems for commercial, institutional, and light industrial facilities in northwest Indiana and throughout the midwest. The firm is known for its quality professional engineering services and creativity. Based in Munster, Indiana, the consulting firm has provided "MEP" (mechanical, electrical, and plumbing) engineering design services for hundreds of buildings in the region.

Established in 1975 by Ronald L. Millies, and joined by his son R. Lee Millies in 1984, the company has successfully provided engineering services for more than 2,500 projects and now employs a staff of 25.

The principals and owners of the firm are both alumni of the Valparaiso University School of Engineering. Their pride in Valparaiso University took tangible expression in 1993 when they had the street on which the firm's new home office is located renamed Valparaiso Drive.

State-of-the-Art Systems

Working with architects, contractors, and building owners, R.L. Millies & Associates provides thorough evaluations and innovative design for environmental systems in buildings of all types. A large percentage of the firm's work is in the design of state-of-the-art systems for schools and educational facilities. It is in the design of schools—with their critical need for application of cutting edge technologies in

communication and data, fire protection, space comfort conditioning, lighting, and other systems—that the firm has built an impressive track record.

School facilities in the region for which R. L. Millies & Associates has provided engineering services include Whiting High School, Munster High School, Pulaski Middle School in Gary, Harrison Elementary School in East Chicago, Kankakee Valley Middle School in Wheatfield, John Wood Elementary School in Merrillville, Westville Junior High School in Valparaiso, Boston Junior High School in LaPorte, as well as numerous school districts in Illinois, junior colleges, and universities.

Also on the company's resume are MEP designs for office buildings, churches, restaurants, theaters, hospitals and clinics, nursing homes, fitness centers, post offices, police stations, fire stations, courthouses, sports facilities, and light industrial facilities. Well known to local citizens and visitors to the region are such R.L. Millies & Associates projects as the Empress Casino and Lake County Visitors Center, both in Hammond; the Porter County Administration Center in Valparaiso; and the 8-story commercial office building of Bank One and the 120,000 square foot Lake County Mental Health Center, both in Merrillville; and St. Margaret Mercy Healthcare Centers in Hammond and Dyer.

Creative Solutions

What appeals to the father and son team—Ronald L. Millies, a licensed professional electrical engineer and R. Lee Millies, a licensed professional mechanical engineer—is the application of creative engineering ideas for building owners and users.

The internal environment of a building—the technology of which has changed immensely in the past few decades—is of critical importance to building occupants. Years ago, air quality was not a major concern and wide fluctuations in building temperature were tolerated. Today, variations of as little as two degrees are noticed by office workers and air contaminants, carbon dioxide levels, are important factors.

"People are more sensitized today to lighting and to temperature," R. Lee Millies says. "Our mission is to design systems that take full advantage of available technologies that create safe, comfortable, functional internal environments in which productivity—whether in an office, hospital, school, or fire station—are enhanced as a result."

In addition to heating and air conditioning systems, power

systems, and lighting, R.L. Millies & Associates also designs the complex systems required for today's high-tech structures: audio-visual-data transmission, computer centers, energy conservation and reclaim, fire protection, and more. The firm also provides life safety surveys that analyze a building's propensity to function appropriately under adverse conditions such as a fire or local power failure. Working closely

with owners, architects, and contractors, R.L. Millies & Associates stresses the importance of communication between all members of the team to arrive at the best possible solutions.

"Each project involves challenges that engineering logic combined with imagination can resolve," explains Ron Millies. "Our goal is always to achieve the highest functional efficiency within the budget while not sacrificing the aesthetics of the architecture."

The full slate of services offered by R.L. Millies & Associates includes HVAC, plumbing, electrical, lighting, and fire protection design for both new and renovation projects; computer-based mechanical/electrical load calculations; computer-based operating and life cycle cost evaluations; CAD drafting; audio-visual-data system layout and design; performance contracting acquisition assistance; electrical distribution system surveys and documentation; budget cost estimating; engineering drawing peer review; construction observation and shop drawing review; and MEP system problem evaluations and recommendations.

Over the past 25 years, R.L. Millies & Associates has built a reputation forged of competence and creativity. It is a recipe for success that has worked not only for hundreds of buildings, but indeed for the firm itself.

The well-engineered MEP systems include esthetic integration of HVAC and lighting systems with the building architecture as accomplished at Lake County Vistor's Center (D.O. Architects), (above) and Empress Casino Hammond facility (left) (L.G.I. Architects).

The new central air conditioning chiller plant for St. Margaret Mercy Healthcare Center North Campus (bottom) designed and developed by R.L. Millies and Associates was a team effort with the hospital staff and H&H Architects.

R. L. MILLIES & ASSOCIATES, INC. CONSULTING ENGINEERS

9711 Valparaiso Drive
Munster, Indiana 46321
(219) 924-8400
(708) 474-0104
www.rlmrlm.com

MINER ELECTRONICS CORPORATION

M INER ELECTRONICS CORPORATION ILLUSTRATES AN IMPORTANT BUSINESS LESSON. THE COMPANY STARTED IN 1948 AS A HIGHLY SKILLED TELEVISION AND TWO-WAY RADIO REPAIR FIRM. TODAY, IT IS KNOWN AS THE REGION'S PREMIER RADIO COMMUNICATIONS COMPANY. WHILE ITS FOCUS CHANGED OVER TIME, ITS STATUS AS A FAMILY-OWNED COMPANY SURVIVED AND ITS

Miner Electronics opened its doors in 1948 under the leadership of Jack Miner (top). Since then, the company has remained on the cutting edge in electronics and communications.

Service with a smile (center) is a hallmark of Miner Electronics Corporation.

Joel Miner, Janet Miner, and Bill Dow (l to r, bottom) are at the helm of the 52-year old company, established in 1948 by the Miners' grandfather and father, Harold E. Miner and Jack Miner.

commitment to customer service never wavered.

The lesson is that well-managed companies that work hard to serve clients can survive though marketplaces and products change over time. Miner Electronics' promotional message—"new technology from an old friend"—underscores the point.

Harold E. Miner and Jack Miner, a father and son team that saw potential in the new technologies, founded Miner Electronics. The first practical television system began operating in the 1940s and there were rapidly growing numbers of television owners. Also, two-way radio technology was making mobile communication possible—a logical next step in the evolution of communications from morse code to telegraph to telephone to radio transmission. The two men had a knack for repairing the cutting-edge equipment and for trouble shooting technical glitches. They opened their own store in Hammond, where they remained until building a new facility in Munster in 1980.

Miner Electronics maintains its store and service center in Munster, as well as offices at 7 Arthur Industrial Park on Route 50 in Bradley, Illinois.

Today Miner Electronics is still a close-knit, quality-focused, family-owned company. Janet Miner and Joel Miner—Harold Miner's grandchildren—serve as president and vice president, respectively. William Dow is vice president and general manager.

"Customers come to know we never got into this business to make a fast buck," says Joel Miner, reflecting on the decades-long history of the company. "We have established business relationships with clients who can count on us to provide the right systems and the service they deserve."

Respected Supplier

Miner Electronics has been providing effective business communications strategies for more than 50 years. Since its beginnings in the Miner's basement workshop, the company has grown to become a respected supplier and service provider for Motorola two-way radio systems, paging systems, and Nextel digital cellular telephones.

Working as a partner to ensure quality and reliability in mobile communications, the company assists corporations such as LTV Steel, BP Amoco, and Praxair as well as many municipalities in the region. Agencies like the Indiana State Police—for which a reliable communications system is a critical necessity—turn to Miner Electronics. The company's clients now include many of the region's largest corporations and organizations in a territory that stretches throughout northwest Indiana and northeast Illinois.

From police and fire departments to petrochemical companies and from transportation and trucking businesses to security

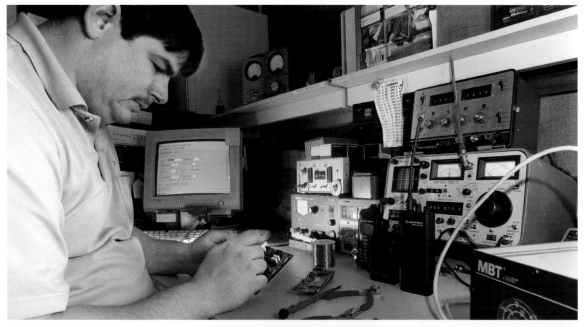

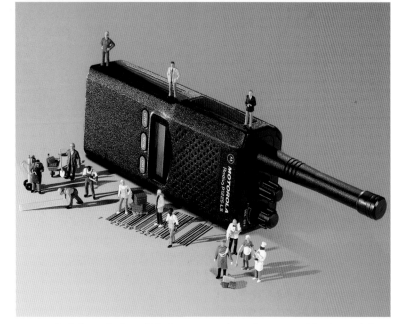

firms, Miner Electronics provides expertise in the design of two-way radio and cellular communications and repair services that keep systems running.

Reliability is Key

Clients who choose Miner Electronics value the firm's experience in both systems design and service and support. Partnering with Motorola, the company ensures businesses have access to the latest and best technology available in two-way radio equipment. Staff consultants and technicians design systems based on each company's needs and budget. A key component of systems design is built-in flexibility that permits later expansion or reconfiguration as a client grows or alters its operations. Reliability, and also adaptability over time, are hallmarks of Miner Electronics systems.

At Miner Electronics, customers find every component of the communications systems they require: system design, product selection, installation expertise, and 24-hour service and repair.

Nothing is more devastating to a company's day-to-day operations than communication systems failures. Failures are handled quickly and dependably by Miner Electronics' highly trained crews. Licensed, certified technicians participate in on-going training programs to

ensure their knowledge of design and repair is top-notch. They also are expert in the use of state-of-the-art diagnostic equipment which speedily pinpoints problem areas and aids in timely repair. The company's fully equipped vans, transporting an extensive inventory of parts and tools, allows on-site solutions for almost any situation. Miner Electronics also provides 24-hour service for clients who need around-the-clock protection. That kind of back-up support is increasingly important in a global marketplace where communication never stops.

"We're a partner in keeping the lines of communication always open," explains Bill Dow. "From the original design to installation

and repair, we consider it our job to make sure each and every customer is satisfied."

Poised for Future

Change is constant. Technology never rests. Management and staff at Miner Electronics know new systems—from wireless Internet to mobile data transmission systems—are on the horizon. The company is poised to welcome future technologies, master their intricacies, and help customers stay on the cutting edge.

This philosophy, together with a passion for customer service, has helped the company grow and change to meet the marketplace for more than five decades and will be key in years to come.

Trained and experienced repair personnel (top left, center) ensure Miner Electronics systems serve customers well. The company's client roster includes a host of major corporations and government agencies that require high reliability and maximum flexibility in two-way radio communication.

A technician at Miner Electronics (top right) uses his expertise to install a state-of-the-art Mobile Data System in an Illinois State Police car.

Miner Electronics has enjoyed a relationship with Motorola since 1948. Today the company is a respected Motorola radio systems design and repair firm (bottom).

MINER ELECTRONICS CORPORATION

500 45th Avenue
Munster, Indiana 46321
(219) 924-1765
(708) 474-7720
www.MinerElectronics.com

N ATIONAL METAL SERVICES CORP. IS A PREMIER EXECUTIVE SEARCH AND RECRUITMENT COMPANY SERVING HEAVY INDUSTRY AROUND THE GLOBE. THE INDEPENDENT NORTHWEST INDIANA FIRM, ESTABLISHED IN 1978, HAS BUILT A TRACK RECORD IN THE RECRUITMENT OF EXPERIENCED MANAGEMENT PERSONNEL FOR THE STEEL, STEEL PROCESSING, METALS, MINING,

machining, fabricating, and other heavy industries.

Recruitment Track Record

National Metal Services Corp. assists established and new companies in locating personnel whose education, talents, experience, and professional goals make a good match with the client firms' needs and strategic plans. Owner John Penrod and his staff, who bring to the task combined experience of more than 60 years in the recruitment field, serve markets in the U.S. and overseas. With an active roster of about 450 client companies and approximately 500 recruitment requests at any given time, the corporation currently handles about 90 percent of the personnel search and recruitment needs of the country's fully integrated steel mills. People are recruited for jobs in manufacturing, marketing, and sales with major industrial companies.

Clients trust National Metal Services Corp. to find the best available people for any position.

According to Penrod, two factors have contributed to the corporation's success. First, the company has always stressed the importance of long-term client relationships. Because National Metal recruiters know each industry and individual business "inside-out," they are able to quickly and effectively assess client needs and understand client goals.

"We have served some of our longstanding clients for 30 or more years," Penrod explains. "Our knowledge of the customer's business—from the nitty-gritty, day-to-day operations to the long-range corporate vision, helps us locate prospective employees who fit the industry, the experience model, and the personality of each client firm."

A second spur to the corporation's success is a commitment to the field of employee recruitment. The world of business offers an ever-changing and growing marketplace. National Metal Services staffers keep abreast of industry trends and study the new technologies that impact personnel search and recruitment.

"The manufacturing environment has changed vastly in the last decade," Penrod says. "One of our goals is to integrate what we know about the complexities and technologies of industries today and apply that knowledge to serve customer needs."

Penrod and his staff also draw upon their experience in industrial settings. For instance, before entering the recruitment arena, Penrod—who earned a degree in electronics engineering—worked in instrument repair, engineering, and on industrial development projects for companies involved in everything from steel manufacturing to aircraft engine design in the Chicago metropolitan area. In 1967, he became a partner in Robert D. Hughes & Associates, beginning a career in executive placement that would lead to the formation of National Metal Services Corp. in 1978. Originally located in Homewood, Illinois, the company moved its offices to Dyer in 1988. It has been a strength of the company, Penrod says, that he and other staff members have spent time on production floors in a variety of industries.

Bill McGinnis, John Penrod, and Eleanor Woods (top, l to r) bring more than 60 years experience in heavy industry (bottom) to the task of executive recruitment for a host of companies around the globe.

Wide Client Base

Clients of National Metal Services Corporation represent a wide cross-section of the steel, metals, and machining industries. To help steel giant Nucor gets its Crawfordsville, Indiana scrap-processing mini-mill off the ground, the company searched its database and personnel files and located 40 percent of the mill's hired management staff. It helped find workers for PMX, a Korean-owned Cedar Rapids, Iowa company that produces copper-clad sheet used by the U.S. Mint in Denver to make coins. Sheffield Forging in the United Kingdom, a division of Atchison Castings of Atchison, Kansas, turned to National Metal Services for national sales and marketing staff capable of promoting its special quality rolls to flat rolled sheet mills.

An average executive placement requires about three months of searching, according to Bill McGinnis, a senior consultant with the firm who has been in the recruitment field for 24 years, 17 of them with National Metal Services. But that's not the end of the process. A licensed and bonded firm, National Metal Services also arranges for the psychological testing, reference and financial background checks, and other analyses that qualify a candidate for ultimate placement.

"Our aim is to make certain the prospective employee will perform as expected on the job," says McGinnis. "Our clients save time and money when the match is right and they don't have to go through another search."

Every position requires a certain special candidate whose qualifications for the job make him or her "the right one." Since every company has its own ambience, and every position its own dynamics, the professionals at National Metal Services know only meticulous effort can produce good results.

"We can search and find a left-handed, red-headed person born in Newfoundland, who now lives three blocks from the plant and speaks Urdu," says Penrod, displaying a sense of humor honed by years of experience seeking the perfect people for specific jobs. "Our business is about intangibles, which means we're in the expectations business. And we always aim to meet or exceed expectations."

The company is accustomed to getting calls for recruitment assistance around the clock. Clients telephone during the day, but also send out requests via fax (219/322-2957) or e-mail 24 hours a day.

Advice From Pros

While National Metal Services has built a solid reputation among companies who rely on it for recruitment services, the firm also assists prospective employees. People with management level and senior operations experience in industrial settings turn to the company to learn of new and exciting positions.

Keeping tabs on the best steel marketers, production chiefs, fitters and welders, metalworkers, engineering and maintenance specialists, and others who have talent and superior initiative is part of the job of a recruitment firm catering to industry.

"We're on top of the marketplace," explains Eleanor Woods, who spent 38 years in the steel industry before joining National Metal Services. "It's our job to know exactly what companies are doing today and what skills are needed."

▶ Tom Hocker

For prospective employees who know steel or metal fabrication or mining like the backs of their hands but find interviewing nerve-wracking, Penrod has good advice. In fact, Penrod produced an audio tape specially designed to help good workers first become accomplished applicants.

National Metal Services Corporation stands at the crossroads where growing companies and good people meet. Its reputation as one of the most knowledgeable, thorough, and effective of industrial recruitment firms has made the company an asset for hundreds of businesses in the region and around the world.

The firm serves the recruitment needs of industries including steel and steel processing companies, metals and mining firms, and fabricating plants. In addition to employee searches, National Metal Services Corp. also handles psychological testing, financial and background checks, and reference calls that save its clients time and expense.

Each day brings new challenges at National Metal Services Corp. (bottom). The company's clients include an active roster of 450 firms and about 500 recruitment orders at any given time.

NATIONAL METAL
SERVICES CORP.

211-A Matteson Street, POB 39
Dyer, Indiana 46311
(219) 322-4664
NTNLMTL@concentric.net

WITH THE SHOT OF A CANNON, NATIONAL STEEL'S MIDWEST OPERATIONS WAS BORN IN THE NEW TOWN OF PORTAGE ON AUGUST 18, 1959. SINCE THEN, THE NORTHWEST INDIANA STEEL PRODUCER HAS PROVED THAT WHAT STARTS WITH A BANG CAN KEEP GOING WITH GUSTO. NATIONAL STEEL'S PORTAGE PLANT HAS BECOME A STANDARD BEARER IN THE STEEL INDUSTRY FOR QUALITY,

technology, and efficiency. It has also earned a well-deserved reputation as an environmental partner and exemplary corporate citizen.

Headquartered in Indiana

National Steel's Midwest Operations are part of the Regional Division of National Steel Corporation, headquartered in Mishawaka, Indiana. The company began with the merger of Weirton Steel, Great Lakes Steel, and the M.A. Hanna Company in 1929. Though based in Pittsburgh, the new National Steel saw opportunity in the Great Lakes region. The finishing mill at National Steel's Midwest Operations was built in Portage in 1961, on land it had purchased decades earlier. Currently, NKK, the second largest steel maker in Japan, is the principal owner of National Steel.

Throughout its history, National Steel has been a force for growth and progress in the region. The first steel mill in Porter County, Midwest Operations not only provides jobs for local residents, but pursues a course marked by technological innovations and community partnerships that positively impact the region.

A case in point is the recognition Midwest Operations earned in 1999 as winner of a U.S. Senate Productivity Award. Given to honor productivity gains, the award was the first ever presented to a steel facility in northwest Indiana. The plant, a producer of flat rolled steel products for automotive, container, construction, and sheet mill industries throughout North America, was cited for increased productivity and shipments, enhanced product quality, and reductions in costs that translated into savings for customers.

Positive Partnerships

What is compelling in the story of National Steel's Midwest Operations—and the entire corporation—is its commitment to building partnerships. Its all-time high rating in customer satisfaction grew not only from quality steel shipments, but also from the company's efforts to understand the needs of its customers. Today, Midwest Operations engineers and mill employees routinely visit customer facilities to observe first-hand how they can serve clients better. National Steel's Midwest Operations has been the recipient of numerous awards for its achievements from major manufacturers such as Ford, General Motors, Toyota, and Mitsubishi.

A teamwork attitude with the Midwest Operations workforce has returned benefits, too. Since 1984, when the United Steelworkers of America and National Steel Corporation signed a Cooperative Partnership Agreement, the company and its employees have worked together to satisfy customers and create an environment typified by

National Steel's Midwest Operations in Portage, Indiana has become a model of efficiency, technology, and service since opening in 1959 (top).

From partnership-building to investment in technology and training (bottom), National Steel has pursued strategies to maximize efficiency. Its efforts earned the company a U.S. Senate Productivity Award in 1999.

In its gleaming lakefront facility, National Steel produces flat rolled steel for the automotive, container, construction, and sheet mill industries (top).

goodwill, open communication, and results-focused initiatives.

Partnerships with the community also distinguish Midwest Operations. When the discovery of a Karner Blue Butterfly—a butterfly on the federal government's list of threatened species—put construction of an expanded landfill in jeopardy, the company took steps that brought it recognition and appreciation from citizens and conservation groups. National Steel initiated a three-year project to build a suitable environment for the endangered butterfly and opened its Training Center to students who come to learn more about the butterfly and the environment. The company has donated 38 acres, the butterfly's

new habitat, to the Indiana Dunes National Lakeshore so that efforts to restore the Karner Blue's numbers and chances of survival can continue. Now, through a program offered by Indiana Dunes rangers, students and others have the opportunity to tour the Karner Butterfly habitat and talk to park staff about the environment.

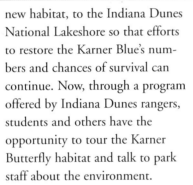

Innovation is Hallmark

Innovation—the impulse to try new ideas and accomplish greater feats—remains a hallmark at Midwest Operations. In 1999, the company opened its new Training Center. The 17,000 square foot facility will play an important role in the future of National Steel, training and upgrading the skills of workers from throughout the organization. From technical skills and computer technology to safety training, the new center is designed to help Midwest Operations employees achieve even greater job and personal successes.

Looking to the Future

When the cannon ball zoomed through the sky at Midwest Operations' christening in 1959, then Indiana Governor Harold W. Handley hailed National Steel as an exciting new chapter in the industrial development of northwest Indiana. Since then, many chapters have been added to the story of the company's own success. National Steel's Midwest Operations has proven to be one of the nation's high-quality, high-technology steel producers. Along the way, though, it took time to focus on customers and employees—and even to save a little blue butterfly.

National Steel's plan to expand a landfill took a new direction when the Karner Blue butterfly (center), on the federal endangered species list, was discovered on the property. The company earned accolades from environmentalists and citizens when it donated land for a Karner Blue habitat and welcomed naturalists and students to visit (bottom).

NATIONAL STEEL

Midwest Operations
U.S. Highway 12
Portage, Indiana 46368
(219) 762-3131
www.nationalsteel.com

NiSource Inc.

ONE OF THE FASTEST-GROWING COMPANIES IN THE ENERGY MARKETPLACE, NISOURCE INC. IS NOW THE LARGEST NATURAL GAS SUPPLIER EAST OF THE ROCKIES. AND ITS ROOTS ARE IN NORTHWEST INDIANA. THE MERRILLVILLE-HEADQUARTERED, PUBLICLY TRADED FAMILY OF COMPANIES SERVES MORE THAN 3.6 MILLION GAS AND ELECTRIC CUSTOMERS PRIMARILY IN NINE

states and employs about 15,000. With impact in states from Maine to Texas and an indefatigable drive to make a positive difference in the energy industry, NiSource is evolving into a model company equipped to meet the needs of a rapidly changing marketplace. NiSource also supports the communities in which it does business through environmental, economic development, and neighborhood initiatives that routinely bring the company high marks as a committed corporate neighbor.

NiSource's primary business is the distribution of electricity and natural gas in the Midwest and northeastern United States. NiSource made a major leap forward in February 2000 with its announced merger with Columbia Energy Group, one of the nation's largest integrated energy companies with gas distribution facilities, major interstate gas pipelines, and Appalachian exploration and production assets.

Positioned for Growth

The NiSource/Columbia merger creates the second largest gas distribution company in the nation in number of customers with 19,000 miles of gas pipelines, 700 billion cubic feet (bcf) of gas storage, 4,000 megawatts of power generation, and 965 bcf of proven natural gas reserves. The acquisition, shepherded by NiSource chairman, president, and chief executive officer Gary L. Neale, fulfilled the firm's well-defined strategy of building a super-regional energy company capable of delivering cost-efficient energy to customers, making wise investments in high technology, and returning value to shareholders.

"Our new company is positioned for the explosive growth projected for the competitive natural gas industry," Neale explains. "The flexibility imbedded in the operation of our combined assets will allow us to create a virtually unlimited number of high-value energy packages."

NiSource's substantial presence in the industry has been built upon the foundation of what it does best. In a deregulated, newly competitive marketplace, NiSource is focused on the efficient, reliable, and cost-effective energy commodity distribution to its growing customer base.

NiSource is also working toward technological advances that benefit employees and customers.

The company employs several technologies including computer-aided dispatch for service vehicles, infrared identification of electrical failures, and on-line purchasing and billing options via the Internet. NiSource is also involved in partnerships to advance cutting-edge distributed electricity generation products, which put power-producing facilities at the site of consumption.

Environmental Efforts

Protection of the environment is a core concern at NiSource. The company views preservation of habitats and efforts toward business sustainability as important elements of its growth plan. NiSource environmental professionals are broadening their roles to integrate business activities and pursue alliances with customers, communities, and stakeholder groups. The Environmental Challenge Fund, an employee-driven, nonprofit corporation, enables employees to show their environmental commitment while offering organizations a funding source for activities that help restore the environment.

NiSource's Lake Erie Land Company is restoring the native prairie and watershed within Coffee Creek Center in Chesterton. The 640

NiSource's corporate headquarters are located on a beautifully landscaped site in Merrillville (top).

NiSource workers ensure natural gas gets to more than 700,000 customers and electricity gets to more than 416,000 customers in northern Indiana alone (bottom).

acre mixed residential/retail/commercial neighborhood is earning national acclaim for its traditional neighborhood design combined with energy efficiency and environmental sustainability. Salmon now swim in a waterway where there was earlier mostly rubble and a diminished fish population.

Service Area is Key

The high-demand energy corridor stretching from the Gulf of Mexico to Chicago to New England, where 40 percent of the nation's energy is consumed, is the expanded service area for the new NiSource. Regionally, in northwest Indiana, NiSource owns a regulated utility providing natural gas to nearly a million customers and electricity to 426,000 customers across 32 northern Indiana counties. One of NiSource's primary subsidiaries, Northern Indiana Public Service Company (NIPSCO) has a net electricity-generating capacity of 3.4 million kilowatts, provided by four generating stations located in Gary, Michigan City, Chesterton, and Wheatfield.

Due to improved operations, NIPSCO's fuel cost to produce a kilowatt of electricity has been reduced by 33.5 percent since 1986. Because of this and other cost-saving measures, NIPSCO

has maintained the same electricity rates in the region since 1988. In addition, the company has constructed a generating system that achieved compliance with the Clean Air Act amendments of 1990 a full two and a half years early and without a rate increase. NIPSCO was also the first utility company in the nation to comply with the sulfur dioxide provisions of the Act with innovative flue gas desulfurization control technology.

Exciting New Ventures

An exciting new avenue for growth is typified by Primary Energy, another NiSource subsidiary. Dedicated to the provision of on-site power generation for industrial users, Primary Energy is setting a new standard of service in delivering cost-effective and environmentally supportive energy solutions. For the last several years, the subsidiary has been helping large industrial customers use waste gases and production by-products to become more energy self-sufficient.

Primary Energy finalized agreements in 1999 to develop, engineer, and construct two major co-generation facilities in northern Indiana. Construction began in 2000 on a 525-megawatt natural gas-fired facility at the BP (formerly BP Amoco) refinery in

Whiting, Indiana. Primary Energy will also operate and maintain the $250 million facility when construction is completed in 2001.

A similar facility is planned for LTV Steel's manufacturing complex in East Chicago, Indiana. The "inside-the-fence" power source will enable LTV to generate electricity using by-product fuels from blast furnace operations. The $60 million project is slated for completion in 2001.

These projects are enabling the company to expand clean power technologies without building significant new infrastructure. Moreover, the existing generating capacity freed up by the two facilities will be used to supply electricity for NIPSCO's expanding customer base in northern Indiana and the expanding midwest wholesale energy market.

Poised for Prosperity

The prospects for NiSource Inc. and its subsidiaries are very good indeed. The company—committed to fueling the future—has made significant investments in the regions and technologies where growth is expected to be strong. The new millennium will be a proving ground for the energy powerhouses of the future. If recent history is any indication, NiSource Inc. will be a premier competitor.

A Walgreens store in Chesterton (top) hosts a prototype of NiSource's microturbine-based total energy package, which is designed to provide reliable, efficient, clean energy for its operations.

Protection of the environment is a core concern at NiSource. The company promotes alliances with environmental organizations and regularly sponsors projects from local tree plantings (bottom) to habitat restorations.

NiSource Inc.
801 East 86th Avenue
Merrillville, Indiana 46410
(219) 647-6200
www.nisource.com

AT THE DAWN OF THE 20TH CENTURY, SAND DUNES AND SWALES WERE MOVED TO MAKE WAY FOR SOME OF THE LARGEST STEEL MILLS EVER SEEN. WITHIN DECADES, NORTHWEST INDIANA WAS KNOWN WORLDWIDE AS A STEEL-PRODUCING POWERHOUSE. A CENTURY LATER, THE AREA'S ECONOMY HAS GROWN AND STRETCHED IN WAYS UNIMAGINABLE WHEN THOSE FIRST STEEL

Tom Hocker ▼

Forum representatives tout northwest Indiana's status as the nation's premier steel producer (top), but also equally important qualities like its national and local parks, excellent schools, and well-managed municipalities.

Northwest Indiana Forum president Thomas McDermott (center) regularly speaks to business and citizen groups about the region.

Business skills and know-how are taught to budding entrepreneurs through the Forum's Small Business Development Centers (bottom).

ingots were poured. Today the region is also a manufacturing giant, a transportation crossroads, an agricultural marvel, a health care center, and a tourist destination.

Region of Riches

Just as a booming business needs a strong marketing department, the region required an advocate for economic growth and diversity—an organization dedicated to the task of spreading the word that northwest Indiana was tough enough to produce steel, but also rich in the resources needed for a multitude

of businesses. Since its incorporation in 1979, the Northwest Indiana Forum has been that advocate. A private, not-for-profit, economic development organization funded largely by regional corporations, the Forum has for 21 years served as a catalyst in introducing businesses to northwest Indiana and helping existing companies to flourish. It is governed by a Board of Directors representing a wide variety of northwest Indiana industries.

It's often said "marketing is a dirty job, but someone's got to do it." No sentiment could be further from the thoughts of Forum officers and staffers who relish the daily opportunity to tout the region's major selling points. Partnering with area businesses and government agencies, the Forum has helped attract more than $1.25 billion in new capital investment and 12,000 jobs to the region since 1993.

The Whole Pie

Northwest Indiana has an amazing array of benefits for businesses and residents," Forum president Thomas M. McDermott

explains. "In addition to its prime transportation hub location, favorable business climate, and committed workforce, the region has the kind of amenities that attract top employers. That's because we also focus on Quality of Life—from the preservation of the Dunes to the building of parks and support of local schools."

In other words, according to McDermott, the seven-county (Lake, Porter, LaPorte, Jasper, Newton, Pulaski, and Starke) region offers prospective businesses not just one slice, but the whole pie.

"We're not promoting one advantage," he said. "We've got

ia menu of them—and that makes a difference in this new world of competitive, high-tech, global economic development initiatives."

The Northwest Indiana Forum uses a three-part strategy to achieve its goals. First, it works to improve market fundamentals in the areas of taxation, environmental quality, transportation infrastructure, workforce development, health care, and regional image to better position existing businesses for expansion of their operations in the region. Second, the Forum attracts new industries to northwest Indiana that offer workers good incomes and the economy a healthy diversification. Third, it stimulates business development and growth among local companies through its Small Business Development Centers that provide no-fee marketing and financial consulting, technical assistance, and access to sources of competitively priced capital.

A Beautiful Place

More than 550,000 tons of steel are still produced in northwest Indiana every week—almost twice what any other area turns out. But what the Northwest Indiana Forum touts goes beyond that "tough exterior" to the colorful and creative. It is an image expressed in the series of posters the Northwest Indiana Forum introduced in 1997. Based on the 1920s posters commissioned by South Shore railroad magnate Samuel Insull, the popular posters bring attention not only to a commodious business climate, but a cultural climate enriched by universities, symphonies and art organizations, Lake Michigan waves and historic farmsteads, and an internationally known port and a growing airport, among other highlights.

Once a "well-kept secret," northwest Indiana is now celebrated via the award-winning posters in homes and offices worldwide. That just proves, says McDermott, that when it comes to the region's promising future, the writing is on the wall.

The South Shore posters, a new series based on the historical posters commissioned by railroad magnate Samuel Insull in the 1920s, have provided high-impact promotion for northwest Indiana. The colorful and creative posters (top) are a huge hit, and have earned top marks for their ability to convey regional assets like the Indiana Dunes National Lakeshore (bottom).

NORTHWEST INDIANA FORUM

6100 Southport Road
Portage, Indiana 46368
(219) 763-6303
www.nwiforum.org

WORLD WAR II WAS OVER, AND THE CIRCUS HAD COME TO TOWN. AND AS HE SAT ONE DAY IN HIS OFFICE, PROFESSOR HAROLD WILLIAMSON SENSED A STRANGE PRESENCE. PURDUE CALUMET'S REGIONAL PRESENCE IN THOSE POST-WORLD WAR II DAYS WAS A SMATTERING OF ROOMS AND AFTER-HOUR LABORATORIES IN A HODGEPODGE OF BUILDINGS THROUGHOUT THE AREA.

The circus was making its annual appearance at Hammond's Civic Center the morning Professor Williamson didn't quite feel alone in his office. There was a ticket window in the wall above his desk. It happened to be open, prompting the good professor to poke his head through for a look-see. Legend has it that Professor Williamson's curiosity found him face to, uh, trunk with an equally curious elephant.

Professors—and, for that matter, elephants—have come and gone during Purdue University Calumet's half century-plus existence. But the Hammond-based university's influence on the Calumet region never has been greater.

World War II Roots

The region's largest institution of higher learning was conceived during the specialized training demand years of World War II. Eager, after the war ended, to extend its educational facilities to residents unable to attend the main campus in West Lafayette, Purdue introduced degree credit courses in the Calumet region in 1946.

By late 1951, the construction in Hammond's Woodmar neighborhood of what is now the Gyte Science Building marked a permanent campus home for Purdue's Calumet extension. Today, Purdue Calumet is a sprawling, 14-building, 167-acre campus that serves more than 9,000 students from 17 to 70 years of age.

Complete associate, baccalaureate and master's degree programs are offered in some 100 fields of study. Classes also are taught off-campus in Merrillville, Crown Point, and St. John.

Academic programs feature traditional Purdue strengths in such professional fields as nursing and management/business; as well as natural, behavioral, and social sciences; liberal arts and the humanities; and—of course—engineering and technologies. Purdue Calumet's commitment to technological instructional resources is unprecedented locally. Northwest Indiana's industrial nature has prompted the introduction of various academic programs in fields and disciplines specific to regional needs.

The campus' Donald S. Powers Computer Education Building, with its impressive collection of computing resources, has helped cultivate Purdue Calumet's reputation as a regional computing center.

Alumni Verify Quality

Another reputation—for delivering quality education—was verified in a recent survey of alumni four, seven and 10 years out of school. Some 97 percent indicated that they consider their Purdue Calumet education as good as or better than the education of alumni from other colleges/universities.

Beyond degree offerings, some 15 short term, professional certificate programs have helped workers in the region bolster job skills.

Leveraging university resources and expertise to provide training for local business and industry through the Purdue Calumet Resource Center typifies the university's commitment to region-enhancing outreach.

Purdue Calumet also reaches out to the region with services, expertise, and learning opportunities through these campus-based centers of excellence: The Entrepreneurship Center, which offers unique, specialized training with a track record of helping small business owners succeed; the Charlotte R. Riley Child

Academic programs at Purdue University Calumet feature university strengths in science and technology (bottom).

Center, an accredited child care facility for 3-to-12-year-olds which doubles as a teaching lab for Early Childhood Development degree program students; the Gerontology Center, with information, instruction, and assistance for older citizens and area professionals; the Head Start XXI Resource Center, offering resources, expertise, and training for Head Start families and teachers; the Marriage & Family Therapy Center, with help for families and couples provided by supervised marriage and family therapy graduate students; the Total Fitness Center, a multi-faceted, time-efficient exercise facility, staffed by exercise physiologists; International Business Development, known for its programs and opportunities for those who conduct business abroad; and the aforementioned Resource Center, providing professional development and personal enrichment training.

Impact In the Region

Additionally, outreach is conveyed through the university's Professional Development Schools initiative, in which university faculty and students interact with area school systems to enhance teaching and learning.

Purdue Calumet also partners with the Challenger Learning Center of Northwest Indiana to provide a campus home for the Center's simulated, multi-faceted outer space-based learning experience, geared primarily for upper elementary and middle school students.

What's more, scholarship dollars continue to increase; more than 30,000 degrees have been awarded; and outside the classroom, men's and women's varsity basketball teams provide a region-wide source of sports pride.

The circus still comes to town... and Purdue Calumet is playing a center stage role in its impact on the Calumet region.

Students enjoy the lovely campus in Hammond (top and bottom), but may also study at off-campus sites in Merrillville, Crown Point, and St. John.

Short term, professional certificate programs offered by the university help the region's workers bolster their job skills (center).

PURDUE UNIVERSITY CALUMET

2200 169th Street
Hammond, Indiana 46323
(800) HI-PURDUE
www.calumet.purdue.edu

Since 1986, Pollution Control Industries (PCI) has been providing responsible waste management for business, industry, and municipal clients that conserves valuable resources and shows respect for the environment. PCI operates nationwide with three major full-service waste processing facilities, one of which is in East Chicago.

POLLUTION CONTROL INDUSTRIES

4343 Kennedy Avenue
East Chicago, Indiana 46312
(800) 388-7242
www.pollutioncontrol.com

Partnering with communities, Pollution Control Industries sponsors local household waste collections and contributes to neighborhood initiatives like a recent outdoor mural project in East Chicago (top).

Computerized tracking systems at PCI monitor all waste handling from intake to disposal (right).

Advanced facilities allow the company to safely process a wide range of waste materials and recycle many for use as fuel (bottom).

PCI offers a valuable service that benefits all citizens of the region. Effective, safe recycling and treatment of waste materials—a natural by-product of the manufacturing of goods that make life better—is key to healthy communities.

The company's expertise is wide-ranging. PCI is the firm of choice for handling, recycling, and treatment of hazardous compounds like paints, inks, and plastics at industrial and manufacturing sites in the region. The company also helps many local communities develop and conduct massive household hazardous waste collections. These "Save the Earth" community waste drives ensure that paint cans and other solid waste find their way into cement kilns for use as fuel rather than spoiling the landscape or jeopardizing public health.

One of the nation's most experienced hazardous and non-hazardous waste handlers and processors, PCI offers a variety of services and waste management options for consumer product manufacturers, businesses, and municipalities. The East Chicago facility is not an incinerator or final disposal site for any materials. Instead, materials are shipped from PCI to other regulated facilities. PCI strives to conduct every aspect of its business in an evironmentally sound manner and to stand as a role model for other companies in the environmental management industry. As PCI continues to prosper, they will continue to create local job opportunities and also remain active in community organizations—giving back to the city where PCI was founded— East Chicago.

Advanced Technology

Licensed and trained professionals adept at the handling of hazardous materials are at the heart of the operation. So are specially designed facilities for the recycling and treatment of collected waste. For example, PCI's "shredding tower," an automated drum processing tower that shreds and separates metal containers and other solid wastes, produces liquid and solid fuel products. The company's unique aerosol can recycling system reclaims propellants, contents, and containers without waste. This technology allows PCI to accept and recycle virtually any commercial aerosol product. Much of the waste PCI recycles is sent off site for use as fuel in cement kilns, minimizing the use of precious fossil fuels like coal or natural gas.

An advanced Lab Pack/Depack facility at PCI makes the processing of small quantity laboratory waste efficient and affordable. While modular work areas ensure worker safety and protect the environment by containing vapors, a special bar code tracking system closely monitors the entire process from intake to disposal.

According to Robert Campbell, president and CEO, it may look like a dirty job, but his company is glad to do it. "For many years, industry has had no place to turn for the safe and efficient recycling of waste materials," he says. "We view our work as an important part of the partnership when it comes to safeguarding human health and the environment."

RADIO ONE
COMMUNICATIONS

Radio One Communications president Leigh Ellis (center) with members of the staff at the company's Valparaiso headquarters (top).

Covering a territory that stretches from Chicago to South Bend, Indiana 105 has earned status as the midwest's longest-running, continuous Country format radio station (bottom).

that—is today known as the preeminent voice of northwest Indiana. The family-owned communications company has not only built a committed listenership in a territory that now extends from Chicago to South Bend, but also has received a trophy case of awards for its high ratings, news coverage, and creative advertising. Moreover, it is keeping the region

at the forefront of radio technology, switching from analog to bring the first fully digitally-operated station to northwest Indiana.

One Company, Four Entities

Radio One Communications may be more precisely described as four businesses in one. In addition to WLJE-FM, widely known as Indiana 105, the company also operates WAKE Radio (AM 1500), TimeTemp, and Indiana On Hold. WAKE-AM serves primarily Porter County and sections of Lake, LaPorte, and Jasper counties with adult format music, news, and information. Its adult pop standards format—from Frank Sinatra and Bing Crosby to the big band sounds—brings timeless favorites into mature households. TimeTemp provides advertiser-paid, accurate time and temperature via telephone, while Indiana On Hold offers regional businesses top-quality studio production of targeted marketing messages for customers temporarily on hold.

Under the direction of president and general manager Leigh Ellis, Radio One Communications operates from offices and studios at 2755 Sager Road. The Valparaiso location has been home to the company for just under four decades and through six additions to the facility.

Don't Go Changin'

As the popular song advises, Radio One Communications hasn't gone through changes spurred by toadying to every passing trend. For instance, its flagship Indiana 105 boasts status as the longest-running continuous Country format radio station in the midwest. The commitment hasn't just been to country, but to customers. Radio One research proved listeners like what they hear on Indiana 105. If music is a main focus, so is local news. Indiana 105, and WAKE Radio, too, are deemed the hot spots on the dial for definitive coverage of northwest Indiana news, sports, weather, and traffic. From commuters on the highway battling rush hour jams to parents wondering if a snowstorm has closed local schools, the company's stations command high numbers of regional listeners.

Leigh Ellis and his crew of about 20 radio personalities, technicians, writers, salespersons, and support staff listen to the customers—both the general public and the advertisers—with a keen ear. According to Ellis, "listening to customers gives us the data we need to make sure they'll keep listening to us." That's undoubtedly an important reason why a 1999 Arbitron listenership audit showed Indiana 105 knocked the socks off all competitors in its seven-county market area.

Many listeners in that market area—Lake, LaPorte, Jasper, Newton, Porter, Pulaski, and Starke counties—have grown up with Indiana 105. According to Ellis, they appreciate the focus on "all things local." Popular programs, like the station's A.M. drive time "Dawn Patrol," have grown listenership in recent years.

Commercial Success

Since 1964, Radio One Communications has continued to build its rapport with the business community. The success of its stations, as well as TimeTemp

and Indiana On Hold, have created advertising venues regional businesses use to further their own fortunes. Radio One counts more than 250 northwest Indiana product and service companies among its regular advertisers. The company offers its award-winning creative staff and studios for production of radio advertisements. An increasingly popular advertising buy for area businesses are Indiana 105 remote broadcasts, conducted live and on-site by studio personalities and personnel.

Regional businesses, says Ellis, appreciate being able to invest in cost-effective advertising targeted to the northwest Indiana marketplace. Businesses also appreciate Radio One's commitment to pursuing the latest technologies—technologies that are now digitalizing the firm's stations and that earlier earned the company kudos as one of the first communications organizations in the region on the Internet and providing Internet access.

An Unbroken Record

Radio One Communications has an unbroken record of success in its marketplace. It also has an unbroken record of succession. It was Leonard J. Ellis, father of the current president, who envisioned a radio station tailored to the local market. Ellis started his business as Porter County Broadcasting with the WAKE 1500 AM frequency in 1964. It was the county's first homegrown and home-focused radio station. Within three years, he applied for and was granted a second license. The 105.5 frequency, awarded in 1967, gave Porter County—and the whole of northwest Indiana—its first FM stereo radio station.

Leonard Ellis worked at Radio One Communications—the more regionally-tailored name to which the company switched in 1994—until he retired in 1984. During his tenure, the business grew year over year, and won awards for its news and commercial writing. Ellis

himself brought home one of the biggest trophies of all—an award in 1978 as DJ of the Year from the Country Music Association. He was inducted into the Indiana Broadcaster Hall of Fame in 1996.

At the helm of day-to-day operations and masterminding the vision for the future is Leigh Ellis. Leonard Ellis still serves the privately-held, family-owned business as chairman of the board; his wife, Bernice, acts as secretary-treasurer.

Future-oriented Company

Leigh Ellis knows the history of Radio One Communications like the back of his hand. But he's focused on its future. Though the company still operates from the same Valparaiso offices as it did decades ago, its marketplace has grown to include all of northwest Indiana. Radio One is intent, Ellis stresses, on keeping its number one radio station status. He also sees opportunity to expand the company's asset base in electronic media, drawing upon the experience, talent, and high standards for which Radio One Communications has become known.

When it comes to northwest Indiana media, Radio One Communications is a major player. And that does impress the market much.

Remote broadcasts, conducted live at advertiser locations, draw customers to regional businesses (top).

Radio One's certified marketing consultants help clients design effective radio promotion programs (center).

Local news, weather, and traffic reign at Indiana 105. Regional listeners depend upon the station for up-to-date information 24 hours a day (bottom).

RADIO ONE COMMUNICATIONS

2755 Sager Road
Valparaiso, Indiana 46383
(219) 462-6111
www.indiana105.com

LOCATED IN THE HEART OF THE CALUMET REGION IS THE MIDWEST'S PREMIER HEAVY AND HIGHWAY CONSTRUCTION FIRM, RIETH-RILEY CONSTRUCTION CO., INC. THE 100 PERCENT EMPLOYEE-OWNED COMPANY HAS A LONG HISTORY OF DELIVERING COMPETITIVELY PRICED, QUALITY WORK IN A TIMELY FASHION. THIS HAS EARNED RIETH-RILEY A SOLID REPUTATION AMONG PUBLIC OFFICIALS, COMMERCIAL

and residential developers, and industry leaders. Since 1916, Rieth-Riley has been satisfying customers by providing a wide range of diversified construction services.

Proven Track Record

Residents throughout Rieth-Riley's primary service areas of Indiana, Illinois, and Michigan know the company's work well. The company has built thousands of miles of streets and highways on which they travel, runways at airports from which they depart, and roads and parking lots they use to access residential developments and shopping centers. Much of the infrastructure at commercial centers and steel mills where area residents work has been built by Rieth-Riley.

Rieth-Riley is the company of choice for clients building major projects, particularly those that require fast track construction. The company is uniquely positioned to self-perform work which would typically be subcontracted out to a number of different contractors. In-house sitework capabilities

include earthmoving, storm and sanitary sewers, water lines, hot mix asphalt and concrete paving, curbs and gutters, concrete flatwork, and material recycling. Heavy construction capabilities include footings and foundations, pile driving, and bridge construction.

New Challenges Welcome

Most of the company's in-house abilities were utilized during the construction "frenzy" which took place during the race to open the region's gaming facilities. Facility operators took notice of the advantages gained by contracting

with Rieth-Riley, a firm that consistently delivers as promised. Rieth-Riley has an established history of exploring new frontiers where others have never been. Knowledge gained through such experience gives the company an edge over their competitors. In 1916, the company had the honor of receiving the first contract ever awarded by the Indiana Department of Highways. Nearly 50 years later, Rieth-Riley built the first segment of the Indiana Toll Road, and in 1998 the company completed the first design/ build construction project initiated by the Indiana Department of Transportation.

Multiple, permanent hot mix asphalt plants and operational facilities located across the Calumet region enable the company to service customers' needs

expeditiously and competitively, regardless of where the project is located. The company owns and operates several portable concrete plants that are often set up on the job site, reducing the cost to the customer and increasing productivity. Company-owned portable asphalt plants are also available for use on projects.

State-of-the-art, high production plants and equipment are staple marks of Rieth-Riley. Heavy investment in technology has contributed significantly to the company's place at the top of its industry. Engineers, estimators, and surveyors are outfitted with the latest computer hardware and software, while field personnel operate computer-controlled equipment and plants.

Investing in the Future

The impact of Rieth-Riley's investment in equipment and technology, however, takes a back seat to its investment in people. Since 1986, Rieth-Riley has been employee-owned. Today, it is one of the few large construction companies in the country to be 100 percent employee-owned. Ownership has resulted in employees taking personal pride in the work of the company and exhibiting

unparalleled enthusiasm and productivity. In its drive to be the best, Rieth-Riley has keyed on training and educating its employee owners. Personnel frequently attend workshops to learn new construction techniques, and master the latest job scheduling and estimating software. They also obtain updates on innovations in materials and quality control issues. The highest education and training priority within the company is reserved for safety-related issues. The company's safety and risk management departments hold regularly scheduled awareness programs for personnel. They accept nothing less than strict adherence to Rieth-Riley's comprehensive safety policies.

Honesty and integrity are the primary building blocks of Rieth-Riley Construction Co., Inc. Company employees, at all levels, are expected to perform ethically and to treat customers fairly. The company's sense of "doing the right thing" extends beyond its relationship with customers. The desire to be a good corporate neighbor has resulted in Rieth-Riley contributing funds and volunteer hours to dozens of local charitable organizations.

**RIETH-RILEY
CONSTRUCTION CO., INC.**
301 North Cline Avenue
Gary, Indiana 46406
(219) 977-0722
www.rieth-riley.com

THE ROMAN CATHOLIC DIOCESE OF GARY IS BUILT UPON THE DEEP FAITH OF THE NEARLY 186,000 CATHOLICS IN LAKE, PORTER, LAPORTE, AND STARKE COUNTIES IN NORTHWEST INDIANA. OURS IS A CHURCH STRENGTHENED BY DIVERSITY—RACIAL, ETHNIC, GENDER, AGE, AND VOCATIONAL. THIS DIVERSITY IS SEEN IN OUR 79 PARISHES, WHERE THE PEOPLE OF GOD WORSHIP

and nourish their faith. Each Sunday, and throughout the week, the Church of the Diocese of Gary gathers to exercise its primary responsibility, to give praise and thanks to God—Father, Son, and Holy Spirit. The celebration of the Eucharist (Holy Mass) is both the summit of our faith and the source of our outreach to the world.

Outreach to the World

This outreach is seen in the faith formation that we provide to all, especially Catholics. Besides Calumet College of St. Joseph, 27 Catholic elementary schools and three high schools provide strong religious, moral, and ethical formation for more than 10,000 students. That same formation is provided to nearly 13,000 students who are enrolled in parish religious education programs.

In partnership with the diocese, parishes provide religious formation to adults through Bible study programs, faith-sharing groups,

missions, and the weekly Northwest Indiana Catholic newspaper.

Justice and Charity

Our Christian outreach mirrors the justice and charity Jesus demonstrated for us. Parish Peace and Social Justice commissions and conferences of the St. Vincent de Paul Society feed the hungry, clothe the naked, comfort the ill, and visit migrants and the imprisoned.

Catholic Charities of the Diocese of Gary and its seven Catholic Family Services centers provide counseling and material assistance to thousands of needy people, regardless of religious affiliation.

We promote Gospel-based social justice through the Diocesan Peace and Social Justice Office and through the Heartland Center which, through its research and education, sensitizes people to their responsibility to address systemic injustices such as abortion, euthanasia, assisted suicide, the death penalty, racism, violence, inequities to the poor, and other situations which diminish the quality of life and dignity of people.

Always cognizant that we are a universal Church, we extend our concern for the poor throughout the world through Catholic Relief Services.

Dignity of Human Life

The offices of the Diocese of Gary work with the leadership of the parishes to promote and recognize all segments of the community—youth, persons with disabilities, Hispanics, and

Bishop Dale J. Melczek, the third bishop of the Diocese of Gary, is the spiritual shepherd of the nearly 186,000 Catholics in Lake, LaPorte, Porter, and Starke counties (top).

Catholic schools provide spiritual and academic formation for more than 10,000 students in northwest Indiana. Franciscan Sister Lucy William's relationship with students at Sister Thea Bowman Elementary School in Gary is warm, loving, and joyful (bottom).

African-Americans—to build the kingdom of God.

Our commitment to the dignity of all human life is evident in the care provided by our six Catholic hospitals, three homes for the elderly and infirm, and two protective facilities for youth. Our respect for life is present at each of its stages—from conception until death.

In 2000, the Church celebrated the Great Jubilee, a commemoration of Christ's birth, death, and teachings. At the start of a new millennium, Catholics in northwest Indiana and around the world have joined together to seek greater understanding and to renew their faith. The theological virtues of faith, hope, and charity served as guides in millennium preparations, designed to strengthen Christians in their faith, provide hope in eternal life, and rekindle charity carried out in service to others, especially the weak and the poor.

The Word of God and the Work of God are fulfilled and preached by the Catholic Church in northwest Indiana because of an unbending commitment to discipleship, stewardship, and evangelization. All members of the Diocese of Gary, led and inspired by dedicated priests, deacons, and religious and lay leaders, are called upon to use their gifts of time, talent, and treasure to continue—in word and deed—the mission of Jesus Christ.

Celebration of the Eucharist—the holy sacrifice of the Mass—is both the summit of Catholics' faith and the source of their outreach to the world (top left).

Volunteers from the St. Vincent de Paul Society sort items contributed to the annual Northwest Indiana Catholic "Caps for Kids" Collection (bottom left).

Every spring, Catholics who have been married 25, 50, or more than 50 years celebrate their love during an anniversary Mass at Holy Angels Cathedral (top right).

Holy Angels Cathedral on Tyler Street in Gary is the see church of the Diocese of Gary. All diocesan celebrations—such as ordinations, marriage anniversary Masses, and Chrism Masses (pictured)—are celebrated at Holy Angels (bottom).

ROMAN CATHOLIC DIOCESE OF GARY

9292 Broadway
Merrillville, Indiana 46410
(219) 769-9292
www.dcgary.org

SOUTHLAKE MALL

2109 Southlake Mall
Merrillville, Indiana 46410
(219) 738-2260
www.shopyourmall.com

Southlake Mall, the largest shopping mall in Indiana, attracts customers with more than 150 high-appeal stores.

On a map of the northwest Indiana region, Southlake Mall sits at the crossroads of the community's bustling commercial life. Located on U.S. Highway 30 in Hobart, and serving a territory that extends north to Chicago, east to South Bend, and south to Lafayette, Southlake Mall is not only the largest shopping mall in

the region, but also in the entire state of Indiana.

Southlake Mall is a star in the constellation of facilities managed by The Richard E. Jacobs Group, a Cleveland, Ohio based corporation that owns and operates 38 malls throughout the United States. Built in 1974 with state-of-the-art design, Southlake Mall was ahead of the pack with skylights and large, open public spaces that have allowed for growth and flexibility over time. Investment in the mall, which offers 1.5 million square feet of retailing space, has continued with a major renovation which included a new food court, new restroom facilities, and construction of a central elevator system in 1999.

Hub of Activity

With more than 150 stores, Southlake Mall is a hub of activity at every hour of the day and in all seasons. Anchor retailers include Sears Roebuck & Co., J.C. Penney, L.S. Ayres, Kohl's, and Carson Pirie Scott. Hip new retailers like Abercrombie & Fitch, Rave Girl, and Thomas Kinkade Gallery also find the mall's heavy traffic, broad regional outreach,

and high annual household income rates a boon to sales.

"Southlake is consistently among the top-performing of our centers," says Amy M. Mellett, marketing director at Southlake Mall. "Sales are strong here and we continually strive for greater market share."

Marketing is one of the mall's strong suits. In addition to aggressive advertising in regional media, Southlake Mall has developed or integrated most of the traffic-generating features employed by major shopping centers in the last decade. Its Real Bonus program offers movie passes, gift certificates, and other incentives to committed

customers. The year-round free Gift Wrap program helped customers pretty more than 95,000 packages in 1999. The mall's "Operation Cooperation" encourages staff and customers to work together to create a safe shopping environment for everyone and provides helpful tips to mall visitors. Southlake Mall is also a partner in a host of regional initiatives, such as providing space for local agencies to promote safety, literacy, and other programs. Not only a superior shopping mall, but a stellar neighbor, Southlake Mall donates at least fifty percent of profits from holiday promotions like pictures with Santa to charities such as the Make-A-Wish Foundation.

Never content to rest on its laurels, Southlake Mall has developed a web site at www.shopyourmall.com that lets customers get mall information, new store announcements, details on special promotions, buy mall certificates and send e-mail.

"In this business, the focus isn't on what you did yesterday for consumers," Mellett stresses. "We're always working on what we can do for shoppers tomorrow."

Oregionality

STATE LINE ENERGY

State Line Energy pays more than $6 million in annual property taxes and employs 114 people. In 1997, it was purchased by Atlanta-based Southern Energy, Inc. Southern Energy—with operations in 12 countries on five continents—develops, builds, owns, and operates power production and delivery facilities and provides a broad range of services to utilities and industrial companies around the world. Its Southern Company Energy Marketing unit provides energy marketing, risk management, financial services and other energy-related commodities,

State Line Energy's 114 committed employees help the company produce 2.36 billion megawatts of electricity each year. Using state-of-the-art technology, they also monitor air and water quality at State Line's Hammond plant.

products, and services to customers in the United States and Canada.

A familiar profile on the shores of Lake Michigan, the State Line Energy plant sits on a 66-acre site. It currently houses two coal-fired units where low-sulfur coal is burned in large boilers, turning the water inside the boiler to steam. Each hour, up to four million pounds of pressurized steam turns turbines connected to generators that then produce electricity. The steam is created by boiling millions of gallons of water at temperatures up to 1,000 degrees Fahrenheit.

Engineering, design, and permitting processes are now underway to expand State Line Energy's capacity. The planned construction of a third generating unit is slated to increase output by 550 megawatts by the year 2003. For this unit, the latest, clean-burning natural gas technology will be employed to create one of the cleanest generators of electricity in the region.

Air and water quality figure heavily in State Line Energy's current methodologies and prospects for the future. Technologies employed at the plant include the burning of low-sulfur coal. The

resultant emissions then pass through a bag house where ash particles collect on hundreds of cylindrical bags. In a precipitator unit, the ash particles are subjected to an electrical charge that causes them to stick to giant metal plates. This procedure is used to remove more than 98 percent of particles from emissions.

Lake Michigan water used to cool steam is carefully monitored and controlled to protect quality. In a process known as once-through cooling, water from the lake is pumped into a plant through a condenser, which is basically a network of tubes. As steam passes along the outside of the tubes, the cold lake water absorbs the heat, allowing the steam to change back to water.

State Line Energy is committed to providing ample supplies of clean energy to customers in the region.

As the new century unfolds, State Line Energy is committed to supporting the region by providing the energy that fuels growth. State Line Energy can also be counted on as a reliable energy source, a company that is involved with the community it serves, and a strong supporter of the local economy.

State Line has been a familiar landmark along Lake Michigan since 1929. Plans for a third generating unit will boost the company's energy output by 550 megawatts by the year 2003.

STATE LINE ENERGY
P.O. Box 687
Hammond, Indiana 46325
(219) 473-6400
www.southernco.com

SULLAIR CORPORATION

Montbrison, France and Shenzhen, China. With operations utilizing ISO 9001 certified manufacturing systems on three continents and a worldwide distribution network, Sullair aims for the highest quality standards. Focus on "market-rate-of-demand" manufacturing has helped Sullair maximize operational efficiency and improve its competitiveness in the international marketplace. Sullair, established in 1965, was acquired by Sundstrand in 1984. United Technologies acquired the company in 1999.

"With the acquisition of Sullair, United Technologies has become one of the world leaders in compressed air equipment manufacturing and rotary screw technology," says Ed Laprade, president of Hamilton Sundstrand's Sullair Corporation. "The compressed air market is often referred to as the fourth utility in industry, and Sullair has been a leader in this market since its inception."

In recent years the company has broadened its business definition from a rotary screw technology focus to a broader emphasis on

Sullair is a world leader in compressed air equipment manufacturing and rotary screw technology. Dedicated training centers (top) available to Sullair employees, distributors, and customers combine classroom and hands-on training.

The company's manufacturing facilities in Michigan City specialize in production of rotary screw air ends (bottom). Sullair, part of United Technologies, also operates plants in France and China.

providing the market with compressed air system solutions utilizing a range of technologies," Laprade added. "This opens up new avenues for growth on which we intend to capitalize."

Legendary Reliability

Sullair makes its name in the compressed air industry with the legendary reliability and durability of its rotary screw air end. These qualities allow the firm to offer extended warranties—up to ten years in some cases—on its stationary and portable compressors. Confidence in the equipment is enhanced by Sullair's development of proprietary, life-extending compressor fluids in strategic partnership with Dow Chemical and Dow Corning. In addition to these agreements, Sullair has successfully developed strategic alliances with some of the most recognizable names in industry, including Caterpillar, John Deere, Toshiba, and Cutler-Hammer.

Differentiating itself and adding value in the marketplace, Sullair has dedicated training centers at all three manufacturing sites that includes hands-on training in the proper operation, maintenance, and service of Sullair equipment. Sponsored by Sullair distributors, regional end-user seminars are also presented by the company's training staff for current and potential customers.

Sullair's global network of authorized distributors and field service representatives provides responsive, knowledgeable service—including on-site, factory-based technical assistance, and Sullair replacement parts.

Leading Edge Tools

Sullair's manufacturing complex in Michigan City houses leading-edge machine tools for the production of rotary screw subassembly units used in all rotary screw equipment produced by Sullair in North America. The machining of male and female rotors—the heart of the compressor—requires precision and exactness to achieve the durability and reliability that is a Sullair core competency. To achieve this, Sullair employs a statistical process control system to monitor rotor quality standards.

These rotary screw subassemblies are the integral component in OEM packages sold to other manufacturers for process and gas compressors and drilling applications. Sullair leverages its core competency in rotary screw technology and manufacturing by packaging these units in both stationary industrial and portable construction equipment.

Serving Major Markets

The Industrial Products business unit manufactures stationary rotary screw air compressors from 5 to 600 horsepower yielding 13 to 3100 acfm (actual cubic feet per minute) that are used in a wide variety of industrial applications requiring compressed air. Such applications cover the spectrum of general industry, with the textile, pharmaceutical, carpet, and woodworking sectors representing major markets. Sullair complements its industrial air compressors with a full range of contaminant-removal systems that dry and filter the compressed air prior to its use.

"Sullair is the most likely supplier of equipment that is routinely used in virtually all manufacturing facilities: compressed air and vacuum systems," says Rick Stasyshan, vice president and general manager of Sullair Industrial Products.

For customers whose need for clean, dry air is vital, Sullair offers a range of oil-free rotary screw air compressors. These compressors provide instrument-quality compressed air for critical applications such as food processing, pharmaceuticals, electronics, and hospitals. For customers who require industrial suction, Sullair offers vacuum systems ranging from 5 to 200 horsepower yielding 80 to 3095 acfm. These systems provide the

advantages of pulse-free vacuum for applications such as plastic extrusion, medical suction for patient care, and furniture manufacturing.

To meet specialized customer needs, Sullair has assembled a Specialty Products team that produces customized air systems for markets as diverse as industrial gas separation, railroads, industrial rental, engineering and contracting firms, and OEM's. The common element among these markets is the requirement of compressed air products with specific options, special capabilities, or other modifications.

Sullair has also pursued product strategies to provide energy efficiency advantages for its customers in light of increasing energy costs in many markets. For example, Sullair has incorporated premium efficiency motors into all of its designs. Sullair has also developed a unique tandem two-stage compressor air end that offers 11 to 13 percent energy savings over a single-stage compressor, a spiral valve capacity control that produces part-load savings up to 17 percent, and heat recovery systems that recycle compressor-heated air for supplementary plant heating and process use.

A Leader in Construction

Sullair's construction products serve the building industry with a range of portable compressors ranging in capacity from 110 to 1900 cfm, providing pneumatic power at construction sites and standby plant air for applications where the need for compressed air is critical and immediate.

The portable compressors are complemented by a wide range of pneumatic contractor tools, manufactured at Sullair's plant in Montbrison. Channels to market for construction products include independent distributors and national industrial rental companies.

"The Sullair name has long been recognized for quality and reliability in both the industrial and construction industries," notes Dave Doerr, vice president and general

manager of Sullair Construction Products. "Through the combined efforts of our distributors and the strategic alliances we have formed with key national rental companies, Sullair's range of products are now widely available on both a purchase and rental basis."

Community Outreach

As a concerned corporate citizen, Sullair reaches out to communities in the region through such organizations as the United Way. Its long involvement with Junior Achievement, an organization that encourages businesses to teach young entrepreneurs, has brought the company kudos from parents and educators. Sullair's own mentoring program places employees in local classrooms. From mentoring in a classroom to running marathons for the American Cancer Society, Sullair and its employees are on the front lines, making a difference in the lives of hundreds of youth in the region.

Sullair construction equipment—portable air compressors and air tools—are on job sites all over the world (top).

Long active in Junior Achievement and mentoring programs, Sullair volunteers in 2000 worked with students in Mrs. Kahn's morning kindergarten class at Nieman Elementary School in Michigan City (bottom).

SULLAIR CORPORATION

3700 East Michigan Boulevard
Michigan City, Indiana 46360
(219) 879-5451
www.sullair.com

LINER TITANIC LOST; 1500 SUCKED INTO SEA ... $30 MILLION WHITING FIRE LEAVES 2 DEAD, 26 HURT ... RECORD 18 INCHES OF SNOW STRIKES REGION. FROM HISTORY-SHAPING TRAGEDIES AND TRIUMPHS TO THE SEASONS OF EVERYDAY LIFE IN THE REGION, THE TIMES NEWSPAPER HAS BEEN THERE ... REPORTING, ILLUMINATING, INVESTIGATING, AND CELEBRATING FOR MORE THAN 120 YEARS.

The Times built its Munster headquarters (top) in 1989, employing cutting edge design to accommodate new technologies in newspaper production and printing.

Readers stay in tune with the times—and The Times—with access to an Internet version of the newspaper (bottom) complete with daily stories, special features, classified advertising, and rich archives.

The winner of the coveted Blue Ribbon designation from the Hoosier State Press Association in six of eight years since 1993, The Times consistently garners designation as the state's top newspaper, as well as journalism awards from the Inland Press and other associations.

A newspaper with a rich history, The Times began life as the weekly Western Indiana Tribune, founded in December 1880 by Hammond enterpreneur Porter B. Towle. Seven months later, Towle sold the fledging paper to Alfred Winslow who changed its name to The Hammond Tribune and made it Lake County's first daily newspaper in 1883. In those days The Lake County Times served Hammond and East Chicago, while other small towns had their own newspapers. As the population of these smaller towns grew, many of the smaller newspapers were sold to larger news organizations. The Lake County Times expanded its circulation by buying some of these newspapers.

In 1906, Sidmon McHie, a native of Canada with interests in livestock and grain operations, purchased The Hammond Tribune

and changed its name to the Lake County Times. For the next 86 years, the newspaper was published in downtown Hammond at the Fayette Street plant. Another name change, to The Hammond Times, came in 1933. The McHie family owned the paper until 1962 when it was purchased by Robert S. Howard, president and founder of Howard Publications, Inc. Howard Publications, a privately-held group of 17 daily newspapers located throughout the United States, continues to publish the newspaper, renamed The Times in 1967 to reflect its wide readership and the expanded area it serves. In the late 1980s, the newspaper switched from its traditional afternoon publication to a morning circulation.

Rapid technological changes in the 1980s also created opportunities for The Times to expand its focus and provide even more information for its customers. A state-of-the-art facility was constructed in Munster and The Times moved in October 1989.

Soon after, William Howard, one of Robert Howard's sons, joined The Times as publisher. New computer systems allowed sweeping changes in the newspaper's appearance, introducing reader-friendly design, full-page color, and cutting-edge graphics.

Although zoning of the news for readers has long been a Times tradition, the 1990s saw an even greater push for regional zoning. In July 1990, a Crown Point zone was added to the Illinois, Hammond, Ridge, and Tri-Town zoned editions. In February 1991, a Merrillville zone was created, followed by a Hobart edition in May 1994. A new high-tech facility located in Crown Point was opened in 1994, allowing for a concentration of both editorial and advertising staff in the East Lake area. In August 1995, The Times expanded into Porter County through a merger with the Vidette-Messenger in Valparaiso, creating a new edition called The Vidette Times. In 2001, The Times broke ground for a larger facility in Portage, the

county's largest city, where a zoned edition of the newspaper is produced daily.

Today, The Times reaches more than 220,000 readers every day, delivered to more than 95,000 homes by more than 1,400 carriers and through single-copy sales at stores and newspaper racks. Circulation stretches from the southern suburbs of Chicago east through Lake, Jasper, Newton, and Porter counties in Indiana.

Vital Mix of News and Advertising

The Editorial Department consists of small departments that handle specific news topics. Local news stories are covered by Times reporters, freelance correspondents, and photographers. The features department produces special interest sections including Seniors, Living, On The Go, and

HomeFront. The Sports Department covers national and local sporting events in the paper's nine editions. The Editorial page provides both newspaper management and readers with a forum for discussion of the issues of the day. Designing the way stories, photos, and graphics combine is the work of news display editors.

The Advertising Department handles classified and retail ads. Classified ads fall into two major categories—liner ads, such as want ads, garage sale ads, and Happy Ads; and classified display ads, such as those purchased by car dealers and real estate firms. Retail ads include all other businesses, such as lumber yards, grocery stores, and retailers. Telemarketers, advertising representatives, and graphic artists work in tandem to create advertising campaigns and to serve as an advertising agency for its business customers.

Photography at The Times has become state-of-the-art, utilizing the latest in digital cameras which use computer disks rather than film. Not only can the photos be instantly downloaded into the computer system, the technology is also environmentally friendly because no chemicals are used to develop film.

In the information age, research is vital to The Times. The research center staff categorizes news stories

and photos that appear in the paper, and searches thousands of data bases to obtain information for reporters and other staff members. This department also maintains The Times' archival microfilm. Every issue of The Times ever printed since 1906 is on that microfilm.

When designing The Times plant in Munster, newspaper officials ordered the latest platemaking and printing equipment. Today, the paper's computer system can send completed pages directly to the plate room where a negative is made or where a laser will etch the image onto the plates, eliminating the need for negatives. Each week more than 3,000 plates are created to publish The Times. Each of the negatives and plates produced contains recyclable material which is captured for reuse.

The Pressroom boasts a $9 million 8-unit Goss offset press capable of running 75,000 papers in 45 minutes. The press' main computer panel runs more than 23 onboard computers, allowing pressmen to control how fast each unit is running as well as the color level and positioning of each page.

Today Times maintains its position as the number one newspaper in the Calumet region by honoring its past and constantly focusing on what's important to the people of this area.

Twenty-three computers allow press operators (top right) to control newspaper production and monitor printing speed, color levels, and page positioning. The pressroom boasts a $9 million Goss offset press capable of turning out 75,000 newspapers in 45 minutes.

In addition to blue ribbon editorial, The Times also produces a wide array of special sections, tailor-made advertising vehicles, and brochures for clients (top left). The award-winning advertising staff is expert at helping businesses get their messages to the public creatively and effectively.

THE TIMES

601 45th Street
Munster, Indiana 46321
(219) 933-3200
www.thetimesonline.com

W HAT IS ALMOST 16 FEET TALL, UP TO 80 FEET LONG, AND—EMPTY—CAN WEIGH 75,000 POUNDS? NEED ANOTHER HINT? THIS PRODUCT OF NORTHWEST INDIANA ROLLS AND IS A PACKAGE—BUT IT'S DEFINITELY NOT OF THE THROWAWAY VARIETY. THIS IS AN EASY RIDDLE FOR RESIDENTS OF EAST CHICAGO, INDIANA, WHERE UNION TANK CAR COMPANY MANUFACTURES RAILROAD

tank cars at 151st Street and Railroad Avenue. Of course, railroad tank car is the answer.

On-Track Manufacturing

Almost sixty-five thousand tank cars have rolled out of the gates of Plant No. 1 since it was opened in 1969. Most of those cars are still in use today, transporting products as different as corn syrup and caustic soda, or muriatic acid and chlorine—even unfinished beer. In fact, just about any end product in use today—from popular soft drinks or the latest shampoos to the dashboards of automobiles—probably has ingredients that are shipped in tank cars built at the East Chicago Plant.

Each tank car is designed for the chemical characteristics of a specific bulk liquid product. That product's weight dictates the car's capacity—from about 14,000 gallons for a heavy product like sulfuric acid up to 34,000 gallons for liquefied petroleum gas—so that the total weight of the loaded car is no more than 286,000 pounds on the rail.

Although they look alike, tank cars are very specialized: a car for liquefied gas is built of thicker steel to contain higher pressures, while one for a viscous product that solidifies at summertime temperatures carries heating coils under its insulated steel jacket. Even cars built for the same product often are equipped with special features and are quite different. Some cars are super-insulated, almost like thermos bottles on wheels, to keep their contents at controlled temperatures for days. Others are constructed of aluminum or special alloys. And, inside and hidden from view,

While Union Tank Car's East Chicago plant is one of the most automated and efficient heavy manufacturing operations in the world, much of the credit for the high quality and consistency of the mammoth product is due to the skill and dedication of the highly trained workforce (top).

Continual Quality Improvement takes center stage at Union Tank Car. Tank welds are x-ray inspected and a team of technicians inspects the cars in an ongoing process as they proceed through the manufacturing line (bottom).

many cars are coated to protect their contents from contamination from the tank material—or visa versa.

On the outside, tank cars can be painted a variety of colors, but most are shiny black and are decaled in yellow with Union Tank Car's identifying reporting mark, "UTLX."

Largest Plant is in East Chicago

The red brick office building with the landmark water tower on 151st Street headquarters Union Tank Car's Transportation Operations. Departments responsible for tank car engineering and drafting, environmental compliance, coating development, safety, fleet operations, and repair services

are housed here. The operations of the other U.S. manufacturing facilities, including a valve manufacturing plant in McKenzie, Tennessee; a tank car manufacturing plant in Sheldon, Texas; plus Union Tank Car's North American network of car repair shops, mini shops, and mobile repair units also are directed from the East Chicago offices. But it is the plant behind the office where "heavy" manufacturing takes place. It's there that tank cars are built.

Plant No. 1 is the largest of Union Tank Car's three manufacturing facilities. It is highly automated, with one-of-a-kind machines and custom built fit-up fixtures. Its four story high,

12,000 ton cold forming head press is an imposing example. This unique machine presses steel blanks as thick as 1-1/8 inches into concave tank ends. The press cycles surprisingly fast and delivers incredible repeatability.

"A lot of the fixtures in Plant No. 1 were designed and built when the plant was new," explains Lou Kulekowskis, senior vice president of operations. "They have been improved over the years, but the basic design remains the same. Proof of that design and of the value of frequent maintenance is that they continue to produce components with the exact tolerances we need to make a tank car. Kulekowskis adds, "Even so, the tank cars we build today are certainly improved over the ones we built in the past. That's because Union Tank Car is continually investing in the process. For instance, now we rely heavily on automatic welding equipment. And we've programmed robotic welding equipment to produce a lot of the subassemblies. They turn out pieces that are consistent in quality and dimension."

But more than the machines, it is the people who work here at Plant No. 1 that Kulekowskis believes make Union Tank Car products superior. "We have 700 folks who really care about the job they do," he says. "We give them the tools they need to do the job right and we offer as much training as possible. In return, we get loyalty. It's typical for our employees to retire from Union Tank Car after 30 or 35 years! That kind of experience—and dedication—is our most important ingredient for building the best tank cars in the world."

Unique in Industry

A drive along Railroad Avenue reveals rows of newly manufactured tank cars stretching end-to-end from Chicago Avenue to 151st Street. The shiny ones that have been blasted and painted and have passed their final quality inspection are ready for railroad interchange service. Some Union Tank Car-built cars are sold, but most are leased under a contract that provides for periodic maintenance and running repairs, payment of state property taxes, and administration and record-keeping. Union Tank Car's customers—the chemical, petrochemical, and food-processing giants of the Fortune 500—depend on UTLX facilities and people for their tank car support.

"Union Tank Car Company is the only leasing company with TANK CAR as a middle name," notes company president Frank Lester. "It fits, too, because Union Tank Car is unique among the companies that own and lease

railroad tank cars. We do it all. We design and manufacture, manage, maintain and repair, provide and install interior coatings and linings, re-market and, eventually, recycle our cars." Lester notes that Union Tank Car facilities are located in areas of high tank car concentration in the U.S. and Canada—and that a tank car repair shop in Mexico will soon be operational. So many facilities, but still the focus is on personalized customer service. "Our customers only need one phone number for everything related to their UTLX tank cars," Lester stresses. "That's the number of their regional UTLX service office."

Union Tank Car Company, a member of The Marmon Group of companies, is headquartered on Jackson Boulevard in Chicago. Regional offices are located in Chicago, Pittsburgh, Atlanta, and Houston.

The company's East Chicago facility is a familiar site to residents of the region. Located on 46 acres at 151st and Railroad Avenue, the plant facilities include 735,000 square feet under roof, tracks with tank cars in various stages of completion, and the Transportation Operations building with its signature water tower.

Union Tank Car's corporate vision is to meet its customers' expectations and to be clearly recognized as the preferred designer, builder, and full service lessor of specialized railcars. New leased cars decaled in yellow with the company's reporting marks, "UTLX," are ready for a service life that easily might span a half century.

UNION TANK CAR COMPANY

151st and Railroad Avenue
East Chicago, Indiana 46312
Corporate offices (312) 431-3111
www.utlx.com

T HE UNIVERSITY OF CHICAGO HOSPITALS REPRESENTS THE ACHIEVEMENT OF THE REMARK- ABLE. PHYSICIANS HERE ARE UNITED BY THE DESIRE TO PRACTICE MEDICINE, TO ADVANCE RESEARCH, AND TO EDUCATE THE PHYSICIANS OF TOMORROW, ENABLING THEM TO PLAY A LEADING ROLE AT THE FOREFRONT OF MEDICINE. BRINGING ALL OF THESE ELEMENTS TOGETHER

UNIVERSITY OF
CHICAGO HOSPITALS
CHILD LIFE CENTERS OF
NORTHWEST INDIANA

Physicians, researchers, and scientists (top) have earned the University of Chicago Hospitals a reputation as one of the nation's premier medical institutions.

The University of Chicago Hospitals is the only hospital in the region that has earned a top spot in the *U.S. News & World Report's* annual ranking of medical institutions. It has been at the top of the rankings for several years in a row (bottom).

gives the University of Chicago Hospitals the opportunity to provide unparalleled care to its patients. Here, physicians and researchers combine their expertise to find solutions to a variety of medical problems—both common and rare.

U of C Hospitals:
At the Forefront
of Medicine™

P hysicians, researchers, and scientists here have been pioneers, leaders, and visionaries in medical research and teaching for decades. The University of Chicago has been associated with 11 Nobel prize winners in medicine or physiology.

What sets the University of Chicago Hospitals apart from other hospitals is its ability to deliver innovations from the laboratory to the patient's bedside, bringing advanced care to patients from the Chicago metropolitan area and northwest Indiana more quickly and effectively than at other institutions.

This institution is the only hospital ever in either Illinois or Indiana to be ranked by *U.S. News & World Report* on its "Honor Roll" of the nation's best hospitals—a distinction the University of Chicago Hospitals has earned for the past several years in a row. Ranked among the top hospitals in the nation in cancer, endocrinology, gastroen- terology, geriatrics, gynecology, nephrology, neurology, ortho- paedics, otolaryngology, pulmonology, rheumatology, and urology, the University of Chicago Hospitals is recognized as a national leader in medical research and patient care.

Northwest Indiana
Expansion

A lthough the University of Chicago Hospitals' main campus in Chicago remains the hub

of medical activity, over the past several years they have expanded, offering a growing network of sites in northwest Indiana for conven- ient accessibility to world-class care.

Child Life Centers of Northwest Indiana

Physicians at the University of Chicago Child Life Centers provide general pediatric care in Munster, Merrillville, and Portage. Specialty care for children and obstetrics/gynecology specialty care for adults is also conveniently provided in Merrillville.

The first Child Life Center opened its doors in July, 1974 in Crown Point, Indiana. In March, 1999, the office moved to its current location at 300 West 80th Place in Merrillville. The Merrillville practice includes three general pediatricians. The practice is in close proximity to the University of Chicago Children's Hospital Pediatric Specialty Office.

In January, 1999, a University of Chicago Children's Hospital office opened its doors at 8528 Broadway in Merrillville. At this location, more than 20 University of Chicago specialists in allergy, cardiology, endocrinology, gatroenterology/hepatology, neurology, neuropsychology, orthopaedics, otolaryngology, surgery, psychiatry, psychology, pulmonology, rheumatology, sports medicine, and urology provide outstanding care for pediatric patients. These experts also see patients at the University of Chicago Children's Hospital.

The Child Life Center in Munster opened its doors in 1980 and is currently located at 9305 Calumet Avenue. The Munster practice, staffed by four general pediatricians, accommodates patients in the surrounding communities. Expanding to meet the needs of the community, the

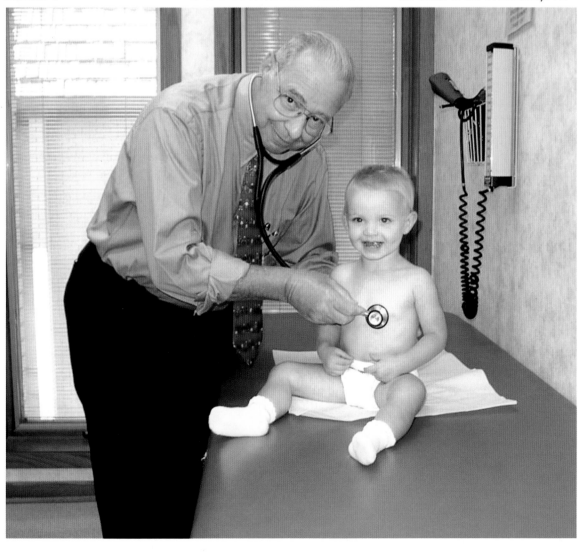

Pediatric care is a University of Chicago Hospitals specialty. Experts like neurologist Kurt Hecox, M.D., Ph.D. (top) bring extensive training and years of experience to the practice of child-centered medical diagnosis and treatment.

Gilbert Givens, M.D. (bottom) is a familiar and friendly face to northwest Indiana patients. Givens and his fellow pediatricians care for patients at the Child Life Center in Munster.

Medical experts (top) at the University of Chicago Hospitals are at the forefront of combatting children's diseases. Innovative treatments and advanced techniques are hallmarks of the nationally renowned institution. They have also helped thousands of northwest Indiana and Chicago metro area couples become parents.

Child Life Center in Portage opened in March 1999. Located at 2710 Willowcreek Road, the practice consists of two general pediatricians and is in close proximity to a major expressway, enabling easy access for patients from throughout the region.

Obstetric and Gynecology Expertise Close to Home

Obstetrics and gynecology experts in infertility and reproductive endocrinology provide care for adult patients at 8520 Broadway in Merrillville. These specialists are the same physicians who see patients on the main campus in Chicago. Here, experts specialize in the most advanced techniques to treat infertility in men and women, and have excellent success rates in helping couples become parents.

Our reproductive endocrinologists provide innovative treatment options for endometriosis and uterine fibroids, offering the latest state-of-the-art surgical techniques,

including minimally invasive endoscopic and laparoscopic procedures. And while these locations make it convenient for patients to see a University of Chicago physician in northwest Indiana, they are all in close proximity to major expressways, making them easily accessible to the University of Chicago Medical Center.

Patients interested in seeing a University of Chicago expert in

THE UNIVERSITY OF

CHICAGO
CHILDREN'S
HOSPITAL

virtually any specialty area come to the Center for Advanced Medicine, 5758 South Maryland Avenue in the Hyde Park neighborhood of Chicago.

The Center for Advanced Medicine enhances multidisciplinary outpatient care by facilitating the collaboration of pediatric and adult specialists. This combination of expert skills and state-of-the-art diagnostic technology results in the most innovative care possible, attracting patients from around the world.

Executive Health Program

The University of Chicago Program for Executive Health, located at the Center for Advanced Medicine, was launched in 2000. This program focuses on the special needs of busy professionals who are highly valuable to their companies, yet often are at higher risk for problems such as heart and lung disease. Consultations with physicians who are ranked among the best in the state, along with comprehensive diagnostic testing, are performed all in one day. Results are often available the same day so that physicians may explain results in great detail and care can begin without delay.

Among the unique services provided to the communities of northwest Indiana by the University of Chicago Hospitals is the

University of Chicago Hospitals' Aeromedical Network (UCAN), a hospital-based air medical transport program. UCAN's main objective is to provide patients throughout the region with the safest air medical environment and the highest quality patient care. UCAN uses one helicopter, a twin-engine Dauphin 2, that flies at speeds up to 180 mph

and can transport two patients with a flight crew of three—a trained flight nurse, a flight physician, and pilot. For more than 16 years, UCAN has provided transport for critically ill or injured patients, connecting small community hospitals with the University of Chicago Hospitals and to other tertiary care facilities.

The University of Chicago Hospitals' Aeromedical Network (top) provides helicopter transport for urgent cases, assuring immediate medical assistance to residents of northwest Indiana.

Unparalled outpatient specialty care for adults and children, as well as unique programs like the Executive Health Program, are provided at the state-of-the-art Center for Advanced Medicine (bottom).

UNIVERSITY OF CHICAGO HOSPITALS

5758 South Maryland Avenue
Chicago, Illinois 60637
Toll free: 1-888-UCH-0200
www.uchospitals.edu

Child Life Center
9305 Calumet Avenue
Munster, Indiana 46321
(219) 836-1301

Child Life Center
300 West 80th Place
Merrillville, Indiana 46410
(219) 791-1580

Child Life Center
2710 Willowcreek Road
Portage, Indiana 46368
(219) 762-7000

University of Chicago Children's Hospital Pediatric Specialty Office
8528 Broadway
Merrillville, Indiana 46410
(219) 756-1200

University of Chicago OB/GYN Subspecialty Office
8520 Broadway
Merrillville, Indiana 46410
(219) 756-1206

G ARY WORKS, THE FLAGSHIP PLANT OF U. S. STEEL, IS THE LARGEST INTEGRATED STEEL PLANT IN THE UNITED STATES WITH A RAW STEEL CAPACITY OF 7.7 MILLION TONS. COVERING ALMOST 4,000 ACRES ON THE SOUTH SHORE OF LAKE MICHIGAN IN GARY, INDIANA, GARY WORKS WAS THE FIRST GREAT CAPITAL PROJECT OF THE UNITED STATES STEEL CORPORATION.

U. S. STEEL
GARY WORKS

The foundations of Gary Works and the City of Gary were laid in 1906, five years after United States Steel was created as the largest corporation in the world. The site was chosen by Judge Elbert Gary, United States Steel's chairman, who was looking for a site upon which to build a modern plant and one which could accommodate a highly efficient facility to serve the growing needs of the middle west.

Today the plant manufactures and sells a wide variety of steel mill products. The plant produces hot rolled, cold rolled, and coated sheet steel, tin mill products, and steel plate used in the automotive, food packaging, appliance, and construction industries.

The 7,200 people who produce the high value-added steel demanded by the plant's customers are essential to Gary Works' success.

Quality steel production, backed by employees committed to continuous improvement, distinguishes Gary Works more than anything else. This quality effort relies heavily on employee involvement to update procedures and monitor processes. Employees regularly visit customer plants to discuss Gary Works' products and quality directly with the people who use them.

Environmental Commitment

E nvironmental protection at Gary Works is a major element of the plant's commitment to continuous improvement. Over the years, more than $600 million has been spent on facilities to protect air, water, and land quality, and the annual operating cost of these environmental control facilities is about $100 million. State-of-the-art technology now controls more than 99 percent of emissions from company production facilities, and the company is increasingly focused on outright prevention of pollution at the source.

Gary Works' environmental efforts are strengthened by ongoing programs that enlist employees to help protect the environment. One program, Continuous Improvement to the Environment (CITE), is an extensive training effort that teaches employees to make environmental decisions a key part of their everyday on-the-job responsibilities. A second program under development is a comprehensive environmental management system based on the ISO 14001 international standard. The fundamental goal of this program is to continually improve the plant's environmental performance as determined by the overall

Designed at the turn of the century to be the world's most efficient and productive steel manufacturing plant, Gary Works continually upgrades processes and technology (top).

Gary Works' environmental efforts are aimed at protecting air, water, and land.

Oregionality

impact operations have on the surrounding environment.

Although recycling has recently become the goal of communities across the nation, it has been a way of life at Gary Works since the plant produced its first heat of steel. The plant recycles more than 5,000 tons of steel scrap each day, some of which comes from the nation's commitment to household curbside recycling.

Community Counts

In addition to its commitment to its customers, employees, and the environment, Gary Works is committed to the community. In partnership with government, civic organizations, and community groups, Gary Works supports programs in the community that contribute to overall economic development in the City of Gary. Among the many organizations that receive financial support are the Lake Area United Way, which benefits 19 agencies in Gary, and the city's Christmas in April initiative. As part of its support of education, Gary Works and the USX Foundation provide four-year college scholarships to area

high school seniors through the U. S. Steel Scholars Program, and to children of Gary Works employees through U. S. Steel Scholarships.

Gary Works employees support the community through personal contributions and volunteer countless hours in community service each year. They have made Gary Works the area's largest supporter of the Salvation Army's Angel Tree program that provides new Christmas gifts for needy children.

While it is steeped in history, Gary Works is a modern steel plant with a modern vision to guide it. That vision includes

being an innovative steel company that clearly distinguishes itself as the industry leader in providing superior quality and service to its customers. Equally important is its goal to be a company that has respect for all employees, creates an atmosphere that motivates employees to fully utilize their talents, encourages all employees to work together effectively, and promptly recognizes and rewards each employee for contributions to the overall success of the company.

Simply put, Gary Works wants to be the best place to work and the best place to buy steel.

Gary Works produces hot rolled, cold rolled, and coated sheet steel; tin mill products; and steel plate used by the automotive, packaging, appliance, and construction industries (top).

Quality steel production, backed by employees committed to continuous improvement, distinguishes Gary Works more than anything else (bottom).

U. S. Steel Group of USX Corporation
One North Broadway
Gary, IN 46402
(219) 888-2000
www.ussteel.com

VILLA CESARE

For sophisticated soirees, ritzy receptions, and posh parties, there's no better venue than Villa Cesare in Schererville. The popular banquet facility, opened in 1989 by Cesare Battisti Lodge, has earned a region-wide reputation as an accommodating and comfortable place for events of all kinds. Villa Cesare was the brainchild of

a northwest Indiana Italian-American fraternal organization, the Cesare Battisti Lodge (#27) of the Italian Sons and Daughters of America (ISDA). The lodge, like many organizations of its type, needed a building in which to house its membership activities. A facility that could do double-duty as both a meeting place and a revenue source was the ideal solution. The members of the lodge moved the group's headquarters from East Chicago to Schererville and purchased several acres of land on which they could construct Villa Cesare. For more than a decade, Villa Cesare has been host to wedding receptions, class reunions, holiday parties, high school proms, chamber of commerce events, and church and civic organization fundraisers.

"It's been a dream come true," says Gino Baldin, manager of Villa Cesare and longtime member of the Cesare Battisti Lodge. "We've built a good home for our organization and a strong business in the community which the people here needed."

Welcome to America

For generations, organizations like the Italian Sons and Daughters of America and the Italian-American National Union (which merged with ISDA several years ago) formed a way for immigrants and their families to make a more comfortable transition to life in America. Established across the country at the turn of the century, fraternal organizations were

Since opening in 1989, Villa Cesare has hosted hundreds of wedding receptions, high school proms, and class reunions (top).

Past president Gino Baldin, president Tony Basso, and committee member Jim Magro (l to r) are longtime members of the Cesare Battisti Lodge (#27) of the Italian Sons and Daughters of America (bottom left).

Elegant rooms, many outfitted with dance floors and bar areas, make Villa Cesare a regional draw for parties and special events (bottom right).

ready-made communities where language and customs were honored, and where help was available to newcomers. In the early days, the groups' aims were simple indeed; the provision of group insurance, for instance, was one important benefit a lodge like Cesare Battisti could offer members.

The genesis of Cesare Battisti dates to 1918, when an Italian tailor named Augusto Vespaziani arrived in East Chicago from Connecticut. Talking with other Italians he met, Vespaziani mentioned an Italian social club he knew in his former hometown and suggested such a club might work in the Calumet region. Within a year, a formal application was made for admission to what was then called the Unione Siciliana. The lodge took the name of an Italian World War I hero and patriot, Cesare Battisti. No one could then predict that the lodge would grow to become the largest in Indiana and one of the largest in the greater Chicago metropolitan area. Nor could anyone predict that the lodge, which for years held its meetings and get-togethers in a small, rented social hall, would someday build and occupy a fine hall all its own.

Today, Cesare Battisti continues to provide a warm family environment and cultural connection for Italian Americans throughout northwest Indiana. At Villa Cesare, third and fourth generation members often take Italian language classes and learn about their mutual heritage. Social events for members build community and offer camaraderie. Scholarship programs established by the lodge support higher education and occupational training for the sons and daughters of members.

Proud to be Italians, the members are also proud to be Americans. Though the lodge rarely "toots its own horn," Cesare Battisti has been a longtime donor to charitable organizations throughout the region. It also routinely

provides discounted rates to not-for-profit groups who book Villa Cesare for fundraisers and events.

Beautiful Banquet Facilities

Villa Cesare is an impressive place. Three huge rooms—the Roma, Venezia, and Palermo—accommodate groups as small as 50 or as large as 900. The rooms feature amenities like dance floors and open bar areas. On-site chef Jack Lencioni and a talented kitchen crew of about 30 prepare elegant meals in Villa Cesare's fully-equipped facilities.

A wide menu of time-honored favorites is offered to customers who have choices ranging from prime rib to roast pork to lobster, as well as Italian favorites like Chicken Picatta served with Fettucine Alfredo and a host of hors d'oeuvres and drinks. Both table service and buffet-style dining are available.

Help with all the extras—from color-coordinated linens and decorations to fine crystal and show-stoppers like ice carvings—are a Villa Cesare specialty.

Villa Cesare maintains a Web site (www.villacesare.com) where information on the banquet hall's facilities, menu selections, and

more can be accessed 24 hours a day and e-mail inquiries may be sent regarding availability dates and special needs.

Home Sweet Home

Villa Cesare is home sweet home for its members. Cesare Battisti Lodge members also hope residents of the region and visitors from throughout the country enjoy the banquet hall's offerings and amenities.

"Every day, we open our door to guests and our goal is to provide an elegant setting and memorable food and service," Baldin says. "This is our home and it gives us a sense of pride to share it with others."

Assistance is available in the selection of table settings, crystal, and coordinated linens (top).

In 1997, the lodge nabbed honors in the Schererville Co-Ed Softball League tourney (bottom).

VILLA CESARE
900 Eagle Ridge Drive
Schererville, Indiana 46375
(219) 322-3011
www.villacesare.com

F OR 25 YEARS, VARIED PRODUCTS OF INDIANA, INC. HAS PROVIDED SPECIALTY PLATE, FLAME-CUTTING, AND FABRICATION SERVICES TO THE NORTHWEST INDIANA STEEL MARKET AND A WIDE SPECTRUM OF INDUSTRIAL CLIENTS. FROM A 40,000 SQUARE FOOT UNDER-CRANE FACILITY IN CHESTERTON, VARIED PRODUCTS PRODUCES METAL PARTS TO CUSTOMER SPECIFICATION USING

VARIED PRODUCTS OF INDIANA, INC.

2180 Highway 149
Chesterton, Indiana 46304
(219) 763-2526
www.variedproducts.com

President Dennis Willard (top) established Varied Products to serve northwest Indiana steel mills, fabricating shops, and other industrial clients.

Automated burning machines at Varied Products manufacture metal burnout parts in 50 standard shapes; custom parts to meet specific needs are a specialty of the company (bottom).

state-of-the-art technology that guarantees consistency and accuracy.

Materials fabricated by the company are shipped near and far. Flame-cut steel parts from this factory may travel to a steel mill minutes away in northwest Indiana. Specialty items, like a recent order for massive steel nuclear containment doors, may be destined for a client in the USSR. The company produces complex parts for OEM's, machine shops, and fabricators.

Dennis Willard, president of Varied Products, believes the company's focus on expert service and speedy delivery have driven the firm's growth.

"Our ability to produce custom parts for specialized applications is critical for fabricators and end-users," Willard says. "Our focus on efficient production and speedy delivery means customers get exactly what they need when they need it."

Consistency is Hallmark

Varied Products has earned recognition for its production burning services. Automated burning machines manufacture top quality metal burnout parts in 50 standard shapes. A CAD

(computer aided design) system allows the firm to create custom shapes to meet specific needs. "Part-to-part" consistency is a company hallmark. Complex parts once difficult to produce are easily handled by Varied Products' trained staff, expert in holding close tolerances and reducing warpage.

Complete in-house fabrication and finishing services include normalizing, annealing, stress relief, shot blasting, beveling, fabricating, drilling, grinding, machining, welding, and 4-sided burning. Company engineers work with each client to determine the design specifications most appropriate for the intended use. All inventory—which includes ASTM A-36 plate material, 1045 steel, abrasion resistant plates, alloys, PVQ material, and stainless steel—is marked with stocking numbers documented with test reports.

Custom flame shape-cutting ranges from gauge material up to 24-inch thick metal. Varied Products houses equipment that can burn with optical tracing or CNC equipment widths up to 120 inches and lengths to 55 feet. All burners are programmed through a CAD system to ensure accuracy and consistency whether the order is for one part, or one thousand. The company's expertise allows for multiple burn parts, a benefit to customers who save time and money on complex parts and who can avoid the expense of machine stock removal.

In addition to plate burning capabilities, Varied Products offers its steel fabricating facilities for projects up to 20-ton welds. The company's certified welders, qualified in AWS-D1.1 Structural Welding Code and ASME-Section

VIII Division 1 of the Boiler and Pressure Vessel Code, are expert in this cost-effective alternative to casting. Individual and short-run parts are fabricated using castings as a model or from design drawings.

Latest Technology Means Top Customer Service

Varied Products employs the latest techniques to assist customers. Orders for custom burns or fabricating may come to the company via DXF or IGES computer files, facilitating quicker response time. In fact, the firm consistently "turns around" rush orders within 24 hours and provides a 24-hour emergency service for its clients. Substantial stock inventory enhances Varied Products' ability to respond with the right parts at the right time to avoid production down-time.

Northwest Indiana's industrial marketplace depends upon the services of companies like Varied Products. Customers see Varied Products as a partner in production, keeping fabricating shops humming and assembly lines rolling in the region.

A HOME IS AT ONCE BOTH A COMMODITY AND AN OBJECT OF PERSONAL AFFECTION. NO ONE UNDERSTANDS THIS BETTER THAN JAKE WAGNER. HIS VALPARAISO COMPANY, WAGNER HOMES, HAS PROVEN ADEPT AT ANTICIPATING MARKET TRENDS WHILE ACHIEVING AN EXTRAORDINARILY HIGH LEVEL OF CUSTOMER SATISFACTION. WAGNER HOMES, ESTABLISHED IN 1985, HAS BEEN

a pacesetter in custom home construction. Built on the premise that clients seeking a residence should get the house of their dreams, the firm has also acted as developer for many of the city's most touted neighborhoods. Consider the Brentwood neighborhood, Wagner Homes' first residential development. Believing the market was hungry for larger, upscale housing with definite personality, Wagner created an enclave of residences inspired by English country home architecture that remains a bestseller neighborhood nearly two decades later.

A home is an investment, but also a living, breathing structure that must meld with the personality, lifestyle, and preferences of its owner. That's where the Wagner Homes staff shines brightly.

"Since our priority is making sure we do what pleases our clients, we spend a great deal of time and energy getting to know them," Wagner says.

The People's Choice

The level of research astounds—then delights—Wagner Homes' clients. The firm goes miles beyond the usual inquiries about favorite architectural styles and colors. Extensive research provides project staff such useful information as whether the main users of the kitchen are right or left handed, how often the family will host formal dinner parties, if a home office might be needed, and more. Homeowners appreciate the attention to detail. This degree of investigation results in a truly custom home. And it has helped the company win 15 first place awards, including People's Choice in Porter County's annual Parade

of Homes over the last 16 years, national honors as a Custom Builder of the Year, and a bevy of community improvement awards.

Wagner Homes has been a developer or builder in the most distinguished community areas in Porter County: Walden, Whitethorne Woods, Quail Ridge, St. André, Sand Creek. The company was a pivotal player in the development of Aberdeen and Keystone Commons, two neighborhoods singular for beautiful homes combined with amenities like preserved open space, walking trails, gazebos and ponds, and exquisite landscaping.

Distinctive Vision

While prospective homebuyers come to Wagner Homes for expertly designed residences, they also appreciate the excitement the firm brings to the task. The company is renown for projects like the Preserve at Aberdeen, where Wagner displayed his appreciation for the arts and crafts period in the mahogany woods, copper cornices, and fine detailing of the residences. The neighborhood also features an intact landscape, with homes

nestled under canopies of trees amid native plants and grasses—an ode to lodge-inspired living.

Bringing distinction, personality, and variety to custom building is a Wagner Homes gift. Luckily for future clients, Jake Wagner has taken a fancy to trout fishing in Canada. On a recent trip, he noticed how street names in the village where he stayed had a simple and literal quality. A street with the name "River View" was bound to run by water; a path marked "Apple Lane" was home to rows of fruit trees. Designed to provide information the way folks used to—by reference to the natural landscape—the names had charm and beauty. In Wagner's newest neighborhood—Harrison West—the streets already have tentative names: Throughwoods Road, Orchard View, Ravine Edge.

It is this kind of vision and "big picture" imagination that has distinguished Wagner Homes in the marketplace. A perfectly crafted home, well tailored to its occupants is the goal. As for delightfully different-from-the-pack ideas, Wagner Homes clients happily discover: they come with the turf.

450 Vale Park Road
Valparaiso, Indiana 46385
(219) 465-1995
www.wagnerhomes.com

Jake Wagner (below) established his custom home building firm in 1984. Since then, Wagner Homes has built not only hundreds of homes, but also a reputation for superior quality and creativity. Homes in the Preserve community at Valparaiso's Keystone Commons feature traditional materials like stone and wood (bottom) and interiors (top) rich in detail.

Celebrating its 120th anniversary, Weil-McLain, a United Dominion Company, is the leading designer, manufacturer, and marketer of cast iron boilers for space heating in residential, commercial, and institutional buildings in the United States and Canada. With headquarters nestled alongside the shores of Lake Michigan

in Michigan City, Weil-McLain has been a fixture in Indiana's business landscape since 1921.

From Baseball Hall of Fame to Mount Rushmore

As the industry leader in hydronics comfort heating, Weil-McLain has never lost the true focus of what business is all about—dedication to providing the best products, customer service, and satisfaction. Following those simple business practices has afforded Weil-McLain the opportunity to provide comfort heating to such prestigious

places as the Baseball Hall of Fame, the College Football Hall of Fame, the Statue of Liberty, and Mount Rushmore.

Weil-McLain's roots travel back to 1881, when founders Isadora and Benjamin Weil created a small plumbing and heating house in Chicago, Illinois under the name "Weil Brothers." In 1918 they acquired their largest boiler supplier, the J.H. McLain Company of Canton, Ohio, and in 1919 the company name "Weil-McLain" was established. In 1921, Weil-McLain moved the boiler operations from Canton, Ohio to its present facilities in Michigan City, Indiana. Together with its manufacturing

operations in Benton Harbor, Michigan, Weil-McLain has facilities that cover more than 600,000 square feet on 36 acres and employ more than 600 people.

Weil-McLain has one of the most modern cast iron foundries in the industry. Environmentally-friendly electric melt furnaces have replaced the old cupola method of melting iron and has enabled Weil-McLain to produce more than 25 tons of molten iron per hour for castings, yielding more than 100,000 boilers per year.

To ensure quality products, the manufacturing process is computer controlled and each step is monitored from melting through

Environmentally-friendly electric melt furnaces have replaced the outdated cupola method of melting iron at Weil-McLain's Michigan City manufacturing facility (left).

Employees work diligently to maintain high quality standards at Weil-McLain. The company is ISO 9001 certified and was the recent winner of an Indiana State Quality Improvement Award (right).

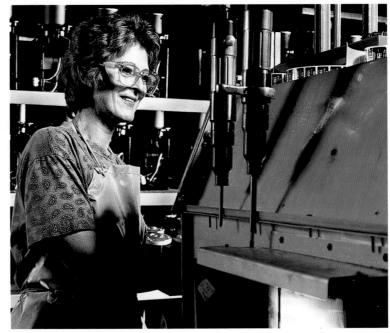

machining. Each boiler casting and block assembly is hydrostatically tested for leaks. Additional testing is performed on packaged units, and Weil-McLain designed and built oil burners are 100 percent fire-tested to ensure reliability.

Industry Leader Sets the Standard

While constantly striving for excellence, Weil-McLain has continued to set industry standards for quality. In 1997, Weil-McLain was the first major U.S. boiler manufacturer to receive the Environmental Protection Agency's ENERGY STAR® Partner of the Year Award. In September of 1998, Weil-McLain achieved ISO 9001 certification, a set of standards recognized globally that provide a common approach to maintaining a quality system for products and services. The total commitment of Weil-McLain employees made this usually 24 to 30 month certification process a reality in just nine months. The certification demonstrates the company's ongoing commitment to providing quality products and services and the tremendous dedication routinely displayed by its employees.

In raising the bar for quality and customer satisfaction even further, Weil-McLain was awarded a 1999 Indiana State Quality Improvement Award. This award symbolizes leadership in helping to establish a culture in which quality and customer satisfaction are incubated and nurtured. Capping a century of success, Weil-McLain was honored to receive the Indiana Century Award for its corporate citizenship and significant contribution to Indiana's economic growth.

Clear Global Vision

With a clear global vision for the new millennium, Weil-McLain has developed a UDXcellence plan to achieve world-class performance in four critical areas: customer service, operations, product development,

and total quality. "Our overall objective is to make the company world-class with the best customer satisfaction of any company in the world," says Tom May, president of Weil-McLain. "Throughout its history, Weil-McLain has been successful because it remained loyal to its core beliefs and values," he notes. "That holds true today in the ethics and pride of our workforce, and will carry our company forward into the exciting challenges of the new millennium."

Weil-McLain, a United Dominion Company, produces the high-efficiency boilers that heat such prestigious landmarks as the Statue of Liberty (top).

Weil-McLain's multiple boiler system allows schools and other institutions to efficiently create separate zones of comfort and to maximize efficiency— both when the building is full or unoccupied (bottom).

WEIL-MCLAIN
500 Blaine Street
Michigan City, Indiana 46360
(219) 879-6561
www.weil-mclain.com

PBS affiliate WYIN has been serving northwest Indiana and the Chicago metropolitan area for more than 13 years. It's unique among public television stations due to its alternative PBS program schedule that features an extensive commitment to local, national, and international news; high school and college sports; the best of PBS

8625 Indiana Place
Merrillville, Indiana 46410
(219) 756-5656
www.wyin.org

Exciting changes are on the horizon at WYIN Channel 56. By 2003, the northwest Indiana PBS station will complete its transition from analog to digital transmission (top).

Special projects manager Nancy Brandt meets with station board member Bob Mummey about upcoming Channel 56 events (bottom left). The station's internship programs train young people for jobs in broadcasting and production (bottom right).

documentaries and prime time specials; plus British comedies and science fiction.

Exciting changes are on the horizon for PBS 56. WYIN is expected to complete its transition from analog to digital technology on January 1, 2003. This will allow the station to broadcast four separate program streams at one time. WYIN is also reviewing an invitation from Mayor Scott King to relocate its studios to downtown Gary, the station's city of license. The proposed state-of-the-art media and technology center will set the architectural tone for the entire downtown Gary redevelopment plan as well as create numerous opportunities for both the station and the region.

At the helm of WYIN is president and CEO James A. Milner, a veteran PBS station manager who has served stints at WFYI-TV/FM in Indianapolis, WFWA-TV in Fort Wayne, and the Corporation for Public Broadcasting in Washington, D.C. Milner, along with an engaged board of directors and committed professional staff, is forging a new vision for the station's future. Reminding viewers to "Keep Your Eyes On Us," WYIN

seeks opportunities for service through partnerships with local organizations including the Lake County Convention & Visitors Bureau and the Northwest Indiana Forum. To help promote the region, WYIN uses the South Shore poster collection—a highly popular series of art posters touting the region's amenities and institutions—for station ID's.

Like all public television stations, WYIN relies on support for daily operations from the local community. Two of three operating dollars come from viewer contributions, program and production underwriters, special events, and local foundations. These funds help cover the substantial utility costs, parts and maintenance expenditures, programming fees, and production expenses.

Station special events are designed not only for fun, but also to build friendships and alliances with volunteer groups and associations. In 2001, an annual spring 56 Sports Auction will cap off the college basketball schedule with more than 250 sports collectibles ranging from autographed baseballs to golf clubs to one-of-a-kind momentos

from legendary sports personalities. Other joint ventures include the WYIN and Times Newspapers salute to area merchants who have earned distinction as the "Best of the Region." The fall 56 Fine Art and Furniture Auction presents a unique collection of fine wine, furniture, and art donated by notable regional vintners and artists. And the social season is not complete until year's end when WYIN presents its annual Fall Gala salute to great music and ledgendary performers. Volunteers from throughout the regional community are credited by the station for ensuring all WYIN events are exceptional.

Community-wide support enables WYIN to meet its mission "to promote and grow a sense of community through locally produced programs" like Indiana Now!, Prep Football Report, Roundball Review, 56 Game of the Week, The Tom Higgins Show, Graveyard Theatre, and the 56 Nightly News.

WYIN-PBS 56 is a valuable component of northwest Indiana's media mix. The station is also a neighbor, a friend, and a force to keep an eye on.

Photographers

We may all, as the apostle Paul says in the New Testament, see through a glass darkly. The contributing photographers in Oregionality, however, have helped us see many things clearly. Credit for the images in Oregionality goes to men and women from every corner of northwest Indiana and from the Times Photography Department who looked through the lens and captured the heart and soul of the region.

KIRK JOHN MITCHELL, *Oregionality* Photo Editor, has been a professional photographer since 1985. Born in Hammond and a graduate of Portage High School, Mitchell holds a degree in photography from the Art Institute of Ft. Lauderdale. He worked as a freelance photographer for numerous publications before joining the staff of the *Times* in 1992. He now serves as director of advertising photography and pre-press manager. Mitchell has also provided photography services to many corporate clients in the region. The winner of numerous awards for his work, Mitchell earned a number of first place honors in the Indiana Advertising Executives Association and Hoosier State Press Association competitions. He also nabbed first place in the 1992 "Capture the Essence of Northwest Indiana" calendar contest as well as three portraiture awards in the 1991 Burrell Expo. His current interests include the emerging field of digital photography and the new technologies of pre-press imaging and photo reproduction.

JON HENDRICKS discovered photography working for newspapers in Pennsylvania. A native of Lockport, New York, Hendricks arrived in northwest Indiana when he enrolled as an art student at Valparaiso University. He focused on photography, an art form he believes has a unique ability to capture hearts and minds, as well as speak to them. Now a freelance photographer for various Indiana publications including the *Times*, Hendricks employs both digital and regular format cameras in his work. He hopes to eventually open a photographic museum. Clicking away in every corner of the region for the past two years, Hendricks uncovered his favorite spot: Lost Marsh golf course in Hammond. "The course illustrates that industry and natural habitat can exist together," he says. His advice to other photographers is to be patient. "Everyone wants an instant picture," Hendricks explains, "but the best come when you have knowledge of your subject."

CRAIG BERG opened a pizzeria in Chesterton nearly three decades ago. But photography is his true love, an avocation he has pursued since he was ten years old. Born and raised in Valparaiso, Berg was smitten early by the limitless photographic possibilities of the dunes and he's a regular there at sunrise and sunset. Area residents and tourists alike snap up his framed photographs and note cards at local galleries, which capture the beauty, uniqueness, and tranquility of the region's most captivating natural landmark. It all began with a Brownie Hawkeye camera Berg was given by his parents. Now he spends time at the Lake Michigan shore each week with his Nikon 35mm camera. An explorer with a camera, Berg (www.dunesphotos.com) looks at every vista as a potential photograph. He tells other photographers to be daring and creative. "Do something different, lay on the ground, stand on something, try the offbeat."

THE TIMES PHOTOGRAPHY DEPARTMENT deserves much credit for the portrait of northwest Indiana presented in Oregionality. In today's world, digital technology allows the images we see to be edited, altered, and transmitted within minutes. The Times photographers represented in this book gave us glimpses of real people in real places. Peering into every corner in the region, they crystallized with cameras moments in time that are meaningful. Times photographers include (l to r) Tracy Albano, John Watkins, Tasos Katopodis, Zbigniew Bzdak, Gregg Gearhart, and Geoff Black. Not pictured: Michael Gard, Natalie Bataglia, John Luke, and Ed Collier.

Jon L. Hendricks

Craig Berg

CAROL BANACH was born in East Chicago, raised in Whiting-Robertsdale, and now lives in Highland. A lifelong resident of northwest Indiana, her earliest memory of photography harkens back to a trip she took to Slovakia when she was 12. Banach's Brownie camera dangled from her neck as she leaned over the rail of the S.S. United States to watch the waves. She took photographs on that trip, and often since. A former elementary teacher, today Banach uses a Pentax "point and shoot" to capture stunning scenery. Favorite haunts include the Indiana Dunes National Lakeshore, the Michigan City lighthouse at sunset, Bailly-Chellberg farm in autumn, and the Whiting Park bike trail. Banach says photography is her way of "capturing images and memories I may never see again—not just for the pleasure of viewing them, but for the wide range of emotions they evoke."

LARRY BRECHNER still remembers his first camera. Brechner received the nondescript roll camera when he was five, took a slew of photographs, then immediately opened up the camera to "see the pictures." Brechner lost those images, but has made up for them since. A director and theatrical lighting designer for the past 25 years, and now auditorium and theater director for the School Town of Munster, Brechner has parlayed his understanding of light and angle into an impressive portfolio of photographic work. A lifelong resident of Highland, he works in both color and black and white mediums. Brechner also uses his talent with the camera in his theater lighting design work. His

favorite northwest Indiana sites include the dunes, Deep River Park, and the Lake County Courthouse in Crown Point. Though he lost that first roll of film, today Brechner (www.brech.com/npIndex.html) offers novices a rule of thumb: "Every roll of film should produce ten useable shots, three good shots, and one really great shot."

TOM HOCKER was born and raised in Texas, but moved to northwest Indiana in 1970. He served as a photographer at Inland Steel for ten years, and taught photography at Purdue University Calumet from 1971 to 1995. Hocker fell in love with photography taking pictures in a railroad switching yard when he was 20 years old. He went on to earn a master's degree in photography from the Institute of Design in Chicago. Today, Hocker says he not only enjoys taking photographs, but finds it "as necessary as breathing." His favorite subject is falling water, but he has captured a world of images throughout his years as practitioner, teacher, and mentor. One treasured place to shoot is the former Atlas Cement plant, an abandoned industrial site Hocker says has "the feel of the Arizona canyon lands." A resident of Hammond, these days he often flies to northern Ireland where he is documenting community reconciliation projects in Belfast.

SUSAN HURLEY would like more time to explore photography. A specialty pharmaceutical representative, Hurley earned a

bachelor's degree in art from Northern Illinois University and enjoys photography and watercolor painting. Her affinity for photography began on her fourteenth birthday when her parents presented her with a Kodak 110 camera as a present. She has been focusing, clicking, and developing ever since. "Photography is magical," Hurley says. "It allows you to freeze a moment in time." She enjoys portrait work the most, and also photographing nature, sunsets, and unusual subjects. One of her favorite northwest Indiana sites is the Carmelite monastery in Munster. Hurley credits the picture-packed *Life* and *National Geographic* magazines of her youth for fostering her vision. A lifetime dream came true for Hurley when one of her photographs was printed in an edition of *Life*. Born in Chicago and a former resident of Milwaukee, Hurley now considers the region home.

JESSE JOSLEYN has worked as a mechanic, an electrician, and a coal miner, but photography is his true profession. Now the owner of a studio in Hebron, Josleyn says his only mistake was not doing photography earlier in his life. A self-taught practitioner who studied others' work, Josleyn today is known for his heartfelt portraits of families, mothers and their babies, and people in general. Born in Tennessee, Josleyn lived in East Gary until he was ten years old, then moved to Kentucky. He returned to northwest Indiana in 1991. He believes that every good picture tells a story. Though his subjects are not famous, he says, the moms and little babies he photographs at his studio

pack a wallop in love and warmth. "It won't save the world or make me rich," Josleyn admits, "but to know I've made people happy with my photographs is a pretty good thing."

ROBERT KAUFFMAN remembers taking his first pictures with a Nikormat camera when he was 13. He entered one in a contest sponsored by the *Detroit News* that nabbed an honorable mention and encouraged the young photographer. A chiropractor by profession, Kauffman was born and raised in Livonia, Michigan but has lived in northwest Indiana since 1989. His preferred subjects in the region run the gamut from historic buildings to barns to churches. "They all have a story to tell," says Kauffman, who has graduated to a Nikon 6006 for his picture-taking. He also appreciates the gritty realism of the area's steel mills and workers. He focuses his lens as well on trees, boats, lighthouses, sporting events, and people of all sorts. When others ask for photography advice, Kauffman (www.kauffmanimages.com) urges them to concentrate on composition. "You have to eliminate all the distractions to reveal the central idea," he says. "Only then should you press the shutter release."

MICHELLE KEIM-MUELLER is a professional photographer and teacher who has taught college photography courses at Columbia College and Wright College, both in Chicago. She earned a master of fine arts degree from the School of the Art Institute in 1997 and a bachelor of fine arts degree from Columbus College of Art and Design in 1993. Born and raised in Ohio in the nation's largest Amish county, today she enjoys capturing "big steel" in the country's largest steel-producing region. Now a resident of Chicago, Keim-Mueller is represented by NFA Space, a fine art gallery that features new and established artists. She likes to have fun with photography; six years ago, she bartered her skills as a photographer for admission to a large Star Trek convention where she met and snapped Scotty, Mr. Sulu, Wharf, and the Klingon sisters.

CHRISTOPHER MEYERS likes to shoot pictures of buildings, architectural details, landscapes, and found objects. Currently Meyers is the American Heritage Home Trust's project manager for the rehabilitation of Wynant House, a Frank Lloyd Wright-designed home in Gary that he discovered, authenticated, and saved from the wrecking ball. Meyers earned a bachelor's degree from Indiana University Bloomington in 1994 and MSHP degree from the School of the Art Institute of Chica-

go in 1996. A lifelong photographer who studied the art form along with French and Art History, Meyers believes photography can often be more real than the reality, helping humanity to reflect on its state of being. Born in Chicago and raised in the south suburbs before moving to northwest Indiana in 1986, Meyers' favorite photographic haunts include the City of Gary and the Indiana Dunes National Lakeshore. He counsels novice photographers to experiment. "Use shadows, lighting, unique perspectives," Meyers advises. "Mix it up. Sometimes the shots you did not initially want to take yield the best results."

CHERYL MILCHAK feels drawn to the water and spends much time photographing at the dunes. Favorite subjects include the lighthouses, sand, boats, and sunsets. Other favorites are her two daughters, old barns, and landscapes. A laboratory technician for a refractory company, Milchak started taking photos as a youngster and has worked as a wedding and personal portrait photographer. A lifelong resident of the region who was born in Gary, she graduated from

Merrillville High School in 1973 and attended Indiana University Bloomington. Though her very first cameras were simple Kodak instamatics, today she uses a manually controlled Canon AT-1 and enjoys the challenge of photographing in black and white with available light. Milchak's dream is to travel the country taking photographs. Though she would like to do more professional work, she admits she wouldn't want photography to become her full-time job. "I love it too much for it to become just work," she says.

JOHN NIEMANN took his first photograph at 10 with an Argus A2 and hasn't stopped since. The subject was a winter sunset over Potawatomi Golf Course in Michigan City. He was drawn to the images he perused in his parents' *Life* magazines, wanting early on to be a war correspondent-photographer. In the late 1960s with the U.S. Army, Niemann did photograph re-enlisting soldiers and those receiving awards and sent the pictures to the soldiers' hometown papers. Today Niemann is a media consultant for Ivy Tech State College and teaches digital

video technology. He holds a master's degree in instructional design and a bachelor of arts degree from Purdue University. He enjoys photographing his children, people in their natural surroundings, sunsets, lightning over Lake Michigan, the South Shore train yards at night. Over the years, Niemann has produced thousands of photographs of the northwest Indiana region. Born in Michigan City, he now calls Porter home.

ROBIN PEREZ is a creative writer with a bachelor's degree in communications who was born and raised in Gary. She is currently authoring a series of books called "Inner Talents" focused on people who express their talents and follow their dreams. Perez received the gift of a Polaroid instamatic when she was just a teen. Since then, she has found photography to be one of her own talents and a way for her to express herself creatively. Self-taught and self-motivated, Perez photographs ordinary or familiar subjects with an eye to "turning opinions upside down." She often turns her lens on the rich inventory of historic buildings in Gary and elsewhere in the region. She also loves photographing Lake Michigan, especially in winter and early spring—a natural landmark she says offers endless possibilities.

Ellen Skye ▼

Oregionality

MARK REMALEY is owner of Precision Aerial Photo. A graduate of the University of South Florida with a degree in cinematography and writing for film, he parlayed his commercial instrument-rated pilot's license and his knowledge of photography into a career. He has also worked as a parachute instructor, scuba diver, and backpacker, displaying a propensity for finding life's more exciting venues. Born in Evanston, Illinois, Remaley came to northwest Indiana in 1980 and settled in Crown Point. Once the proud five year old owner of a Brownie box camera, today he uses a Nikon 35mm and Mamiya cameras for his personal and professional work. He still laments the fate of one of his "luckiest shots," a photo of the grand old Lake County Courthouse in Crown Point after a snowstorm. "It was interesting—it looked like a painting," Remaley says, "but the negative was destroyed in a fire in 1990." After retirement, he plans to fly throughout all 50 states, Canada, and the Caribbean. Remaley's plan is to produce a book of the hemisphere's most beautiful spots and enchanting places as seen from the air.

ELLEN SKYE is an independent professional photographer whose work has appeared in the *Chicago Tribune, Chicago Reader,* the *Times, Indiana Business, Nevada Magazine,* and *Stagebill,* among other publications. Skye's photographs also appear in books including *All About Cats* and *Reno/Tahoe Visitor.* Many of her photographs were selected for exhibition in the Indiana Statehouse in Indianapolis as part of the Hoosier Millennium Collection. A native of Brooklyn raised on Long Island, Skye moved to northwest Indiana in 1987. She earned a bachelor of fine arts degree from Boston University. Skye was nine when she took her first photograph with a Kodak Duaflex IV camera. She still has the camera—and the bug. "The world is so interesting and beautiful," she says, "I can't imagine not photographing it." In between projects for corporate and editorial clients, Skye loves to photograph trains. Her freight train series of photographs will be part of a show entitled "Unexpected Journeys" in the Fine Arts Gallery at Broward Community College in south Florida in 2001.

OREGIONALITY PROJECT TEAM

Oregionality is the brainchild of a special project team at the Times. The first book of its kind about northwest Indiana, Oregionality was conceived by a team of people committed to the region and driven to showcase its strength and beauty. Team members are (pictured left to right) Claudia White, Ami Reese, Tom Kacius, Mike Donley, Lisa Tatina, Dave Savage, George Carl, Joe Gurnak, and Amy Owens.

William Eaton

Principal Writer
JULIA VERSAU

Profile Writing Acknowledgements
JULIA VERSAU
Air Tek, Kenneth J. Allen & Associates, Alternative Distribution Systems, Amarillo Roadhouse, American Renolit Corp., American Savings FSB, American Trust & Savings, Ancilla Systems, AT&T Broadband, The Bachman Partnership, PC, Bethlehem Steel, BP Amoco, Bulk Transport Corp., Calumet Abrasives, Calumet Flexicore, Chicago SouthShore & South Bend Railroad, Chicago Steel, Cicco's Menswear, City of East Chicago, City of Gary, City of Hammond, City of Lake Station, City of LaPorte, City of Portage, City of Valparaiso, City of Whiting, L.I. Combs & Sons, Inc., Dawn Foods, Frances DuPey, Edgewater Systems for Balanced Living, Empress Casino Hammond, Family Care Centers, Five Star Hydraulics, Inc., Gary-Chicago Airport, Hammond Group, Hardings, Inc., Hessville Cable & Sling, HFS Bank, Hoosier Boys' Town, Hospice of the Calumet Area, Ivy Tech State College, Indiana University Northwest, Indiana's International Port, International Longshoremen's Association, Isakson Motors, Lake County Community Economic Development Department, Lake County Convention & Visitors Bureau, Lamar Advertising, Lincoln 'Way Animal Complex, Mercantile Bank, Merrillville Community School Corporation, Methodist Hospitals, R.L. Millies & Associates, Inc., Miner Electronics, National Metal Services Corp., National Steel, NiSource, Inc., Northwest Indiana Forum, Pollution Control Industries, Radio One Communications, Rieth-Riley, Inc., Schererville Chamber of Commerce, Gerry Scheub, Southlake Mall, State Line Energy, Varied Products, Villa Cesare, Wagner Homes, Weil-McLain, WYIN Ch. 56.

Profile Writers
MICHAEL DONLEY
Hyles-Anderson College, Lake Area United Way

LU ANN FRANKLIN
The Brant Companies, The TIMES

TAMARA O'SHAUGHNESSY
Town of Cedar Lake, Town of Griffith, Town of Highland, Town of Lowell, Town of Munster, Town of Schererville

Craig Berg ▼

Index of Photographers

Kirk John Mitchell

Marie Trgovich ▼

Index of Profiles

Kirk John Mitchell

region*ality*